GIAP

GIAP

THE GENERAL WHO DEFEATED AMERICA IN VIETNAM

James A. Warren

palgrave
macmillan

GIAP

Copyright © James A. Warren, 2013.

First published in 2013 by
PALGRAVE MACMILLAN®
in the United States—a division of St. Martin's Press LLC,
175 Fifth Avenue, New York, NY 10010.

Where this book is distributed in the UK, Europe and the rest of the world,
this is by Palgrave Macmillan, a division of Macmillan Publishers Limited,
registered in England, company number 785998, of Houndmills,
Basingstoke, Hampshire RG21 6XS.

Palgrave Macmillan is the global academic imprint of the above companies
and has companies and representatives throughout the world.

Palgrave® and Macmillan® are registered trademarks in the United States,
the United Kingdom, Europe and other countries.

ISBN: 978–0–230–10712–0

Library of Congress Cataloging-in-Publication Data is available from the
Library of Congress.

A catalogue record of the book is available from the British Library.

Design by Newgen Knowledge Works (P) Ltd., Chennai, India.

First edition: September 2013

10 9 8 7 6 5 4 3 2 1

Printed in the United States of America.

To Lynn Ho, for unstinting support on the firing line

and

in memory of Major General Fred Haynes, USMC
friend, colleague, and worthy adversary of Vo Nguyen Giap

CONTENTS

INTRODUCTION

When the Communists finally celebrated their conquest of South Vietnam in April 1975 after thirty years of unceasing conflict, Premier Pham Van Dong pointed to a senior general, a short, slight man with darting eyes, a high forehead, and an air of energetic intelligence, and said, "There is the architect of our victory." The general, Vo Nguyen Giap, wore a simple officer's uniform bearing none of the scores of medals and ribbons earned over more than thirty-four years of war against his French, Japanese, South Vietnamese, and American adversaries. Giap, then the minister of defense and a senior Party Politburo member, had been the commander in chief of the People's Army of Vietnam (PAVN) between 1944 and 1973. The PAVN was the institution that did more than any other to defeat two great Western powers and secure the political and military goals of the Revolution—a feat as remarkable as it was unprecedented. Giap, though, was far more than a field general commanding an entire army. He built the Communist armed forces from a single platoon in 1944 to a twenty-plus-division force, indisputably one of the most formidable armies of the twentieth century.

Giap was not a soldier who suffered fools gladly. Most of the other senior leaders of the Party found him abrasive, overbearing, egotistical, and a tenacious infighter, traits that served him very well throughout his war years. His French and American adversaries characterized him as a ruthless fanatic, a butcher who time and again refused to quit the battlefield after taking losses no twentieth-century Western army commander could have suffered and retained command. A kind of steely defiance and confidence utterly lacking in ambivalence seemed to shape Giap's decisions. As he remarked just before the outbreak of war against the French, "If France is so shortsighted as to unleash conflict, let it be known that we shall struggle until death, without permitting ourselves to stop for any consideration of persons of any struggle." This was not mere rhetoric. In the wars against France and the United States, 1,100,000 Communist soldiers perished.

There was no quit in General Giap, or the army he created. Driven by personal tragedy—his beloved first wife, a sister-in-law who was an ardent Communist in her own right, and several other close family members died at the hands of French jailers during World War II. He made no secret of his opinions of his adversaries: they were barbaric exploiters of the downtrodden masses, manipulators, imperialistic double-talkers whose self-righteous rhetoric of freedom and democracy belied their goal of conquest.

As both theoretician and practitioner, Giap's primary concern was with protracted, or people's war, a doctrine developed by Mao Zedong designed to marshal the human and material resources of a revolutionary movement against an oppressive government that, at least initially, possessed far greater military assets than those of the Revolution. As Giap would write in the most important of his many books, "Only a long-term war could enable us to utilize to the maximum our political trump cards, to overcome our material handicap and to transform our weakness into strength."

Over thirty years of continuous conflict against nations far stronger materially and militarily than his own, Giap refined and adapted Mao's ideas to fit the particular conditions of Vietnam. He brilliantly applied what historian Douglas Pike calls the "two pincers" of revolutionary power, political struggle and armed struggle, placing greater emphasis on one form over the other at various stages of the Revolution.

Perhaps Giap's most important contributions to protracted warfare were his flexible integration of three types of forces (local militia in the villages, regional forces, and full-time main force units), and his creative use of various "fighting forms"—guerrilla warfare, mobile independent operations by battalions, conventional set-piece battles, and political mobilization.

Almost forty years after the war, we still have a great deal to learn about Giap's day-to-day decisions and his exact place within the senior leadership. The Vietnamese Communists assiduously maintained a policy of collective decision making during their conflicts. Documents and recollections of Giap's comrades in arms do not agree on whether the general was the most influential among the half-dozen men who formulated Communist strategy in the period covered in this book. Nor is there a clear consensus on the extent of his responsibilities as commander in chief. Remarkably, the Vietnamese themselves have not yet produced an authoritative biography of the man who clearly played a critical role in the unification of all Vietnam under Communist leadership.

Thus, let the reader beware: in describing Giap's decisions and strategy, I am to a certain degree describing the decisions and strategy of the entire senior leadership in Hanoi. Giap, at least in this book, figures as the embodiment of the Vietnamese Communist way of war in the twentieth century. A biography of Senior General Giap, in the sense that that word is used in the West, is quite frankly impossible. A blow-by-blow of Giap's life and career is beyond our reach, at least for now.

In this book, I make no attempt to address in depth the scholarly debates swirling around the political maneuvering among the senior leadership. I do point out their existence, albeit selectively. To attempt to do more would be to go beyond the central purpose of the book. Claims and counterclaims concerning the power base and influence of one key figure or another at a given time, even among scholars with access to all available Vietnamese language sources, seem to me very sketchy, at times appearing to reflect more of the bias of the researcher than a judicious reading of the historical record. I can only add that after having studied the wars in Vietnam for twenty-odd years and read much of the authoritative scholarship, I have come to the conclusion that Vo Nguyen Giap was almost certainly the most important strategist of the Revolution next to Ho Chi Minh. He was without question the primary architect of the Communist military machine.

This book might best be described as an interpretive history of Giap as a strategist and commander. Because of the formidable limitations of the sources, the reader is advised that many of the "facts" about the trajectory of battles and the units involved are disputed, and any analysis of Giap's decision making—of his thinking about strategy in general—must be somewhat speculative. This is why at certain junctures, my method has been akin to that of a literary critic attempting to interpret a story line through close reading of texts written by Giap, his contemporaries, and scores of historians who have charted the complex history of the wars in Vietnam.

More than in other historical fields, the work of military historians tends to reflect a cultural and nationalist bias. This is understandable. Wars are violent contests of national will, involving moral matters of courage, endurance, and honor. The temptation to favor one's own side in telling the story is very difficult to resist. Thousands of good books have been written about the wars in Vietnam by American and French historians. In the vast majority of these, the writers devote far more attention to their own forces and strategies and to diagnoses of how they lost. This book will have served a useful purpose if it counteracts that bias, showing how the Communists fought and won.

Ho Chi Minh was, of course, the spiritual father and living symbol of independence to the Vietnamese people. His asceticism, charisma, and patient dedication to a unified Vietnam inspired a nation of more than 25 million exploited peasants—rice farmers, fisherman, factory workers, and coal miners. But Giap bore the primary responsibility for meshing Communist organizational techniques with the explosive yearnings of a colonized people for independence, and for forging the primary weapon of the Revolution. Giap defeated the world's supreme military power despite losing almost every multi-battalion battle he fought against the United States between 1965 and 1973. But as a PAVN colonel famously pointed out to US Army Major Harry G. Summers Jr., just before Saigon fell in 1975: while it was true that the Americans had won all the major battles, it was "also irrelevant."

Vo Nguyen Giap (second from left) discusses battle plans in the bush with Ho Chi Minh (second from right) and two senior officers. Early 1954. (Courtesy Vietnam News Agency.)

Giap and Ho Chi Minh discuss plans for Giap's most celebrated victory at Dien Bien Phu. (Courtesy Vietnam News Agency.)

The PAVN Commander in Chief in the closing days of the War of Resistance. (AP Photo, © Associated Press.)

Two PAVN soldiers, a man and a women, meet on the Ho Chi Minh Trail in May 1970. They had grown up in the same small village in North Vietnam. For the Communists, the American War in Vietnam was everyone's war. (AP Photo/Vietnam Pictorial/Trong Thanh, © Associated Press.)

General Giap (second from right) leads a discussion of battle plans for the Ho Chi Minh Campaign in 1975. (Courtesy Vietnam New Agency.)

A PAVN tank breaks through the front gate of Saigon's Presidential Palace, the seat of the government of the Republic of Vietnam, at 11:30 hours on April 30, 1975. (Courtesy Vietnam News Agency.)

General Giap salutes his fallen comrades at a shrine at Dien Bien Phu's Vietminh cemetery on the fiftieth anniversary of the battle (2004). (AP Photo/Richard Vogel, © Associated Press.)

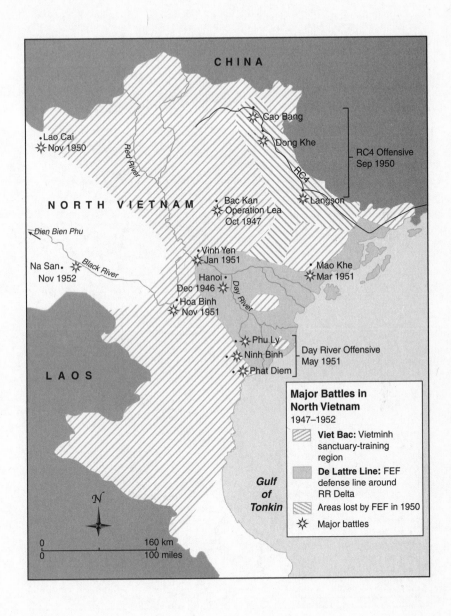

Major Battles in North Vietnam

1947–1952

- Viet Bac: Vietminh sanctuary-training region
- De Lattre Line: FEF defense line around RR Delta
- Areas lost by FEF in 1950
- Major battles

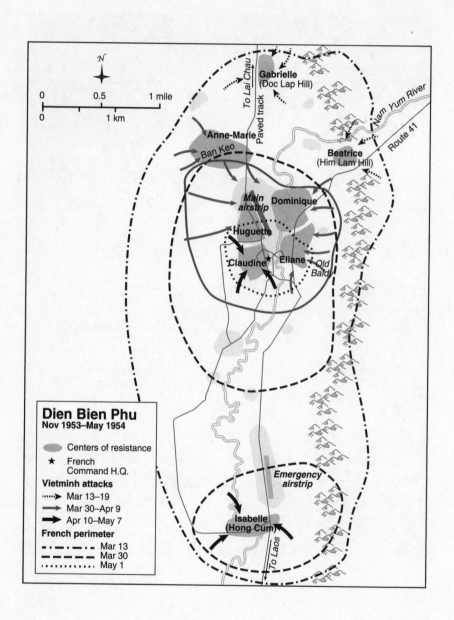

N

| 0 | 0.5 | 1 mile |

| 0 | 1 km |

To Lai Chau

Gabrielle
(Doc Lap Hill)

Paved track

Anne-Marie

Ban Keo

Beatrice
(Him Lam Hill)

Nam Yum River

Route 41

Main airstrip

Dominique

Huguette

Claudine

Eliane

Old Bald

Dien Bien Phu
Nov 1953–May 1954

Centers of resistance

★ French
Command H.Q.

Vietminh attacks
Mar 13–19
Mar 30–Apr 9
Apr 10–May 7

French perimeter
— ⋅ — ⋅ — Mar 13
— — — — Mar 30
⋅⋅⋅⋅⋅⋅⋅⋅⋅⋅ May 1

Emergency airstrip

Isabelle
(Hong Cum)

To Laos

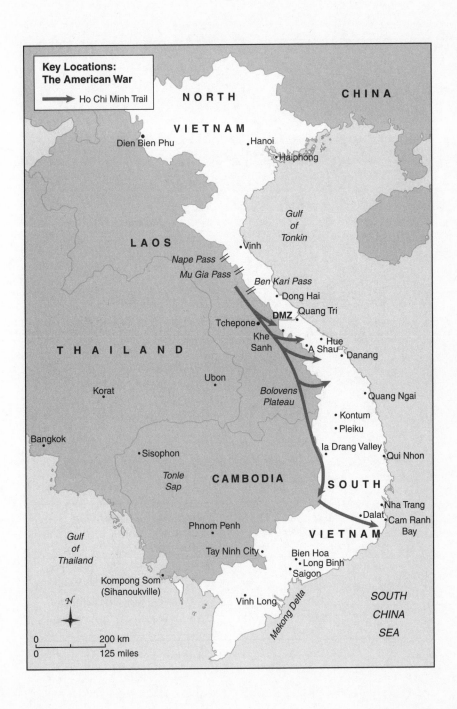

Key Locations:
The American War

→ Ho Chi Minh Trail

NORTH

CHINA

VIETNAM

Dien Bien Phu

Hanoi

Haiphong

Gulf
of
Tonkin

LAOS

Vinh

Nape Pass

Mu Gia Pass

Ben Kari Pass

Dong Hai

Quang Tri

DMZ

Tchepone

Khe
Sanh

A Shau

Hue

Danang

THAILAND

Ubon

Bolovens
Plateau

Quang Ngai

Kontum

Pleiku

Korat

Ia Drang Valley

Qui Nhon

Bangkok

Sisophon

Tonle
Sap

CAMBODIA

SOUTH

Nha Trang

Dalat

Cam Ranh
Bay

Gulf
of
Thailand

Phnom Penh

VIETNAM

Tay Ninh City

Bien Hoa

Long Binh

Saigon

Kompong Som
(Sihanoukville)

Vinh Long

Mekong Delta

SOUTH

CHINA

SEA

N

0   200 km

0   125 miles

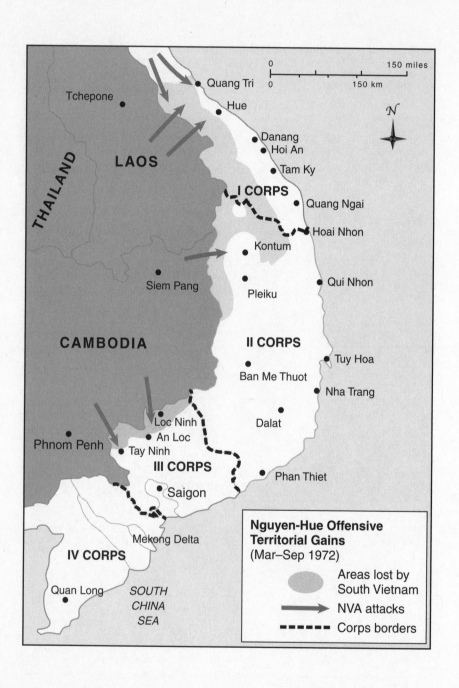

Nguyen-Hue Offensive Territorial Gains (Mar–Sep 1972)

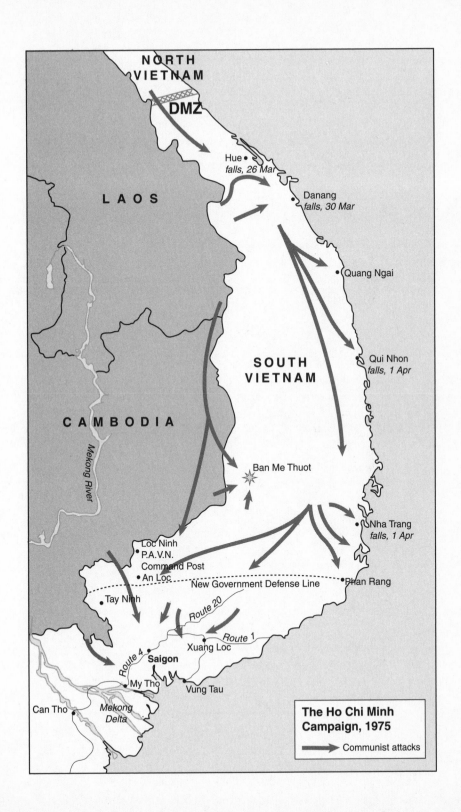

NORTH
VIETNAM

DMZ

LAOS

Hue •
falls, 26 Mar

Danang
falls, 30 Mar

Quang Ngai

SOUTH
VIETNAM

Qui Nhon
falls, 1 Apr

CAMBODIA

Mekong River

Ban Me Thuot

Nha Trang
falls, 1 Apr

Loc Ninh
P.A.V.N.
Command Post
• An Loc

New Government Defense Line

Phan Rang

• Tay Ninh

Route 20

Route 1

Route 4

Xuang Loc

Saigon

• My Tho

Vung Tau

Can Tho •

*Mekong
Delta*

**The Ho Chi Minh
Campaign, 1975**

→ Communist attacks

1

THE VIETNAMESE REVOLUTION AND THE YOUNG REVOLUTIONARY

By the time he was admitted to the most prestigious preparatory school in Hue, the old imperial capital city of Vietnam, Vo Nguyen Giap was already an ardent patriot committed to liberating the country from its French colonial masters. He had an excellent command of Vietnam's 2,000-year history of bold resistance to foreign domination in wars against China and Kublai Khan of the Mongols and a burning desire to make his own contribution. Like other idealistic Vietnamese teenagers at the Lycée National, most of them sons of scholar-mandarins trained in the Confucian tradition who went on to serve as minor functionaries in the colonial government, Giap was well aware of the venalities of French rule, of its crushing and exploitive effects on the lives and institutions of his people. Already he was playing a small part in the burgeoning anticolonial movement led by a small but growing intelligentsia of journalists, teachers, and minor government functionaries in Vietnam's urban centers.

The movement had begun in earnest around 1880, just as France was completing its conquest of Indochina. By the mid-1920s, such political activity as the French allowed was carried out by scores of reformist societies and associations, and several fractious political parties. Many of these organizations advocated collaboration with the French in the hope of developing Western-style institutions and gradual emancipation. Others operated clandestinely, advocating the violent overthrow of Vietnam's colonial administration and the replacement of the country's traditional Confucian elite with Vietnamese intellectuals schooled in the art of modern politics. The French security service, the dreaded Sûreté Generale, viewed the most radical of these parties as a serious threat to French authority. It kept detailed files on thousands of activists and used its vast police powers to crush virtually all forms of political expression. Vietnamese radicals filled the ghastly prisons of Vietnam, where hundreds died from torture, from starvation, or at the hands of executioners. But those who survived the ordeal emerged with a burning determination to break France's grip on Indochina by any means necessary.

One day after school in Hue, a close friend passed along to Giap a copy of an outlawed pamphlet called "Colonialism on Trial." It was written by Nguyen Ai Quoc—"Nguyen the patriot" in English—a much-traveled Vietnamese nationalist who had achieved widespread notoriety at the Versailles Peace Conference after World War I. At Versailles Quoc presented an impassioned demand for self-determination in the colonized countries of Asia and Africa. Quoc had gone on to become a founding member of both the French Socialist Party and the Inter-colonial Union, an organization of radicals from France's various colonies who sought to break the shackles placed on indigenous political expression by France. In 1923 he journeyed to the Soviet Union for formal training as a revolutionary at the Stalin School for Toilers in the East. "At that time," wrote Giap, "for the youths of our age, Nguyen Ai Quoc had become...the object of our dreams. We were so eagerly searching for the truth. To read for the first time a book denouncing colonialism inspired us with so much hatred, and thrilled us."[1]

Reading "Colonialism on Trial" was a pivotal event in young Giap's life, for it was his introduction to the evils of colonialism as understood by a Communist organizer who, over the next fifteen years, would outmaneuver numerous rivals to take up the leadership of Vietnam's crusade for independence. The organization Nguyen Ai Quoc ultimately created to achieve that end in May 1941 was called Viet Nam Doc lap Dong minh, the League for the Independence of Vietnam. The Vietminh, as the League came to be known, was in fact a classic political front organization, meaning that it consisted of various groups and classes of people united around a single objective or platform but led by one party only. In the case of the Vietminh, that objective was clear from the outset: to end French domination and achieve national independence in the name of the people of Vietnam. Over the next thirty-five years, the front would be referred to by different names, but it was always led by the Vietnamese Communist Party, first by Ho Chi Minh, and then, after Ho's passing in 1969, by a dozen or so of his early disciples. Prominent among them was Vo Nguyen Giap.

By the time of Ho's death, Giap had served the Revolution as commander in chief of Communist military forces in Vietnam and minister of defense for more than thirty years. Today, Giap is widely recognized as one of the three most important strategists of the Revolution, along with Truong Chinh ("Long March" in Vietnamese) and Ho Chi Minh himself.

The principal ideas of Vietnamese revolution that Ho led had first come to him by his own account when he was in his Paris apartment in the early 1920s reading Lenin's "Theses on the National and Colonial Questions."

A critical passage of that work follows:

> Above all else we must strive as far as possible to give the peasant movement a revolutionary character, to organize the peasants and the exploited in [revolutionary associations called] soviets, and thus bring about the closest possible union between the Communist proletariat of Western Europe and the revolutionary peasant movement of the east and of the colonial and subject countries.[2]

On reading this passage, Ho recalled in 1960, "What emotion, enthusiasm, clear-sightedness and confidence it instilled into me! I was overjoyed to tears. Though sitting alone in my room, I shouted aloud as if addressing large crowds: 'Dear martyrs, compatriots! This is what we need! This is the path to liberation!'"[3]

Classical Marxism—before Lenin—had assumed that revolution and class struggle could only succeed in industrialized capitalist societies where an oppressed working class, the proletariat, could rise up against the ruling capitalists. Ho took issue with this view. He ultimately came to argue that Communist leadership could generate strong revolutionary momentum in Vietnam only by uniting the rural peasantry with disaffected middle-class nationalists and the small proletariat in a political front movement. To preserve unity of purpose, the Communist nature of the front needed to be obscured under the cloak of an eclectic leadership council with a broad, idealistic platform eschewing Communist doctrine in favor of the goals of self-determination and democracy. Once the front had overthrown the imperialists and achieved control of the state, a disciplined and well-organized Communist Party would break with its non-Communist (and in some cases, even anti-Communist) allies, neutralizing and isolating rivals within the front, and begin to build the workers' utopia Marx had always envisaged.

Ho had a remarkable array of personal and political assets, not the least of which was his ability to recognize the potential capabilities of his comrades. He saw from the outset that Giap was among the most driven and promising of his disciples. Ho also possessed a uniquely appealing personal magnetism. Even his adversaries marveled at his keen intelligence and avuncular modesty. "Uncle Ho's" asceticism contrasted sharply with the arrogance and corruption that swirled around the officials of French Indochina and their Vietnamese minions. Rival Vietnamese nationalist leaders constantly quarreled over platforms and minute questions of ideology and method, while Ho displayed a rare gift for mediating conflicts within his own party, and for establishing temporary alliances with rivals to accomplish short-term Communist objectives.

As a political operator in general, Ho was something of an organizational genius. He also had an almost mystical ability to instill confidence and commitment in the Vietnamese people to a degree that is almost impossible for non-Vietnamese to imagine. Vo Nguyen Giap, like virtually all of the men who worked closely with Ho for a sustained period, revered the man as a visionary and a venerable wise man from the first time he read "Colonialism on Trial."

Far more than any other figure on the nationalist scene in the late 1920s and 1930s, Uncle Ho possessed deep empathy for the plight of the roughly 15 million peasants who comprised 90 percent of Vietnam's population. More importantly, he sensed their explosive revolutionary potential.

Although they lacked what Vietnam's Communists referred to as "political consciousness," they were an extraordinarily resilient and resourceful people. Ho had no doubt that a small group of highly trained Communist cadres could mobilize the peasantry through an intensive indoctrination program designed to create, in effect, a unified way of thinking. As Ho wrote in a 1927 article Giap would surely have read and studied,

> Victory of the proletarian revolution is *impossible* in rural and semi-rural countries if the *revolutionary proletariat is not actively supported* by the mass of the peasant population....In China, in India, in Latin America...the decisive ally of the proletariat in the revolution will be the peasant population. Only if the revolutionary wave sets in motion the rural masses under the leadership of the proletariat, will the revolution be able to triumph. Hence the exceptional importance of Party agitation in the countryside.[4]

Broadly speaking, Communism's growing popularity in pre–World War II Vietnam was inextricably bound up with the corrosive and debilitating effects of French colonialism on the Vietnamese people—on their traditional ways of earning a living and structuring their society. As an American agent active in Vietnam during World War II put it, "French colonialism in Indochina [was] one of the worst possible examples of peonage [and] disregard for human rights...the Vietnamese had been cruelly exploited, brutally mistreated, and generally used as French chattel..."[5] French domination shook the Vietnamese to their very foundations, creating enormous social upheaval and tearing apart the centuries-old rhythms of village life that defined life and work in Vietnam.

France by 1885 had defeated a sustained but disorganized resistance movement led by the Confucian-mandarin elite, leading to the loss of that elite's legitimacy. Meanwhile, the commercialization of agriculture led to a rapid concentration of landownership in the hands of French businessmen and a small number of pro-French Vietnamese, with catastrophic effects for the peasants. Hundreds of thousands of peasants lost their small lots of arable land and were forced to work for pitifully low wages. The poor were further impoverished by high taxes and extortion by local colonial functionaries, most of them Vietnamese.

Peasant farmers on the verge of starvation fled to the few cities by the thousands. Most could find only low-paying work in factories, coal mines, and rubber plantations, where they toiled long hours for a pittance, and were constantly subjected to corporal punishment. The Vietnamese proletariat was in effect enslaved by its venal colonial masters. Communism and the various front organizations it created and led seemed to offer the Vietnamese a clear and inspiring path to liberation, self-determination, and the many benefits of modern life denied them by French exploitation.

The Vietnamese Communist leaders in the 1920s and 1930s were under no illusions that a nationwide uprising was imminent. Patience and discernment on the part of the leadership were essential in building up the political consciousness of the masses and destroying the authority of the oppressors. To act before the time was right was to invite defeat and disaster. Ho and other early Communists employed the ancient Vietnamese notion of *thoi co,* which translates roughly as "opportune moment" but connotes what one leading scholar of Vietnamese revolutionary thought calls a "profound even mystical meaning about the appropriate moment for action."[6] When "the yoke of the ruling classes has become intolerable, and the village masses are in a state of revolutionary ferment and ready to fight actively against the established order," wrote Ho, guerrilla units could be formed to harass government forces, capture weapons to expand the power of the revolutionaries, and protect a shadow government known among the revolutionaries as the political infrastructure.[7] Ho's nascent ideas about guerrilla fighting struck a chord with young Giap, for he had always been keenly interested in the history of Vietnamese resistance—a history in which the themes of protracted war and guerrilla tactics occupied an unusually prominent place.

GIAP'S EARLY YEARS

Vo Nguyen Giap was born on August 25, 1911, in An Xa, Quang Binh Province. Quang Binh itself is located in Annam, the narrow neck of Vietnam between its two great deltas, where resistance to French rule in the late nineteenth and early twentieth centuries had been stronger and more sustained than elsewhere. The future general's father, Vo Quang Nghiem, was a low-ranking but highly respected mandarin in the colonial administration. In addition to his job as a town clerk responsible for preparing and dispensing official government documents, Nghiem worked in the rice paddies as a farmer and volunteered his services as a reading tutor to An Xa's children. Giap's mother, Nguyen Thi Kien, loved to work in the soil, growing rice and sweet potatoes. Like her husband, Kien was passionately committed to Vietnamese independence.

Giap's maternal grandfather had been a rebel commander in the abortive Can Vuong Uprising of 1885. Both his parents recited poems and stories they had learned as children about the resistance and rebellions that flared up with great frequency as France solidified its control over all of Indochina. "Memories of the resistance against the occupation were still very fresh [during my childhood]," Giap has written. "In the evening, in the light of the oil lamp, my mother would often tell me of the grueling trials she underwent during the Can Vuong campaign, in which my father had participated [as a very young man] ... I can still recall my earliest childhood deeply bathed with feelings of love for our country."[8]

Signs of academic brilliance emerged early. Like most of the dozen or so men who would lead the Communist Party of Vietnam, Giap was a member of a tiny minority of young Vietnamese to be educated beyond grammar school. Most of the students at the prestigious Lycée National in Hue were the sons of the French *colons*, bound for university study and careers in government, the law, or other professions, but many future Vietnamese leaders studied there, including Ho Chi Minh, Pham Van Dong, and Ngo Dinh Diem, who led the South Vietnamese government from 1955 until 1963.

Courses were taught in the French language. The curriculum was similar to that of the best schools in Paris: French literature and history, geography, particularly the geography of the entire French empire, philosophy, physics, and chemistry. Vietnamese was taught as a "second" language and literature. By all accounts Giap was one of the best students in the school. He scored the second highest of all the applicants on the entrance exam and consistently ranked first in his class academically.

It was at Hue that the budding radical first began to study contemporary world politics and military history on his own time, establishing a life-long habit of voracious reading and study. After school, he often went to visit Phan Boi Chau, who had led a resistance movement at the turn of the twentieth century. Phan called for the overthrow of French rule, the establishment of a constitutional monarchy on Japanese lines, and the construction of Western social and educational institutions. Phan Ban Chau and his followers had little understanding of how to disseminate their platform to the peasantry or challenge France's iron grip on the nation's political institutions, and the movement faded into history when Phan was arrested for sedition in southern China by the French Süreté in 1925. After confining Phan to house arrest in Hue, the French, for reasons that remain unclear, nonetheless allowed him to meet regularly with admiring schoolboys like Giap who were anxious to learn about the politics of resistance.

At the Lycée National, called the Quoc Hoc in Vietnamese, Giap's penchant for defiance of the French authorities first manifested itself. He joined in numerous protests against government repression of dissent, high taxes and rents, and corruption in the colonial administration. When a fellow student known for expressing anticolonial ideas was expelled for cheating on an examination, Giap claimed that the headmaster had manufactured the charge because he didn't approve of the student's political views. In 1926 he organized a "quit school" demonstration throughout Hue. Not surprisingly, he was promptly expelled from the Lycée and ordered to return to his home village.

Soon after returning to his parents' home in An Xa, he wrote and published his first piece of journalism in a French-language newspaper in Saigon. "Down with the Tyrant of Quoc Hoc" offered readers an account of the quit-school protest and a critical portrait of his erstwhile headmaster. Against the directive of the colonial authorities, Giap soon returned to Hue, where he made new radical contacts, began to read widely in Communist literature, and worked clandestinely in a prominent secret society called the Tan Viet. The organization contained a wide spectrum of anticolonialist activists. Its chief aim, Giap later wrote, "was to carry out first a national revolution, and then a world revolution."[9] Young Giap almost certainly formed the first Communist cell within the organization; the radical wing of the Tan Viet soon splintered off into an explicitly Communist political party, one of three discrete Communist organizations Ho Chi Minh was to unify in 1930 as the Vietnamese Communist Party.

Back in Hue in the late 1920s, Giap found paying work as a political journalist with a moderate reformist newspaper, writing for the underground radical press under various aliases. He participated in a series of protests that turned into a spontaneous uprising in the Annam provinces of Nghe An and Ha Tin in the spring and summer of 1930. A severe famine, coupled with the draconian effects of the Great Depression and government lassitude, prompted one prominent nationalist party, the VNQDD, to attack a French army post. Poorly coordinated, the assaulting force was quickly and brutally put down, but the incident sparked a host of spontaneous uprisings in the factories and in the villages of the region.

At least one of his biographers, John Colvin, claims that Giap formally joined Ho's Revolutionary Youth League (RYL) in 1930, though as with many assertions about Giap's early life, corroboration is lacking. Certainly he would have been favorably disposed toward any organization founded by Ho. By 1930, the RYL, with 1,000 members and cells in all three regions of Vietnam, had become the chief subversive threat in the eyes of the French intelligence-gathering apparatus. Giap's meteoric rise within the Communist Party in the 1930s suggests rather strongly that if he was not formally a member of the RYL, he had at least come to the attention of its founder, and had formed ties to its most promising believers.

Communist agents attempted to capitalize on popular discontent and unrest by orchestrating demonstrations and protest marches, many of which quickly degenerated into violent assaults on colonial authority. Government installations in the villages and cities were overrun and burned, and Vietnamese colonial functionaries and landowners were executed by angry mobs. The French authorities referred to the early 1930s as "the Red Terror." In scores of villages, Communists formed local governing associations, called soviets, to mete out vigilante justice, reduce rents, and redistribute land to the poorest peasants.

The French response was swift and brutal. A march on the city of Vinh by civilians protesting conditions in the countryside was strafed by French fighters, killing about 200 people. Villages and livestock where the Communists had installed soviets were razed by Foreign Legionnaires. Some eighty suspected Communists were executed, and the Central Committee of the Party—its governing body—was captured in Saigon. Vo Nguyen Giap was among the 10,000 radicals picked up by the Sûreté and tried for sedition.

The facts about his imprisonment behind the grim walls of Lao Bao Penitentiary near the Laotian border remain cloudy, as Giap has seldom spoken on record about his time in jail. He was apparently sentenced to two years' hard labor in early 1931 and served at least three months and perhaps as much as fifteen months.

It was in prison that he met a pretty fifteen-year-old girl with radical inclinations and a hatred of French authority that mirrored his own. Her name was Nguyen Thi Quang Thai. In late 1938, about six years after the two were released from prison, Giap married her. She soon bore him a daughter. Those close to Giap have reported that he was never happier than during the brief period, perhaps three years, that he, Quang Thai, and their daughter lived together as a family.

Interestingly, it may very well be true that Giap owed his early release from Lao Bao to the intervention of a powerful figure in the Sûreté Generale, Louis Marty. The Sûreté had started a file on Giap during his Quoc Hoc days; Marty apparently attempted to befriend Giap in an effort to turn him from the path of revolution to the path of service on behalf of France. One US intelligence report found in the Indochina Archives now located at Texas Tech University suggests that Marty sought to use Giap as a liaison between the Communists and the Sûreté in the late 1930s, when a Popular Front government in Paris friendly to the French Communist Party permitted the Communists in Indochina to function in the open. As a result of the Party's expanded activities, the Communists gained a newfound legitimacy in the eyes of the progressive elements in Vietnamese society.

It appears that Marty cleared the way for Giap to resume his formal education. It would have been impossible for a former political prisoner in Indochina with a long record of anticolonial activity to have been admitted to the Lycée Albert Sarraut in Hanoi, the best preparatory school in all Vietnam, and a gateway to graduate study at the University of Hanoi, without an influential sponsor. In 1934, after a year of diligent study, Giap received his baccalaureate from Sarraut, with excellent marks in philosophy. Soon thereafter he was admitted to the school of law at the University of Hanoi to pursue a degree in law and political economy. He obtained the equivalent of a Western master's degree in 1937.

While at university, Giap displayed the explosive energy and drive that would become his trademark in the long wars against the French and the United States. While pursuing doctoral studies, he worked as a history teacher at Thang Long High School in Hanoi in the morning. According to one of his professors, he was the most brilliant student in political economy in the 1938 academic year. Each year a senior economist from Paris selected a Vietnamese student for a prestigious graduate-level fellowship in Paris. In

1938, that economist was none other than Gaeton Pirou, director of French Prime Minister Paul Daumier's cabinet. Pirou offered the fellowship to Giap, who promptly turned it down. He would not desert his comrades in the pursuit of national liberation.

Giap plainly viewed his history teaching duties as part of his contribution to the incipient revolution. Among his objectives at Thang Long, where he taught fourteen- to eighteen-year-old boys, was "to imbue my students with patriotism."[10] One of his students, a future ambassador to the United States named Bui Diem, remembered that the future commander in chief was "possessed by the demons of revolution and battle."[11]

It was through journalism that Giap met two other future giants in the Communist movement: Pham Van Dong, later prime minister of the Socialist Republic of Vietnam, and Truong Chinh, the brilliant revolutionary strategist. All three men contributed articles to the French-language newspaper *Le Travail* in 1937. Giap wrote as well for radical newspapers in Hanoi, several of which were shut down for their attacks on the colonial administration.

As his commitment to the Communist Party solidified and his responsibilities increased, Giap abandoned his pursuit of a doctorate at the university. The exact nature of his subversive activities in 1939 and 1940 remains obscure. He wrote prodigiously for radical reformist newspapers. In 1939, he and Truong Chinh published a highly influential book (using pseudonyms) called *The Peasant Problem 1937–1938*. It offered a nuanced discussion of the role of the peasantry in Vietnamese politics.

Giap was no doubt gratified with the growth of the Party's reputation as an ardent defender of workers' and peasants' interests and as the most disciplined and effective proponent of national liberation. According to French statistics, by early 1939, the Party had 2,000 members and 40,000 followers.[12] Taking its cue from Stalin, the Party in Vietnam had been playing down class struggle against the Western powers in favor of resisting the evils of world fascism (i.e., Germany and Japan). Now, with France preoccupied with the growing threat of German ascendancy, the Party's strategy once again placed the highest priority on national liberation from French imperialism.[13]

Meanwhile, Ho Chi Minh had left Moscow for China in late 1938 and attached himself to Mao's Eighth Route Army, then united in an uneasy alliance with Chiang Kai-shek in a brutal war against the Japanese Imperial

Army. According to one of his biographers, Ho spent about two years writing articles about Mao's war against Japan and digesting the tactics of guerrilla fighting.[14] Given the formidable military responsibilities assigned to Giap by Ho in the 1940s—he would be asked to oversee the development of the revolutionary armed forces—it seems safe to assume that Giap made an in-depth study of Ho's articles on war in China, as well as Mao's brilliant lectures on guerrilla warfare published in 1938, and T. E. Lawrence's account of his time in World War I as an adviser to the Arab insurgency against the Turks. Just before the outbreak of the War of Resistance in 1946, Giap told French General Raoul Salan, "My fighting gospel is T. E. Lawrence's *Seven Pillars of Wisdom*. I am never without it."[15]

Guerrilla war was not, of course, a creation of the Communists or of Lawrence—the Vietnamese people had a long tradition of protracted guerrilla operations in their struggles against China, Champa, and the Mongols. In fact, guerrilla forces (typically small groups of lightly armed, informally trained insurgents) had operated all over the globe for centuries, and guerrilla warfare has played an important role in shaping the outcome of wars within and between nation states since nations as we know them first emerged out of the Middle Ages.

Before the end of the 1930s, Giap had begun to apply what he learned from his study to the highly fluid situation in Vietnam. The looming war against France would require guerrilla units trained not only in military tactics, but in revolutionary ideology as well, for guerrillas would be proselytizers as well as soldiers, living among the people and spreading the methods and doctrines of the revolutionary credo. Political cadres operating under guerrilla protection would work to convert the apolitical peasantry to the revolutionary struggle.

So it was that Giap, assigned the role of educating the Party leadership in military matters, pondered the critical questions: How could guerrilla units be raised and best deployed to expand base areas where the Vietnamese people would provide them with sustenance, moral support, and intelligence on French forces? How, in turn, could the guerrillas be protected from the predations of well-armed and technologically sophisticated French troops? How could military power and political agitation work symbiotically in war against colonial domination?

It seems clear from a reading of Giap's writings and command decisions that, of all the military strategists he encountered before he took up arms and built an army, Mao Zedong was the most influential. Strangely, Giap seldom mentions Mao in his writings on war even though his debt to the man is universally recognized by all serious students of Vietnam's wars in the twentieth century. Mao, like Ho, understood that the greatest asset in the struggle to establish a Communist state was the revolutionary potential of the peasantry. Mao, writes Samuel Griffith, a sinologist who served with the US Marines in guerrilla operations in Central America, "has aptly compared guerrillas to fish, and the people to the water in which they swim. If the political temperature is right, the fish, however few in number, will thrive and proliferate. It is therefore the principal concern of all guerrilla leaders to get the water to the right temperature and kept there."[16] Giap took this notion to heart and never let it go. His way of war would, of course, be refined and modified in light of his experiences in thirty years of continuous battle, but several of his core ideas can be apprehended in the first few pages of Mao's 1938 classic, *On Guerrilla War*:

> Guerrilla warfare has qualities and objectives peculiar to itself. It is a weapon that a nation inferior in arms and military equipment may employ against a more powerful aggressor nation. When the invader pierces deep into the heart of the weaker country and occupies her territory in a cruel and oppressive manner, there is no doubt that conditions of terrain, climate and society in general offer obstacles to his progress and may be used to advantage by those who oppose him.... Because guerrilla warfare basically derives from the masses and is supported by them, it can neither exist nor flourish if it separates itself from their sympathies and cooperation...In guerrilla warfare, select the tactic of seeming to come from the east and attacking from the west; avoid the solid, attack the hollow; attack; withdraw; deliver a lightning blow, seek a lightning decision. When guerrillas engage a stronger enemy, they withdraw when he advances; harass him when he stops; strike him when he is weary; pursue him when he withdraws. In guerrilla strategy, the enemy's rear, flanks, and other vulnerable spots are his vital points, and there he must be harassed, attacked, dispersed, exhausted and annihilated.[17]

In September 1939, Hitler invaded Poland. World War II had begun. The Nazi-Soviet Non-Aggression Pact of August 1939 made it quite clear that Stalin had abandoned his effort to form a united front with the Western democracies against Hitler. Communists in France were transformed from patriotic allies into enemies of the state. The Communist parties inside France and throughout her colonies were declared illegal; several thousand Communists were picked up by the Sûreté in Vietnam though Giap was able to dodge arrest, and Ho was then out of reach, recruiting and organizing in the Vietnamese exile community in southern China.

The Party in Vietnam had to shift rapidly to clandestine activities in the rural countryside and abandon indoctrination work in the urban centers. By the summer of 1940, Germany had conquered France, and the Vichy regime found itself under pressure from Germany's ally, Japan, to permit the Japanese to deploy troops and establish bases in Vietnam in order to carry out attacks on the Chinese and, before too long, to wage war against the United States and Great Britain across the Pacific Ocean. In September 1940, the Japanese entered Vietnam in force. They were the new masters of Vietnam, despite a face-saving agreement France had reached with Japan that officially recognized French sovereignty in Indochina and permitted the French colonial administration police to administer day-to-day political and economic affairs. The Vietnamese Communists welcomed these developments, for they sensed greater opportunities than dangers in the days ahead. For Giap, and for the Revolution, World War II would change everything.

2

UPHEAVAL AND
OPPORTUNITY: WORLD
WAR II

World War II dealt a fatal blow to colonialism by awakening passionate nationalist yearnings among the colonized peoples of Asia and Africa. The great powers envisaged their long war against the Axis as a struggle of free men against the forces of tyranny and darkness. According to the landmark Atlantic Charter signed by Britain and the United States in August 1941, the postwar world was to be shaped according to the enlightened principles of self-determination and respect for the human rights of all, and new governments would be constructed along Western democratic lines. Prewar empires would be dismantled, but circumstances dictated that the dismemberment was likely to take place slowly and deliberately by a yet undefined process. Despite their lofty pronouncements of freedom and equality for all peoples, the old empires were not likely to relinquish easily possessions they had exploited for natural resources, cheap labor, and trade. Their efforts to retain control were bound to clash with the rising tide of nationalism and thirst for unfettered independence that the war had done so much to unleash in the underdeveloped world. In Vietnam, the clash was sure to be particularly complex and stormy, for in very few colonized nations had the war produced an independence movement as resilient, disciplined, or shrewdly led.

As we shall see, by war's end, the Communists under Ho Chi Minh had unified the country's nationalist factions in a classic front organization, established themselves as the voice of the Vietnamese people, and even managed to seize temporary control over the country after the French administration was utterly humiliated militarily in a coup d'état by the Japanese army in the spring of 1945. That the Japanese were clearly on the verge of defeat at the hands of the British and the Americans only confirmed France's weakness in the eyes of Vietnamese patriots of all stripes.

France had been at the outset of the war the second largest empire on earth, covering more than 6 million square miles and containing 80 million souls. Her colonies in Equatorial and West Africa were together as large as the United States. She had important holdings as well in North Africa and the Caribbean, and was a key player in the Middle East. France's humiliating defeat at the hands of Germany and the loss of Indochina—the jewel in the Empire's crown—to the Japanese had a devastating effect on its sense of itself as a great power. To a far greater extent than Great Britain, recovering the most important holdings of its pre-war empire came to be seen as essential in restoring France's honor and its rightful place of influence in international affairs.

The trouble was that with a few exceptions, leading French politicians, especially the imperious General Charles de Gaulle, who emerged from the war as the most powerful figure in France, could not see that, in the words of Fredrik Logevall, the events of World War II had "dealt a blow to [French] imperial authority from which it never would fully recover."[1] As the war approached its dramatic conclusion, "de Gaulle spoke of the cohesion, the unbreakable bond between metropolitan France and her overseas territories. Like so many in the Free French movement, he failed to grasp that the colonial peoples might consider liberation from foreign rule as important as he did."[2] In de Gaulle's view, a few vague concessions by way of political rights and economic opportunities to the Indochinese were certainly within the realm of possibility—perhaps even a kind of limited independence within a French Union—but true independence for Vietnam was unthinkable. France had to remain in ultimate control of Vietnam's economic development and foreign policy and its military.

The remarkable success of Ho's Communists between 1940 and 1945 was due in no small measure to their prescience in reading the trajectory of the world war and in developing an ingenious strategy to take advantage of that trajectory. France's weakness in Indochina was first made clear when she was humiliatingly defeated by Nazi Germany in June 1940 and then, three months later, forced to permit Japan to occupy Vietnam. The Japanese were utterly indifferent to Vietnamese longings for independence—to have granted it would have been a distraction from their overarching plan. They were content to come to an agreement with the French colonial administration, leaving it in charge of governing the country and maintaining law and order outside the main cities, where the Japanese themselves were entrenched.

Ho and his lieutenants early on recognized that these events could lead to a potentially explosive surge of Vietnamese nationalism. That surge would present them with a golden opportunity to establish control over the country's faction-ridden nationalists, and begin to build an alternative political infrastructure among the peasantry. When the war ended in Allied victory—as Ho and Giap had believed it would—their movement could take advantage of the chaos and dislocation bound to result, march in strength out of the hinterlands, and seize the reins of power in Hanoi and Saigon. They earnestly hoped from the earliest days of the war that they would be able to enlist both material aid and moral support from the United States in the wake of the Japanese surrender and a much-weakened and discredited French empire.

To achieve these ambitious ends, it would be necessary to establish a front organization and to keep control, albeit clandestine control, of the front's program in the hands of the Communists. That front would soon be known to the world as the Vietminh. The objectives of the front as Ho and Giap conceived them were really quite straightforward and would remain as such throughout the War of Resistance with France (1946–1954): mobilize the peasantry behind the front and use their collective strength and Communist organizational techniques to build up a politico-military apparatus that would be strong enough to wage war against France should it attempt to re-establish its prewar hegemony.

Vo Nguyen Giap played an enormously important role in the revolutionary movement during World War II, for Ho Chi Minh assigned him primary responsibility for organizing that politico-military apparatus, at first in the jungles and mountains of northern Tonkin—the location of the Communists' first large-scale base area, or "liberated zone"—and then farther south toward the Red River Delta, with its 7 million inhabitants and vast natural resources.

VIETNAM AND THE OUTBREAK OF WORLD WAR II

France's declaration of war against Germany forced Paris to redeploy its Indochinese forces to France to buttress her army for the war in Europe. France's military weakness afforded the well-organized Communists great opportunities. This was not lost on the French commander in Indochina, Admiral Jean Decoux, who called for a "total and rapid" crackdown on the Party. For several months, the Sûreté ruthlessly hunted down its leaders, imprisoning many, and forcing others to go into hiding. Giap himself narrowly escaped imprisonment in the "White Terror." He went underground in Hanoi, albeit temporarily, while most of the leaders of the Revolution dispersed into the northern mountains of Tonkin or south China to regroup and weigh their options.

The Imperial Empire of Japan quickly capitalized on France's weakness. Some 6,500 Japanese troops occupied Vietnam in September 1940, just a few months after France surrendered to Hitler. After forcing the Vichy regime to sign an agreement "permitting" the occupation, the Japanese allowed the French to retain titular autonomy in civil matters, as well as responsibility for maintaining law and order in the countryside. But there was no doubt who held the reins of power in Vietnam: Tokyo called the tune, the French did the singing.

The Japanese army confirmed its dominance in Vietnam by attacking French military outposts throughout the north as it crossed over into the country from southern China, routing many of the French garrisons. The French-Japanese clash was quickly resolved by diplomacy, but not before the Vietnamese Communists opted to take advantage of the ensuing chaos in northern Vietnam by launching a series of uncoordinated uprisings against both the French and the Japanese in the name of Vietnamese independence. The Bac Son Rebellion was the most prominent of these uprisings. It was launched in October 1940, as several Vietnamese guerrilla units attacked retreating French forces in the hopes of gaining a foothold in northern Tonkin. The guerrillas managed to establish some local village and district administrations, but within a matter of a couple of months, the French had crushed most of the guerrilla units or dispersed them deep into the mountains.

Still, the premature uprisings were useful to the Party. Giap took away a valuable lesson from the failed Bac Son uprising: military action without proper political and military preparation was doomed to failure. From the earliest days of World War II until the Communists' seizure of Saigon in 1975, Giap often exhorted local Communist leaders and their restive forces to resist the temptation to pick up arms and launch offensive operations before they were sure that local conditions in the countryside favored success. In fact, during the early years of the war against France, Giap joined Ho in discouraging military adventurism because it threatened the expansion of the movement's political and military forces.

The rebellions of fall 1940 also provided the Revolution with a vital asset: a nucleus of combat-tested guerrilla fighters with a sound grounding in small unit tactics. The most powerful of these were the men of some twenty platoons commanded by a Nung, Chu Van Tan. (The Nungs are non-ethnic Vietnamese who live in the hills of northern Vietnam and practice slash-and-burn agriculture.) Giap, who was at this time just beginning to familiarize himself with the language and culture of the Nung (among other mountain, or Montagnard, peoples), would quickly befriend Tan, already a member of the Communist Party, and rely on his military wisdom and experience to develop the earliest Vietminh guerrilla units. This tough Nung warrior played an indispensable role in helping Giap carve out a remote base area in the contiguous provinces of Cao Bang, Langson, and Bac Kan—all lightly populated, mountainous provinces bordering on China. That base, called the Viet Bac, would by war's end encompass much of the territory of northern Tonkin.

GIAP'S RISE TO POWER

Vo Nguyen Giap's rise to the senior leadership of the Revolution, and to the awesome responsibilities that came with his appointment as commander and chief of the Vietnam People's Army (VPA), really began in May 1940, when he and Pham Van Dong were ordered by Ho to journey via railway and truck from Hanoi into southern China. Their mission: make contact with Ho Chi Minh and help him work out a strategy for the Party to achieve dominance of the independence movement that was sure to emerge once the world war could be brought to an end with Japan's defeat—a development Ho and the other senior leaders believed to be inevitable.

Giap's journey to Kunming was a harried one. At several junctures he and Dong had to jump off trains to escape capture and certain imprisonment, or even execution, by the Sûreté. Sometime in June, the two budding young Communist leaders were taken to the banks of the Tsuy-Hu River in Kunming just as Ho approached the river bank—in disguise, as he almost always was in the days before 1943. The three men spent several days in earnest conversation about the Revolution's prospects, as well as the role the two younger men were to play in the impending drama.

Ho had just returned to Kunming in southern China after a long absence in the Soviet Union and northern China. He could sense that France's position in Vietnam was increasingly tenuous. Ever the political bridge builder and shrewd operator, Ho had just begun in April 1940 to organize a new front among at least four discrete parties of Vietnamese nationalists in exile in southern China. It seems that while in northern China the previous year, Ho had received a first-class tutorial in guerrilla warfare while serving with Mao's Eighth Route Army. Beginning with the first meeting along the Tsuy-Hu River Ho passed on what he had learned to Giap, who for all intents and purposes would remain among Ho's favorite colleagues for the rest of Ho's long life.

Giap was deeply impressed by Ho's simplicity of manner and quiet charisma. "I found him immediately close to me, as if we were old acquaintances."[3] By all accounts, Ho was deeply impressed by Giap's intelligence and commitment. Taking note of the former school teacher's keen interest in the martial history of Vietnam and his fascination with Napoleon's campaigns, he suggested that the young revolutionary journey to Yenan to study Communist organizational techniques as well as military strategy and tactics at a Chinese Communist Party school. Giap was joined once more by Dong, and the two men traveled to Kweiyang, where they waited for transport to the school for some time, perhaps as long as two months.

By his own account, Giap used the time well.[4] Like Ho, he attached himself to the Eighth Route Army, and spent a great deal of time devouring

substantially expanded the Viet Bac, Giap would be responsible for extending the revolutionary administration southward into Thai Nguyen Province on the edge of the Red River Delta. Additional smaller base areas inside the Delta as well as along the central coast of Annam and in Cochinchina would also be developed.

After Pac Bo, Giap returned to the daunting task of building up military and political forces among the Montagnard peoples, learning as he went. In his own mind, building up a way of thinking among the villagers and instilling in them a profound commitment to the cause formed the bedrock of military training. He learned, in short, how to build up "revolutionary consciousness." He became, writes Douglas Pike,

> extremely well skilled in the art of gaining access to the enemy's sources of supply and in knowing how to make do when such war materiel was unavailable. He learned how to move men and supplies around a battlefield far faster than anyone had a right to expect....He and his cadres learned the importance of advertising the guerrilla's cause and of creating the proper image. Finally, he learned how best to work with villagers without being betrayed by them....Giap...knew he needed something far more sophisticated than a simple combat force, so he sought...[a] military mechanism that would place a premium on organization and motivation and thus harness social pressure, the strongest force in any society.[8]

Even at this early stage, when his thinking on the relationship between political mobilization work and armed forces was inchoate, Giap seems to have been convinced that the Revolution's success would require the formation of several types of armed units, both permanent and mobile and part-time and local, and a flexible, yet responsive apparatus for coordinating their operations. It would take several years of trial and error to establish the proper relationships between guerrilla units, propaganda teams, and the traditional regular forces of an infantry army. In practice, it happened that the roles of these varied types overlapped considerably, but with remarkably little friction among commanders of the different tiers of the military forces.

In Giap's thinking from the early 1940s on, the relationship between military work and political work was understood to be symbiotic. Giap and his ever-growing number of young cadres and guerrilla units established village and district chapters of Quu Quocs or "mass salvation associations." These civilian organizations were composed of various segments of society that shared a particular function, activity, or gender—for example, farmers, factory workers, women, or students who met regularly to participate in group consciousness raising sessions led by Party members, to plan community improvement projects, and to demonstrate against French legislation or repressive treatment. The associations were also recruiting organizations, encouraging the reluctant to become directly involved in such tasks as gathering intelligence, joining guerrila units, or digging trenches and tunnels in fortified villages.

The mass salvation associations were formed in this way: Giap's cadres began by entering a village and befriending a few young men who were already keenly interested in the resistance movement. The cadres then presented a cogent critique of colonial exploitation and explained the revolutionary Vietminh program designed to liberate the nation from French and Japanese oppression. Soon thereafter, village salvation associations were introduced, along with liberation committees consisting of sympathetic village elders and committed local sympathizers. The committees bore responsibility for administering village civil and legal affairs and improvement projects. Giap described the process of creating the overarching revolutionary administration as follows:

> A duality of power came into being in nearly all the localities where the Party had its branches. Village authorities sided with the revolution, became members of organizations for national salvation and, in whatever they did, Vietminh committees were consulted beforehand. In reality our own administration already dealt with nearly all the people's affairs. The inhabitants came to us for marriage registrations and to settle their land disputes. Orders were given by French...military authorities to set up guard posts in every village as defense measures against revolutionary activities. But unfortunately for them, there existed right in the village revolutionaries for whom both militiamen and villagers had sympathy. As a result, the majority of these guard posts did not yield their authors the expected results. In many localities they were turned into our own communication links or guard posts.[9]

During the war years, the network of salvation associations came into prominence first in the Viet Bac and later, farther south in Tonkin and along the coast of central Vietnam roughly from Nha Trang in the south to Danang in the north. In the south, they functioned essentially as underground clandestine groups because the French security forces were much stronger in Cochinchina, particularly around Saigon. The people who joined the salvation associations were not, technically speaking, part of the nation's armed forces except in the sense that in Giap's mind, as well as in that of the other Hanoi leadership, the army and the people "were one."

Every mass association was organized in a pyramidal structure: village associations elected one or two of their number to serve on district association committees; district associations elected members from their group to serve in provincial association committees, all the way up to the national level of the hierarchy. Each echelon had wide latitude to respond to issues and concerns within its territorial purview, but the national association issued general directives and policies down through the echelons, that is, from regional association to provincial, to district, and so forth. So it was that all the village associations were integrated into a national structure, controlled in the end by the Vietnamese League for National Salvation—in effect a governing body of all mass salvation organizations—tightly regulated by the Central Committee of the Communist Party.

The extent of each echelon's authority in operating within the Communist political infrastructure is unclear, and in many cases there were redundancies of authority and overlapping responsibilities. Even today, the Vietnamese have never explained clearly the chain of command or the exact distribution of responsibilities within the mass salvation associations. The redundancy ensured smooth functioning even when association leaders were killed or captured.

But the most important point to be made about the system was that it worked, and very well. The associations were responsive to changes in local areas and provided the senior leadership with excellent information on the ground throughout the country, enabling the central authorities to adapt their indoctrinational techniques and marching orders all the way down to the villages. It was an ingenious and highly effective system of political organization. And it was exceptionally resilient.[10]

Giap established his leadership skills in this work in the year between summer 1942 and summer 1943, when Uncle Ho was placed under arrest by Zhang Fakui in China because he was suspected of being a Communist operative. During his imprisonment, he was able to communicate with the Party leadership only intermittently.

It was sometime during 1943 that Giap received some devastating news. He had known that his beloved wife, Quang Thai, and her Communist operative sister, had been imprisoned in the French crackdown on the Communist party in 1939–1940, but he had been unable to contact them for more than two years. He now learned that his wife had died after suffering the tortures and depravations of a French prison. His sister-in-law had been summarily executed.

The revolutionary political and military apparatus continued to grow impressively throughout 1943 and 1944. Personal loss only strengthened Giap's resolve to accomplish the vital work that Ho had entrusted to him. As Giap recalled, "Our Southward March was steadily progressing. It drew in ever greater numbers of cadres and enjoyed an even mightier response from the youth. Hundreds of boys and girls in Cao Bang province left their families and took part in various armed shock-operative groups."[11]

The growth of the apparatus is all the more impressive when one considers that it occurred during a period of intense oppression. French patrols penetrated deep into the Viet Bac, issuing proclamations of reprisals against families whose members joined the Vietminh and offering handsome rewards to those who turned in guerrillas. "Many villages and hamlets were razed to the ground," recalled the future commander in chief long after the War of Resistance. "Those arrested who had revolutionary papers on them, were immediately shot, beheaded, or had their arms cut off and exhibited at market places."[12]

By early 1944, though, it was increasingly clear that the declining fortunes of the Japanese in the Pacific war and the impending fall of the Vichy collaborator government to de Gaulle's Free French organization would lead inevitably to a Japanese *coup de force* against the French in Vietnam. The long-awaited moment for the revolutionary forces to take up arms and attack the imperialist forces of the French and perhaps the Japanese— though how Japan would react was very much open to debate—seemed to be imminent. But when should the Vietminh take up arms? It would not be an easy decision to make.

At a conference of the Cao-Bac-Lang interprovincial committee (in effect the governing body of the Viet Bac) in July 1944, Giap was the driving force for a motion that called for taking up arms as soon as possible and fomenting at least a localized uprising in northern Tonkin. This was the rare case when Giap seems to have abandoned his penchant for extensive preparation for military action. The committee was generally receptive. After spirited debate, it approved a resolution to initiate the uprising by launching a guerrilla offensive in the Viet Bac within a couple of months.

Uncle Ho had not been able to attend the meeting. He was still interned in China. When he finally reached Vietminh headquarters in the Viet Bac in late August, he reversed the committee's decision. He gently but persuasively explained to Giap that his call for a regional uprising was premature. More work needed to be done to build up revolutionary fervor in the liberated zone and elsewhere. Giap recalled Ho's advice in a memoir: "Now, the period of peaceful development of the revolution is over, but that of the nationwide uprising has not yet begun...The present struggle must necessarily proceed from the political form to the military form. But for the time being more importance must be given to the political form."[13]

Ho went on to say, however, that the time was right to form a regular army of full-time soldiers recruited from across all Vietnam, out of the various guerrilla units that were operating more or less independently throughout the country, but most effectively in Tonkin. He entrusted this great honor to Vo Nguyen Giap. On December 22, 1944, Giap formed a single platoon of thirty-one men and three women, drawing on seasoned personnel from his own guerrilla units and others that had been operating in Cao Bang, Langson, and Bac Kan Provinces. This platoon was a fighting unit, but its primary responsibility was to move among the population, spreading the word, seeking recruits, and on occasion protecting unarmed political cadres in their work.

Two days after the first Armed Propaganda Unit was formed, the platoon, wielding ancient rifles, pistols, and machetes, successfully attacked two small French outposts manned by French officers and a handful of Vietnamese militia troops. The officers were killed, and the militia troops quickly surrendered to their countrymen. Giap later reflected on the creation of this first platoon as a turning point. After a bewildering series of name changes, this force became known as the People's Army of Vietnam—PAVN, or simply the People's Army. We shall refer to it as such for the remainder of the book.

And indeed it was a decisive turning point. These first [armed propaganda] units were set up during the upsurge of the people's armed *dau tranh* [struggle]. They were composed of Party members or revolutionary elements, highly conscious politically and carefully selected among members of the workers' and peasants' [mass] associations...and other revolutionary organizations. Their main activities consisted in carrying out armed propaganda and fighting to raise the masses' revolutionary spirit and encourage them to armed insurrection.[14]

Working with one or more district guerrilla platoons or companies, the first Armed Propaganda Units were designed to carry out political work, mobilizing the minds of villagers through public speeches and meetings and urging them to refuse to give rice and taxes to French forces, in addition to "repression of traitors, puppet notables and ruffians."[15] As it gained strength, the PAVN was to spearhead the Revolution in its fabled "March to the South." Since the Armed Propaganda Units and the guerrilla units that soon joined this fledgling national force placed a premium on building up combat strength rather than deploying regular units in battle, they usually attacked only when success was virtually guaranteed, and when the situation lent itself to recruiting disaffected indigenous militia members who were currently attached to the French Expeditionary Force (FEF). An operation resulting in the capture of a handful of modern weapons was more valuable than one that inflicted heavy casualties. In fact, during World War II Giap's army saw precious little combat. It trained rigorously, but outside of training, its work was predominantly political and organizational.

From the formation of the first platoon of the People's Army in December 1944 through August 1945, Giap worked with herculean effort to build the fledgling army; in doing so, he further refined his methods for waging protracted war through the dual pincers of *dau tranh*—armed struggle and political struggle. The pincers intertwined to create an extremely powerful and resilient social force that amounted to a great deal more than the sum of its parts. The dynamic cross-fertilization of political and military work during World War II would pay enormous dividends during the thirty years of war that lay ahead. "Significantly," scholar John McAlister points out,

it was the demands created by military preparation and operations which eventually offered the greatest stimulus to political mobilization. Through the physical mobilization of villagers into the nascent Viet Minh armed force, the coordination of local guerrilla efforts of village self-defense units, and organization of the [armed] propaganda units, the capacity of this structure was tested. Without the military threat posed by the French reoccupation, the Viet Minh would have had to devise other forms of participation and psychological motivation for the political mobilization of the village population. Moreover, as the military requirements of the Viet Minh increased, efforts were made to expand its local organizational capacity.[16]

In keeping with Communist doctrine, the People's Army's structure and training regimen evolved in accordance with changing circumstances. But from the very beginning, Giap instilled in his soldiers the notion that the army and the people must be inseparable and that political work among the people must be continuous. Mistreatment of civilians—stealing, or fraternizing with village women—was severely punished. To a far greater extent than in Western armies, the regular army in Vietnam depended on local civilians for sustenance, shelter, and intelligence on enemy activity.

Political indoctrination occupied more of a Vietminh soldier's training time than small arms tactics. The two missions of the army as given in official publications of the 1940s were, first, to spread propaganda among the people and attract recruits, and second, to wage armed struggle against the enemy. Giap himself was often heard to say that the soldier's work as a political agent was at least equal in importance to his work in combat.

When, on March 9, 1945, the Japanese, fearing that the French would turn against them as defeat loomed at the hands of the Allies, and hoping to improve their bargaining position when the war ended, staged a *coup de force,* killing, disarming, and imprisoning virtually all the French forces in Vietnam. Many outposts in northern Vietnam were deserted by French troops fleeing through the mountains toward China, and Japan declined to man these positions in the countryside with its own forces, thus creating a vast power vacuum on the ground in Vietnam and fueling revolutionary militancy in the countryside.

The ignominious defeat of a great Western power by an Asian military establishment that was itself about to be defeated in a world war was exactly what historian Fredrik Logevall says it was: a "pivotal moment" in Indochina, as "it dealt a blow to colonial authority from which it never fully recovered."[17] Giap at that time had only 1,000 full-time regulars in his People's Army, but he fully recognized that he had a golden opportunity to build up its strength and prestige.

The swell of militancy in the countryside in the wake of the coup was exacerbated by a devastating famine that struck northern Vietnam in late 1944 and early 1945, resulting in the deaths of at least 500,000 people. The Japanese refused to ship desperately needed rice from the south, and the French refused to release their own stores of hoarded rice to the Vietnamese people, heightening peasant desperation. Revolutionary forces were able to capitalize on this tragedy, as thousands of angry and starving peasants joined its ranks. In short, conditions were ideal to foment the long-anticipated uprising.

By April 1945, Giap's PAVN had reached Tran Tao in Bac Thai Province. There it linked up with Chu Van Tan's guerrilla units, which had been operating to the southeast of Giap near Bac Son. Tan's units, informally associated with Giap's PAVN, were now formally incorporated into the People's Army of Vietnam. At Tan Trao, the Central Committee of the Indochinese Communist Party established a Revolutionary Military Committee responsible for both "the political and military command of the resistance bases in north Viet Nam."[18] Giap was its senior officer. Chu Van Tan and Van Tien Dung, Giap's chief of staff in the American War, were the other members of the committee. In May 1945, Vo Nguyen Giap was promoted to commander in chief of the army, and the entire country was divided into seven resistance zones for military planning purposes.

The collapse of the French presence in the countryside proved a boon to Giap's campaign to expand the army as he consolidated Vietminh control over ever-larger swathes of territory in the Red River Delta. Around this time the six contiguous northern provinces of the Viet Bac were formally consolidated into a single "Liberated Zone." In June 1945, the PAVN's first infantry battalion of some 500 soldiers was formed. The People's Army was gaining in strength, expanding its capabilities to fight in engagements involving only a few platoons at once.

By July, it was clear to everyone on the ground that Ho and Giap had been correct in their thinking that the impending defeat of the Japanese in World War II would provide the ideal moment to launch the national drive to seize power. But it was equally clear, as William Duiker points out, that "due to the convulsiveness of events as well as the modesty of [Vietminh] military organization and cadres, emphasis [should still be] placed on psychological preparation of the population."[19] And indeed, Giap's mushrooming armed forces engaged in only perfunctory combat operations—so much so that even sixty years after the events Communist sources seldom mention a specific battle or location of sustained combat.

Throughout the summer of 1945, mobilization proceeded at break-neck speed. Wherever Liberation Army units marched, young men were recruited into village self-defense sections of twelve men each—these units were not technically part of the PAVN. Rather, they were one of the three types of forces developed to foment revolutionary fervor and defend the revolutionary political infrastructure within the villages. Typically each liberated village put forward five men for service in the full-time People's Army.[20]

In Cochinchina, where local fiefdoms, religious sects, and the Binh Xuyen, a sort of Vietnamese crime syndicate, controlled large pockets of terrain, revolutionary strength lagged behind that of the north. The southern revolutionists, too, lacked a large liberated zone or a major base area for conducting guerrilla operations and training. The Vietminh committee overseeing development of the movement in southern Vietnam operated for a variety of reasons with a high degree of autonomy, although it recognized Ho and the Central Committee as the senior leadership of the Revolution. Its initiatives were often judged to be too adventurous by the Central Committee in Tonkin. Still, as summer approached, revolutionary activity in Saigon and the Mekong Delta accelerated. In the cities in the south, clandestine liberation committees readied themselves for action in anticipation of Japan's defeat.

The American Office of Strategic Services (OSS) had established a friendly relationship with Ho and Giap in the last year of the war, exchanging small arms, radios, and a limited amount of war matériel in exchange for intelligence on the Japanese and the return of rescued American pilots who had been downed in their attacks on Japanese installations throughout Indochina. Both Ho and Giap formed warm personal contacts with American agents. They hoped to exploit those friendships in the negotiations concerning the fate of Indochina after the war ended.

On August 14, the Empire of Japan surrendered to the Allies. The next day the Japanese installed an "independent" government in Hue under Bao Dai, the titular emperor of Vietnam, but it was a hollow institution that simply added to the confusion that gripped the French as they looked on anxiously from Paris. Just a day earlier the Central Committee of the Indochinese Communist Party had called for a nationwide uprising and

the establishment of an independent republic under a provisional government dominated by Vietminh representatives, with some representation of
other nationalist parties. On the morning of August 17, Armed Propaganda
Units joined by special assault teams moved into the center of Hanoi. By
the end of the day, major government buildings in the capital had been
seized. Much to everyone's surprise, the Japanese put up very limited resistance, and that only in isolated locations on the approaches to Hanoi. The
frightened Vietnamese militia of Bao Dai's puppet administration assembled by the Japanese after the March coup put up no resistance at all. Many
dropped their weapons and joined the throngs of Vietminh supporters
flooding into the heart of Hanoi. Vietminh paramilitary forces took control of a meeting at the National Theater organized by the puppet regime
of Emperor Bao Dai, and within a few days, Bao Dai assented to Ho Chi
Minh's demand that he abdicate.

Soon, the crowd dispersed into the streets chanting, "Support the
Vietminh!" In Hanoi, at least, the Japanese troops remained stoic specta-
tors, as several hundred thousand people entered the city from the villages
and suburban towns. On the morning of August 19 Giap and his People's
Army troops, about 1,000 strong, marched into the city. On that day, for
the first time since 1873, Hanoi was under the complete control of the
Vietnamese people.

Elsewhere in the country, the seizure of power took a bit longer.
Within a week, most of the towns and cities were firmly under the control
of Vietminh liberation committees. The provisional government declared
September 2 a national holiday. A wave of excitement and joy swept over
most of the nation that day, and nowhere more than in Ba Dinh Square in
Hanoi, where Ho Chi Minh presided over a moving ceremony, famously
quoting the American Declaration of Independence as he declared his own
nation free of foreign domination. Uncle Ho concluded his remarks with
a question: "My fellow countrymen, have you understood?" Vo Nguyen
Giap, standing next to Ho on the rostrum, recalled that a million people
cheered in unison.

CONCLUSION

The complexity and fluidity of events in Vietnam beginning with France's
decision to outlaw the Communist Party in 1939 and continuing through

the fabled August 1945 Revolution posed enormous challenges to all politically active Vietnamese who sought to exploit the convulsions wrought by the Second World War. If the Communists' August Revolution was incomplete and open to challenge from the Allied occupation forces en route to the shores of Vietnam, it was nonetheless an extraordinary political and organizational achievement.

Of course, Ho Chi Minh was unquestionably the visionary, the father figure of steel will and humble manner who inspired millions. His extraordinary ability to work with potential rivals, even anti-Communists, to achieve his revolutionary ends stands out as the greatest individual contribution to the success of the August Revolution, an event the Vietnamese people celebrate to this day.

Next to Ho, however, Vo Nguyen Giap was surely the most important of the revolution's senior leaders. A sound argument can be made that he remained so during the next 25 years, as he built on the promise of his brilliant political and military organizational work during World War II, perfecting and applying a distinctive way of war that would baffle and defeat two advanced Western nations with military establishments that dwarfed his own. If Ho was the visionary, Giap was the driven politico-military captain. "Over time," historian Fredrik Logevall writes insightfully, Giap "made himself more and more the indispensable man—capable and efficient and ruthless in equal measure."[21] Over the next years, through all the trials and sorrows of a highly destructive war, Giap seldom left Ho's side. In the years to come, Giap's ferocious tenacity, his refusal to consider defeat despite seemingly insurmountable obstacles, served as the engine of the revolution's military power, and a symbol of the Vietnamese people's resolve to secure freedom through victory.

3

THE WAR OF RESISTANCE AGAINST FRANCE: 1945–1950

Amid the tumultuous upheaval and uncertainties that shook Vietnam between the end of World War II and the beginning of the War of Resistance against France in December 1946, Vo Nguyen Giap solidified his reputation as one of the Revolution's indispensable men. In looking back at his performance during this excruciatingly tense prewar phase of the struggle, one comes to understand why he was chosen to serve in the dual roles of commander in chief of the armed forces in the field and minister of defense. As the storm clouds of war swept across Indochina, Giap was at once a leading politician and diplomat, a creative military strategist, the chief practitioner of Vietminh strategy, and the architect of the army. Through a combination of prodigious energy and no small measure of ruthlessness, he succeeded admirably in all these roles.

POSTWAR DEVELOPMENTS AND THE RETURN OF THE FRENCH

The August Revolution confirmed definitively the Vietminh's claim to represent the self-determination movement in the eyes of the Vietnamese people. Whether Ho's government would be recognized as the legitimate authority in the nation after World War II by the world powers was another question altogether.

At the Potsdam Conference in the summer of 1945, the Allies had agreed that upon Japan's surrender, the British would occupy Vietnam south of the 16th parallel, disarm the Japanese, repatriate their forces, and maintain order. The Nationalist Chinese forces would do the same north of the 16th parallel. In southern Vietnam, the commander of British occupation forces, unfortunately for the Vietminh, was an ardent believer in colonialism and an unapologetic racist. General Douglas Gracey took his brief to mean that his division of Indian troops should oust the Vietminh upstarts from their positions of newly earned power, disavow Ho's claims of independence, and open the floodgates for the return of the French government and its army. Gracey's troops summarily freed the interned forces of the French and the Japanese. He then rearmed French soldiers, who were almost delirious at the prospect of pushing the Vietminh, who had disgraced their honor and seized their colony, out of the cities and towns and into the countryside by force of arms.

On September 21, 1945, mobs of French troops went on a wild rampage through the streets of Saigon, beating and killing scores of Vietnamese citizens and reserving their special wrath for the Communists, hanging several in gory public spectacles. On September 23, the French easily overpowered the lightly armed Vietminh militia security forces, occupied the government buildings, and hoisted the tricolor over Cochinchina's capital city. Although the Vietnamese people mark the beginning of the War of Resistance as December 19, 1946, it could well be argued that the revolution's first war for independence began on September 23, 1945, for the French action, coming after a week of seething emotion and political volatility, demanded a response.[1] The Vietminh obliged. Tran Van Giau, head of the Vietminh in southern Vietnam, who worked somewhat independently of the Central Committee in Tonkin, staged massive demonstrations and a strike. Finally, on September 25, Saigon exploded with what seemed like hundreds of attacks by armed Vietminh squads on French-manned buildings and neighborhoods throughout the city. Tensions had already reached a fever pitch, and the French section of Saigon, the Cité Hérault, was flooded with enraged Vietminh and their sympathizers. They began to massacre French nationals, women and children prominently among them, with antique rifles, pistols, and machetes. The killing persisted for several days before Gracey's forces restored order and disarmed the French once again.

On October 12, a powerful, 25,000-man French expeditionary force under Philippe LeClerc, spearheaded by an armored regiment, landed in Saigon and quickly removed the new government's officials from all public buildings. Charles de Gaulle, now installed with full powers in Paris, took a hard line. Minor concessions to the Vietminh might in time be negotiated, but for the time being, France was to reassert full authority. The French, with the aid of British forces and even some rearmed Japanese units, quickly went on the offensive and captured most of southern Vietnam's strategically important cities and towns, including the gateway to the Delta, My Tho, and Bien Hoa, the key communications and trading center in Vinh Long Province. Fighting was fierce with several hundred casualties on both sides, and the Vietminh fell back, but its forces quickly established themselves as tough, resilient fighters, "adept at withdrawing and regrouping, then, under cover of night, striking back."[2]

More than 150,000 Chinese troops had swarmed like locusts into northern Vietnam above the 16th parallel to take the Japanese surrender and maintain order. Instead, they pillaged the countryside instead, and Vietnam's centuries-long domination by China prompted Ho and Giap to see the removal of the Chinese as a more pressing issue than attempting to come to an understanding with the French. As Ho famously remarked at the time, "As for me, I prefer to sniff French shit for five years than eat Chinese shit for the rest of my life."[3] In any case, the Vietminh desperately needed time to build up their strength before they could hope to challenge France militarily. The French wanted the Chinese out of Vietnam just as much as the Vietminh. Working with the French to remove the Chinese bought the Vietminh time.

Demonstrating once again his ability to work with one adversary to achieve his ends against another, Ho worked closely with the French in fall 1945 to ease the Chinese out of the north. The French, for their part, wanted the Chinese to withdraw for the most obvious of reasons: they stood in the way of France's quest for reestablishing their colony in Indochina. The Chinese, more and more preoccupied with Mao's Communists in their own country, agreed to withdraw in spring 1946 in exchange for some economic and diplomatic concessions from France.

As the Chinese began their withdrawal and French forces began to pour into Tonkin, Ho and Giap turned their attention to the French. Vietminh soldiers resorted to the tactics that were their stock and trade throughout the next eight years: the well-executed ambush, extensive sabotage of the precarious bridges and roads that the French forces needed to maneuver, and general harassment and obstruction of French authority in whatever guise they encountered it.

A number of battalion-size engagements erupted between French and Vietminh troops, including a fierce nine-hour fight following a Vietminh ambush of a French convoy resulting in heavy casualties on both sides. These attacks occurred frequently enough to heighten feelings of resentment and distrust to the point where progress at the negotiation table became all but impossible. As the year progressed, it became increasingly clear that the yawning divide between the two governments was simply too great to be crossed. Intransigence was general on both sides, and good faith vanished in an endless cycle of accusations and counteraccusations.

While negotiations stalled, Ho and Giap worked feverishly to consolidate their power as the only voice for the people of Vietnam. The task of neutralizing potential nationalist rivals fell to Giap. How could this task be accomplished? Through the tried-and-true Communist method: discredit, discourage, and eliminate rival parties through any means necessary. The chief rivals of the Vietminh were the VNQDD and the Dai Viet parties. Until spring 1946, they had been protected by the Chinese occupiers, who had hoped to use them for their own purposes. Now that their protectors had departed, Giap launched a vicious and decidedly effective campaign of terror and intimidation against these groups. Specially trained Vietminh security units—in effect, Giap's secret police force—pounced on rival nationalist political figures and their chief adherents, killing several thousand and forcing others to flee north to China. The revitalization campaign cemented Giap's growing reputation for ruthlessness in the quest to consolidate Communist power. In Giap's eyes, dissenters, even if they were sincere patriots, were by definition traitors to be silenced for the good of the Revolution.

Already, the demands of preparation for war were beginning to transform the idealistic Vietminh front into a spartan Communist police state with an unstated policy of crushing all internal dissent. Even before the first sparks of fighting in Hanoi in December, recalled one Vietnamese nationalist, "there seemed to be no way of resisting Communism except by the unpalatable means of accepting French control, or the formation of a government inspired and beholden to the Paris master."[4]

Meanwhile, Giap stepped up the indoctrination and proselytizing program in the villages with a view to consolidating the Communist hold over the population. His success in the elimination campaign planted the seeds of his reputation in the many years of war to come. "Even his enemies, men who were notoriously anticommunist," observes historian Stein Tonnesson, "showed respect for him. They seemed to lose some of their aggressiveness when they were in his presence."[5]

Meanwhile, after six months of intransigence, on March 6, 1946, Ho and the French emissary, Jean Sainteny, signed a letter of understanding, hoping to avert war. Under the terms of the agreement, France would be permitted to deploy 15,000 troops in Vietnam for five years; to enjoy favored economic status in trade relations; and to maintain a permanent cultural presence throughout Indochina. For its part, France recognized the legitimacy of the Democratic Republic of Vietnam (the DRV, the formal name adapted by Ho's government) "as a free state having its own government, parliament, army and treasury, and belonging to the Indochinese Federation and the French Union."[6] Crucially, the French retained overarching political control of the Union—an organization akin to the commonwealth of Great Britain—and total control over Vietnam's foreign relations and armed forces.

More troubling for the new government was the failure of the letter of understanding to include Cochinchina as a part of the DRV. The French sought to maintain complete control there, offering to grant but a few cosmetic concessions for Vietnamese participation in its governance. Cochinchina was an integral part of Vietnam and had been so since time immemorial. A Vietnamese state without Cochinchina was completely unacceptable to either Ho's government or the Vietnamese people. In the end, the parties agreed to leave the status of Vietnam's most economically developed region temporarily unresolved. A plebiscite at a later date would decide whether it would join the DRV or enter into a separate agreement with France. In the eyes of the hardliners in the Communist Party the agreement was a nonstarter for obvious reasons. Soon thereafter, the governor of Indochina, a hardline reactionary named Admiral Thierry D'Argenlieu, enraged the Vietminh by unilaterally declaring Cochinchina an independent republic allied with France.

The fledgling government of the DRV was now between the proverbial rock and hard place. Ho's government desperately sought the help of allies on the international front and pressed forward with little hope of gaining critical concessions at conferences at Fontainebleau and Dalat with the French in summer and fall 1946. That fall, a frustrated and defiant Ho had an oft-quoted exchange with American correspondent David Schoenbrun. "How can you hope to wage war against the French? You have no army, you have no modern weapons. Why, such a war would seem hopeless to you," said the journalist. Ho's reply would be echoed time and time again by his commander in chief once the battle had been joined:

> No, it would not be hopeless. It would be hard, desperate, but we could win.…The spirit of man is more powerful than his own machines. It will be a war between an elephant and a tiger. If the tiger ever stands still the elephant will crush him with its mighty tusks. But the tiger does not stand still. He lurks in the jungle by day and emerges only at night. He will leap upon the back of the elephant, tearing huge chunks from his hide, and then he will leap back into the jungle. And slowly the elephant will bleed to death. That will be the war in Indochina.[7]

Giap's hopes of gaining the military and diplomatic support of the United States as a result of Vietminh cooperation with the OSS were soon dashed, in part due to the Americans' not-unfounded belief that a strong French presence in the Western coalition was an essential asset in the looming conflict against the Soviet Union known as the Cold War. Consistently throughout the War of Resistance, the United States supported France's effort to regain its hold over Vietnam, despite America's longtime advocacy of self-determination for colonized peoples. Mao, for his part, was too deeply engaged in civil war with Chiang's Nationalists to offer much help to his fellow Communists—at least for now.

THE MARCH TO WAR, STEP BY STEP

As the French Expeditionary Force (FEF) rose in strength to 100,000 men, including thousands of troops from France's African colonies and the units of the French Foreign Legion, Giap labored nonstop to build up Vietminh military power on the ground. Between September 1945 and the formal start of the War of Resistance in December 1946, Giap essentially doubled the size of the Vietminh's main base area in northern Tonkin, and established several other smaller bases in Tonkin, and along the coast in northern Annam. The regular army expanded from perhaps 5,000 to 50,000 troops, with 30,000 north of the 16th parallel, and about 50,000 trained guerrillas throughout Vietnam.[8]

Throughout the remainder of 1946, local French and Vietminh military units shared responsibilities for preserving order throughout the country, but their interactions were increasingly beset by misunderstanding and mistrust. In such a climate local commanders took matters into their own hands. Murders, ambushes, and atrocities were committed by both sides in the summer and fall of 1946. On September 24, an intense clash between Vietminh and French troops in Saigon degenerated into a riot. Enraged Vietnamese broke into the European sector of the city and killed 150 Western civilians, most of them French.

By early November, General Jean Valluy, the new FEF commander in chief, began contingency preparations for a major operation against Giap's forces in Tonkin. The operation's objective: to crush Giap's forces before they had a chance to redeploy from the environs of Hanoi to the Viet Bac. On November 20 he sent several units into Haiphong to seize control of the customs house along the waterfront, where Giap's troops had been collecting vital customs fees. More importantly, the Vietminh had been receiving critical arms shipments through Haiphong. Some Vietminh Tu Ve—local militia—apparently fired on the French and took one or more soldiers prisoner just as the French moved in on the customs office.

Hostilities quickly escalated. Valluy knew he would need control of the port in order to land fresh expeditionary forces for a mobile campaign in Tonkin. Accordingly, he ordered all Vietminh to evacuate the area around the port. A defiant Giap refused to budge. Valluy answered in a manner that French commanders, to their detriment, would repeat time and time again. On November 23, a French cruiser approached the port and bombarded the Vietnamese areas of the city indiscriminately, setting off a host of firefights all over the town, and leaving 6,000 civilians dead.

It took French reinforcements from the Red River Delta until November 28 to clear out the Vietminh units. Covered by militia and regional forces, Giap's regulars withdrew into the countryside with few casualties. "Although the French government in Paris seemed anxious to achieve a settlement [thereby averting war]," writes Duiker, "its representatives in Vietnam were taking matters into their own hands."[9]

The march toward full-scale war continued. Both sides took measures to strengthen their positions in Hanoi, twenty miles from the port of Haiphong. On December 7, Giap called on all militia and regional forces in the vicinity to prepare to launch attacks on French military installations and government offices within five days. Civilians joined Vietminh forces to prepare defensive positions throughout the city, constructing roadblocks and firing positions in buildings and digging tunnels to facilitate maneuvering out of the line of fire. Believing these forces could stand up against the French in Hanoi for perhaps a month, Giap made plans for the withdrawal of the main forces surrounding the city to the north and west, where he believed he could hold on in the countryside indefinitely. Meanwhile, more than 1,000 Legionnaires landed at ports in Tonkin and Annam in order to take the fight to the capital city.

On the night of December 18, the War of Resistance began with a Vietminh sapper team attack on Hanoi's main power station. The Tu Ve struck French outposts in many Vietnamese cities and towns that night. Urban fighting, typically fierce small unit clashes, erupted sporadically for the next two to three weeks in most cities; in Hanoi, the Vietminh regional forces put up a spirited defense until late January, suffering about 6,000 killed in action, but gaining time for Giap to withdraw his precious regulars. According to his protracted war paradigm, it was essential for these forces to avoid battle and remain in secure base areas for expansion and further training. Today, the Vietnamese celebrate December 19 as the anniversary of the outbreak of their War of Resistance against France.

VIETMINH DOCTRINE AND STRATEGY

A few days after the outbreak of hostilities, the Party's Central Committee issued a strategic directive, laying out their understanding of the war that was to follow. A theory, a way of thinking about how the war should unfold, was required to guide decision making. Giap himself surely had a strong hand in shaping the document, and his strategic thinking on the application of the three-stage model of protracted war in Vietnam, which he had been contemplating since Mao's lectures on the subject were published around 1938, is clearly in evidence in the directive itself.[10]

In the first stage, the revolutionary forces would find themselves on the strategic defensive. Base areas needed to be expanded and strengthened for training and sanctuary purposes; political work had to intensify in order to lay the groundwork for recruiting and intelligence networks. Meanwhile guerrilla units, still lightly armed, could harass the French forces' lines of communication through sabotage, ambush, and raids.

In stage two, the equilibrium stage, the French would reach their peak military strength and consolidate their hold on the cities and towns. Simultaneously, the Vietminh would shift gradually from the defensive to offensive operations by whole regiments, and then divisions, engaging in combat in places and times of their own choosing, grinding down French strength by protracting the conflict. Mobile operations by regular units would be coordinated with guerrilla warfare both within the enemy's rear—the areas under his control—and, to a lesser degree, in offensive campaigns.

The objective of military operations in this stage was not to gain and hold territory, but to force the French to disperse their forces into small units to conduct static defense duties. Once the FEF had been spread thin, they would be vulnerable to battalion and regimental attacks by Vietminh regulars. It was essential that PAVN units develop proficiency in hit-and-run attacks, in which units would disperse before the French could bring artillery or air power to bear. Then they could re-form as a complete unit at a prearranged point, typically in a remote area inhospitable to France's mobile armored groups and air attacks.

Stage three was called the counteroffensive. In theory at least, it culminated in the "general uprising," meaning the point at which the power of the people and the army together was so great that spontaneous rebellions would erupt all over the country.

By the third stage, the regular PAVN would have formed full divisions equipped with modern weapons, including artillery and engineers (in 1946 the PAVN was capable of fighting only at the battalion level of about 600 men in any one engagement) and would be sufficiently trained and seasoned to engage in sustained conventional warfare.

Truong Chinh, writing in *The Resistance Will Win* early in 1947, elaborated on the war strategy of the senior leadership, particularly on the thinking of Giap, who had co-authored with Truong Chinh a prominent book on the Vietnamese peasantry as a force in revolutionary politics. (Indeed, one finds passages in *The Resistance Will Win* that are virtually identical to Giap's earlier writings.) Chinh embraced Mao's doctrinal framework but took exception to his assertion that for protracted war to succeed, insurgents needed one vast sanctuary to develop regular forces and launch major multidivision (i.e., corps-level) campaigns. Vietnam was a small country, but its revolutionaries could compensate for its lack of terrain by developing a large number of small, isolated base areas through the kind of assiduous clandestine mobilization work that Giap's guerrillas had been conducting within villages and districts since 1940.

Mao believed that a successful insurgency could not rely on external developments or allies to win; revolutionaries ultimately had to build an army capable of defeating its adversary in conventional warfare using their own resources. Chinh joined Giap in believing that external factors, especially the growing strength of Communism in the world and the effect of prolonged military action on public opinion in France, could shape the direction of the war in all sorts of ways. Perhaps most significantly, *The Resistance Will Win* argued that in the end Vietminh military forces did not need to achieve clear superiority over French forces in order to achieve victory. Political factors within Vietnam and France, as well as international political trends, might very well result in French withdrawal. This could not be called a military victory in a conventional sense. But it would be a victory nonetheless, because it would mean that the war's objective had been reached.[11]

During the next six years of the War of Resistance, Giap would further refine and adjust Mao's theory of protracted war to reflect his reading of events on the battlefield, as well as the political and moral pressures at work on his own forces and those of the enemy. It is a remarkable tribute to Mao's paradigm, as well as to Giap's refinement of that paradigm, that the conflict, broadly speaking, followed the three-stage trajectory.

The application of the Mao-Giap doctrine would have failed if Giap had been intimidated by the vast superiority of the military forces he confronted. What explains his audacity, his refusal to be daunted and discouraged? A speculative answer, which is really the best we can do with the limited sources at hand, is that he saw the Revolution in almost religious terms and himself as the devoted apostle of Ho Chi Minh. He could brook no compromise and was always ready to die for the cause. A tireless exhorter and teacher as well as a general, he was also willing to give over the lives of his soldiers for the cause in ghastly numbers. He earned his reputation as a butcher, but he was a butcher who always believed that the ends of the Revolution justified horrendous casualties. After all, as Douglas Pike pointed out, Giap understood that people were his major weapon, not firepower.[12] And in war, one uses one's weapons to maximum effect. Therefore, they are essentially expendable.

Giap survived as the commander in chief of the PAVN by discerning with uncanny accuracy not only his own strengths and weaknesses, but also those of his adversary. For Giap, the three-stage model was no procrustean bed; it had to be applied to the war in Vietnam with confidence, discernment, and flexibility.

THE WAR OF RESISTANCE: THE FIRST PHASE

For the first nine months of the conflict, French operations were surprisingly restrained and cautious. FEF commander Valluy had only 40,000 troops at the outbreak of the war—too few in his view to undertake major offensives in the Viet Bac. There, under the watchful eye of Giap, the Vietminh were busily engaged in building up their military and political infrastructure. Meanwhile, Valluy contented himself with ousting the Vietminh from the towns and cities in the most populous regions of Tonkin—the Red River Delta and the coastal lowlands—and gradually re-establishing administrative control in the villages. This was called pacification. In the south, guerrilla fighting was the order of the day and continued to be so with a few exceptions throughout the war. The Vietminh never had the strength there to launch sustained campaigns by regulars.

Pacification operations in Tonkin were conducted by the "oil slick" method, meaning that French control extended outward from a central point, usually a city or a large town, in an irregular pattern. On a map, the areas of French control appeared something like an oil slick gradually expanding on top of the sea over time. Pacification operations worked as follows: Mobile units would clear out Communists from a particular district, set up small defensive posts, then move on and repeat the process in adjoining areas, leaving indigenous (and notoriously unreliable) Vietnamese troops under French control to man the district on a permanent basis.

The core purpose of pacification was to deny the Vietminh guerrillas and propaganda teams access to their critical sources of strength: the people and their provisions, particularly rice. As Mao famously put it, the "fish had to be kept out of the sea." The guerrillas had to be kept out of villages, away from the people.

In Cochinchina, French pacification efforts worked very well, as Giap's forces were weak and had only small sanctuaries from which to mount operations. In Tonkin and northern Annam, it was another story entirely. French gains were far more limited, and even those gains proved tenuous. Inside the Red River Delta and along the central coast, the nights belonged to the Vietminh, as cadres and soldiers alike crept silently into the village centers and began to do their proselytizing and recruiting. In this political work, they had been trained up to the highest standard, and they achieved impressive results. The percentage of territory under Vietminh control expanded slowly but steadily between 1947 and 1950, in large part due to the ever-growing number of guerrillas and political cadres coming down from the Viet Bac, many of whom had just finished their training in southern China.

France's response to the insurgency, much like that of the Americans who came after them, suggests a general failure among those at the highest levels of command to grasp the *political dynamics* of the war and the nature of the adversary. By 1948, the French, aware of their lack of popularity and legitimacy in the eyes of the population, had cobbled together an "independent and free" government under the former Vietnamese emperor Bao Dai. The old emperor was presented in French press releases and briefings as a legitimate alternative to the Vietminh. True, Bao Dai was an ardent patriot. But he had little of the common touch. He was dissolute, a playboy who loved wine, women, and the luxuries of Parisian life. His interest in the welfare of the peasantry of Vietnam was entirely perfunctory. Thus, the "state" of Vietnam, its seat of government in Saigon, had precious little legitimacy in the eyes of the population, or indeed, in the eyes of the world powers.

The French colonial administration itself made no serious effort to address the needs of the peasantry, or to provide them with some measure of political participation in their own affairs. Indeed, the people were exploited by French officers, abused by enlisted soldiers, and often made to feel like prisoners in their own villages. The best the ordinary peasant could hope for from the French colonial government, its civil or military arm, was indifference. The French reaction to advocates of political reform and progressive economic policies for Vietnam ranged from indifferent to hostile. Meanwhile, the Vietminh were intensely focused on cultivating the loyalty of the populace, in addressing their needs, in running literacy programs, in participating in village projects. And the cadres continually hammered away at the venality and indifference of the French.

From Paris to Saigon to Hanoi, the lion's share of French senior officers and colonial officials saw the Indochina war as one of low-intensity combat against resourceful bandits and insurgents. General Valluy and his officers were oblivious to the revolutionary nature of the struggle, and to the tenacity with which their adversary held on to both territory and the people's allegiance. What documentary evidence we have makes it clear that neither the French army nor the colonial administration in Saigon took Mao's ideas on protracted war seriously. In the eyes of the French command, Giap was only an amateur, given over to romantic notions of a Marxian utopia. The idea that he could wage a successful war against French general officers who had distinguished themselves during two world wars and sundry colonial campaigns in Africa was absurd, even preposterous. So it was that a combination of ignorance and arrogance pervaded the French command and its strategic decision making throughout the conflict.

General Valluy appeared particularly ignorant of his adversary. He confidently predicted in September 1947 that his expeditionary force "could eliminate all organized resistance in three months."[13] On October 7, 1947, he launched Operation Lea, the war's first major offensive, with some twenty battalions (15,000 troops) of the FEF. Valluy ordered an elite parachute battalion to drop on Vietminh headquarters in the mountains near Bac Kan with the intention of killing or capturing the senior leaders of the Vietminh. Meanwhile, mobile armored forces as well as amphibious troops would penetrate the heart of the Viet Bac along three axes, encircle the bulk of Giap's growing army of regular troops and his recruits in training among the limestone karsts and caves of the Viet Bac, and inflict sufficient casualties to render most of Giap's regiments and battalions ineffective— perhaps even extinguish the resistance entirely.

In dramatic fashion, the French paras landed directly on top of the Vietminh's headquarters, forcing Giap and Ho to seek refuge in a covered pit for several hours before making a harrowing escape by crawling into the jungle. Ho Chi Minh's mail was confiscated from his small field desk. Several German and Japanese army instructors, who for various reasons sought refuge with the Vietminh after the defeat of their own nations, were captured. Despite catching the Vietminh by surprise, the French force became bogged down and disorganized as they attempted to ferret out the PAVN's larger units in the difficult terrain around Bac Kan. Soon the jungle paths of the Viet Bac were littered with the corpses of French paras who died attempting to extricate themselves from slashing ambushes or to break through the Vietminh's prepared defensive positions. The hunters had become the hunted.

Meanwhile, the main FEF force of ten motorized battalions prepared to launch their attack from the east, marching northwest into the heart of the Viet Bac along a narrow road in the middle of mountainous terrain. Repeatedly ambushed by Vietminh guerrillas and stalled by blown bridges, the French took six full days to reach Giap's outer defense positions ten miles north of the town of Bac Kan. There the Vietminh main force units took heavy casualties, but they fought with resolution and bravery, gaining the respect of professional French soldiers and Legionnaires. The main task force never succeeded in rescuing the paras, many of whom stumbled out of the dense jungles in groups of three or four exhausted men.

A French river-borne amphibious attack force attempted to partially encircle the Vietminh base area from the southeast. It, too, bogged down, first on river sandbars and then against increasingly stiff resistance in the dense jungle near Tuyen Quang. Finally the two pincers of the attack—the amphibious force and the motorized one—met at Chiem Hoa, more than one hundred miles inside the Viet Bac. "The main Communist redoubt in Indochina had become a vast pocket [meaning it was surrounded by enemy forces in every direction except the north] but...in this kind of war and that kind of terrain, the term 'encirclement' was of course totally meaningless," writes Bernard Fall, perhaps the greatest contemporary reporter-scholar of the war. "Between the towns and key points the French now garrisoned...there were vast stretches where the Viet-Minh regiments could slip through, and did."[14] Giap's forces suffered perhaps 3,000 casualties, but they had gained invaluable experience against French conventional operations.

Operation Lea failed to achieve its objectives. So did Operation Ceinture ("Belt"), an attempt to destroy PAVN Regiment 112, the elite "Capital" Regiment that would soon form the heart of Giap's "Iron" Division—the 308th. Operation Ceinture was a major land-sea-air effort involving an attack by eighteen French battalions against the southern edge of the Viet Bac. The FEF succeeded in besting the PAVN in several sharp engagements, prompting Giap to break off contact and retreat to his sanctuaries in the mountains. The PAVN surrendered a number of small supply depots on the Viet Bac's perimeter, but they were expendable.

In late December 1947, the French pulled their mobile units out of the Viet Bac, leaving behind lightly defended garrisons to man a string of old forts along the China-Vietnam border. The forts, however, were not in close enough proximity to one another to be mutually supporting. Therefore, they were all vulnerable to attack by a superior Vietminh force. But Valluy didn't believe Giap's forces could ever mount a sustained and coordinated attack by a force as large as even one regiment.

By early 1948, the PAVN was growing at an impressive rate in both size and skill, while the French command seemed to fall back on the defensive. French support at home for the "dirty war" (as it was called by the French Left) was already beginning to falter, albeit slowly, and the government refused to send reinforcements in the numbers requested by Saigon.

In light of these developments, Giap began to increase guerrilla operations and clandestine organizational work in the Red River Delta aggressively. He also continued to professionalize and expand the PAVN, adding new training camps, and expanding his control in the north well beyond the Viet Bac into some strategic areas in the Red River Delta.

In frustration, the French soldiers inside the Red River Delta coined a new term to describe the slow but steady breakdown of government authority at the hands of the Vietminh cadre: *pourissement*. It meant "rotting away."[15]

GENERAL CARPENTIER ARRIVES

A new French commander, Lieutenant General Marcel Carpentier, arrived in Saigon in the summer of 1949. He possessed a superb combat and command record over two world wars. He claimed to know little about Indochina, but he was well aware that the steady increase in guerrilla attacks in the Red River Delta was a very ominous development. Even as the size of the FEF grew steadily toward 150,000, French troops were spread perilously thin in static defense duties. This severely restricted Carpentier's ability to launch mobile offensive operations against Giap's largest units at the time—his regiments. These early problems would dog the French as the war dragged on. As Bernard Fall observed, "Once full-scale hostilities had broken out, the French, for budgetary and political reasons, could not…make the large-scale effort necessary to contain the rebellion within the confines of small-scale warfare."[16]

Realizing that another massive offensive operation like Lea was unlikely to inflict serious damage on the enemy, Carpentier focused on the same sort of pacification operations that had dominated the early phase of the war. His maneuver battalions (that is, mobile offensive as opposed to static defense forces) could usually clear out Giap's guerrillas and cadres from a cluster of villages, or even a whole provincial district. Yet the government's "control" was both evanescent and cosmetic. The French never had enough troops to garrison the newly won ground and respond effectively to Giap's roving guerrillas as they struck small posts and communication lines.

Meanwhile, the Vietnamese who had joined the fledgling French-led Vietnamese national army were dependably undependable. Desertions were general, and the maneuver forces, such as they were, lacked the critical ingredient in all military organizations: fighting spirit.

On the other hand, Giap and his cadres offered the villagers something they had never had in nearly one hundred years of French rule—a sense of belonging to something important, a national crusade for self-determination, and a bright future in which every soul, even women and children, played an important role. Whether hostile or indifferent to colonial rule, most villagers could not be coerced into providing intelligence on Vietminh operatives to the French, and so, sooner or later, even in villages where political cadres had been caught and killed, the Vietminh returned, and re-established control, whether covert or overt. In the War of Resistance, as in the American War, Giap seldom lacked highly motivated, well-trained replacements. When the French planned to return to a district or village, Vietminh operatives were usually tipped off and faded into the countryside until the threat had passed. In describing this phase of the war in Tonkin, Giap wrote:

> Realizing the war was being prolonged, the enemy changed their strategy. They used the main part of their forces for "pacification" and for consolidating the already occupied areas…They gradually extended their zone of occupation in the North and placed under their control the major part of the Red River delta…. [w]e then advocated the wide development of guerrilla warfare, transforming the [enemy's] rear into our front line. Our units operated in small pockets, with independent companies penetrating deeply into the enemy-controlled zone to launch guerrilla warfare, establish bases, and protect local people's power. It was an extremely hard war generalized in all domains: military, economic and political. The enemy mopped up; we fought against mopping up. They organized supplementary local Vietnamese troops and installed puppet authorities; we firmly upheld local people's power, overthrew straw men, eliminated traitors, and carried out active propaganda to bring about the disintegration of the supplementary forces. We gradually formed a network of guerrilla bases. On the map showing the theater of operations, besides the free zone [the Viet Bac], "red zones," which ceaselessly spread and multiplied [Vietminh-controlled zones], began to appear right in the heart of the occupied areas.[17]

Between early 1948 and September 1950, neither the French nor the Vietminh attempted to engage in major conventional operations. On the Vietminh side the fighting was conducted by regional guerrillas and a limited number of operations by regular PAVN battalions operating independently of the regiments to which they belonged. These operating battalions typically broke down into companies of about 150 men who planned and executed raids or ambushes of short duration. These were the "fighting forms" Giap favored in stage two of the people's war.

Giap's forces invariably returned to Communist base areas after a period of sustained combat operations. As the war ground on, new base areas emerged, most of them on the fringes of population centers. The majority were small, often little more than a cluster of villages. A prominent student of Giap's fighting methods aptly describes the characteristics of a typical base area as "a closely integrated complex of villages prepared for defense [containing] a politically indoctrinated population in which even children have their specific intelligence tasks; a network of food and weapons dumps; an administrative machine parallel to that of the legal authority, to which may be added at will any regular [army] unit assigned to operations in the area."[18]

BUILDING UP THE PEOPLE'S ARMY

Throughout the first three years of the War of Resistance, Giap worked assiduously to expand and improve all three echelons of the revolution's military forces and the political infrastructure that sustained them. And he had to do this while simultaneously frustrating the efforts of tens of thousands of French troops to pacify the Vietnamese population with the limited operational forces at his disposal. This expansion would not have been possible without the conflation of disciplined military and political activity across ever-widening swathes of territory from the Mekong Delta to the Chinese border, a process that was spearheaded in large measure by small Armed Propaganda Teams ranging from a section of eight to ten men (a squad in American parlance) to a platoon of about thirty men (and sometimes women).

As early as 1941, the senior leadership of the Indochinese Communist Party understood that independence could not be achieved without the creation of a full-time, regular army that was equipped with standardized modern weapons, both infantry and artillery, along with engineers, logistical support, and technical specialists. That army, given the nature of the Vietnamese terrain and economic and social structure, needed the support of militia. The most basic militia unit consisted of untrained peasants, including women. Their role was strictly defensive and informational, i.e., they provided intelligence on government activities and offered very limited resistance against French patrols near their villages. The other type of local militia, often of platoon size, had limited military training and was capable of cooperating with the regional units—the second-tier military forces of the revolutionary armed forces. Regional units were typically companies or battalions, trained well enough to plan and execute sabotage and ambush operations. The PAVN regulars, the full-time fighters, would assume greater and greater importance as the war progressed toward stage three of protracted war, the counteroffensive stage. Their role was to engage big-unit combat operations of significant complexity, typically of battalion and regimental size and, beginning in late 1950, division level.

As Giap began to plan for regimental-size operations around 1949, it was clear that his regular army had to continue its expansion, its potpourri of out-of-date small arms had to be replaced, and new heavy weapons, especially mortars and recoilless rifles, had to be integrated into their units. Despite the enormity of the challenge, between the outbreak of war in 1946 and mid-1949, Giap transformed a poorly armed, loosely organized regular force that was formed into battalions into a first-class light infantry force of five 10,000-man infantry divisions, each of which had its own small artillery, antiaircraft, engineer, and logistics elements. In 1949, these divisions lacked a full complement of the weapons and specialists they were meant to have on paper, but they were functioning divisions nonetheless. This was a major achievement, considering that it occurred in a time of general war.

This leap in organizational development had implications of enormous importance, as General Phillip Davidson, an American officer who served with distinction in the Vietnam war, explains: "In every modern army, the division is the basic operational formation, the smallest unit to combine all ground arms, to maintain itself, and to fight independently if need be. In the history of every developing army, the advance to the divisional structure is the move from the minor leagues of warfare into the 'the majors.'"[19] The distinguishing characteristics of the Vietminh's regular army were its high level of esprit, its extraordinary mobility in jungle and mountainous terrain, and, once it began division-level operations in late 1950, its capacity to endure severe hardship and heavy losses while retaining its effectiveness in combat.

While the senior strategists of France and the US advisers who joined them in 1950 continuously underrated Giap's strategic acumen and the capabilities of his army, the junior officers and enlisted men who fought against Communist Vietnamese regular troops and guerillas over thirty years did not. The consensus among Western combat infantrymen was that their adversaries were well trained, tenacious, and resourceful. Much of the credit for their excellence surely lay in the intensive indoctrination sessions and ideological education that soldiers underwent throughout their time in service. Few armies in the twentieth century possessed such unity of purpose and commitment as the People's Army of Vietnam, and certainly no army built on an agrarian peasant base came even close. One of Giap's cardinal principles, perhaps his *first* principle, was that military training had to produce soldiers who understood the nature of the war, and the nature of the enemy, with one mind, one type of "political consciousness." "Correct thinking" was far more important than firepower. Giap was a relentless and passionate advocate of political education within the army. He himself wrote or co-wrote many of the pamphlets and training manuals used by instructors during both wars for independence.

In Giap's mind, political indoctrination remained the only surefire way to compensate for the inevitable material disadvantages the PAVN fought under when engaging professional Western military establishments. "Profound awareness of the aims of the Party, boundless loyalty to the cause of the nation and the working class, and a spirit of unreserved sacrifice are fundamental questions for the army," Giap wrote in 1959. "Therefore, the political work in its ranks is of first importance. *It is the soul of the army.*"[20]

Studies conducted by the Rand Corporation and the American intelligence establishment during the American War make it clear that the average officer in the PAVN knew little about Marxist Leninism's vision of a classless society. It is safe to assume this held true for the soldiers who fought in the War of Resistance as well. Political education within the PAVN was far more concerned with instilling a commitment to one's fellow soldiers, to the army as a whole, and to the Party as a vehicle for national liberation. Giap's success in building an effective army is all the more remarkable when one considers that the average Vietnamese recruit entered army service with little education, no experience with "team building" activities such as team sports, a distrust of outsiders, particularly strangers who exercised authority, and virtually no experience with the world outside his or her home village.

The main force units consisted mainly of men who had received some military training in the village militia and/or regional forces before they were promoted into the regular army. PAVN training of regular infantry units was similar to that of Western forces. Close-order drill and small-unit tactics took up much of the recruit's time at first. Later, great emphasis was placed on camouflage and concealment—far more so than in US Army or Marine training during the same era. And unlike regular French and American infantry, the Vietminh soldiers were well trained in night operations.

A unique feature of PAVN's approach to war concerned its extensive logistical preparation. Western forces on the offensive are typically supplied via motorized vehicles from the rear, or from the air. PAVN supply officers, however, developed ingenious ways of preparing a battlefield and its approaches with supplies and fortifications *before* the arrival of maneuver forces. This required superb planning and highly disciplined bunker and supply depot construction units, often working under sustained time pressure.

Combat operations in Giap's regular army were exceptionally well rehearsed. Soldiers in tactical units were typically briefed on their mission in detail in classrooms around a sand table. Carefully choreographed "walk throughs" of maneuvers within training camps followed. For major assault operations, the PAVN often built replicas of installations and fortifications they could expect to meet in combat.

Statistics concerning the size and makeup of the PAVN in the early years of the War of Resistance are scarce and remain rough estimates. Australian historian Robert O'Neill offers a reasonable estimate that the main forces expanded from 32 battalions of about 600 men each in 1947, to 117 battalions in 1951.[21] Most of those battalions were, of course, composed of infantryman. Perhaps 15 percent were light artillery, combat engineer, and supply units. More specialized units were formed toward the end of the conflict.

The PAVN lacked standardized small arms at the beginning of the French Indochina War, possessing a motley assortment of French, Japanese, American, and Chinese weapons secured during and after World War II. Until the People's Liberation Army of Communist China (the PLA) began to supply weapons and war matériel in limited quantities in 1949, the PAVN had to make do with a handful of 37mm antiaircraft guns and 75mm field howitzers as heavy weapons, but they were able to produce primitive mortars, hand grenades, and small arms ammunition in makeshift armories within the Viet Bac from around 1947 on. No Western army could function with such a limited supply of heavy weapons and no aircraft support whatsoever. No responsible Western commander would have initiated operations with such limited assets.

Everyone within Vietminh-controlled territory was part of Giap's resistance machine. The entire country was divided during the war into approximately a dozen military zones—their boundaries and number changed over time—each of which had its own command group, as well as sub-commands at the provincial and district levels. Giap, of course, had final authority over major combat operations in all the military zones, but his subordinates in the field had the authority to revise and reverse plans depending on the ebb and flow of battle.

Giap's general staff was initially organized on the American model, with four core functional divisions: personnel, intelligence, operations, and logistics. In the latter stages of the war, it was reorganized along the more byzantine and redundant lines of Mao's PLA, where Party and military responsibilities overlapped in a way that is difficult for an outsider to decipher. As in many Communist armies, each echelon from division down to company level had a political officer, or commissar, who looked after morale and political training, in addition to a military commander who was responsible for operations and the combat readiness of his troops.

At the beginning of 1947, 50,000 political cadres were actively working within towns and villages throughout the country with a heavy concentration in Tonkin and Annam. A year later that number had risen to over 100,000.[22] How they fit into the army scheme of organization is unclear. They might have worked in close cooperation with the army commissars, or they might have been formally attached and under the command of those commissars.

Specialist and technical officers were in desperately short supply during the first half of the War of Resistance. Giap's first officers had received limited staff training with either the Nationalist Chinese army—which was at various junctures friendly to the Vietminh during World War II—or the PLA.

Until late in 1950, the PAVN had little in the way of motor transport. The logistical system depended on the resources Giap had in hand: people, reinforced bicycles, and pack animals. Porters were conscripted from the civilian population to ferry food, ammunition, and heavy weapons from one battlefield to another. It took anywhere from two to four porters to transport food, heavy weapons, and other supplies for one infantryman.[23] By the time Giap launched his first major military offensive in the fall of 1950, he had expanded Vietminh regular and regional forces to 250,000 soldiers, not including porters.

With the sage guidance of Ho Chi Minh and Truong Chinh, Giap developed a highly nuanced and sophisticated understanding of how to use socio-political activity—organization, mobilization, and thought control or "consciousness raising"—to focus the energies of the entire population under Vietminh control on achieving the Revolution's objectives. Taken together, these techniques of political *dau tranh* allowed Giap to mobilize an astonishing amount of on-going human activity, choreographed in minute detail, toward (1) building an alternative society and government, marked by revolutionary fervor, high morale, and unity of purpose as defined by the senior leadership; and (2) the breakdown of the legitimacy of the colonial puppet government in the eyes of the entire country. Thus, political *dau tranh* was at once a constructive and a corrosive activity. In the apt words of Douglas Pike, the essential concept of *dau tranh* is

> people as an instrument of a war. The mystique surrounding it involved the organization, mobilization and motivation of people....Violence is necessary to it but is not its essence. The goal is to seize power by disabling the society, using special means [i.e., assassination, propaganda campaigns, sabotage], chiefly organizational. In fact, organization is the great god of *dau tranh* strategy and counts for more than ideology or military tactics. The basic instrument is a united front [the Vietminh, that is], an organization of organizations, casting a vast web over the people, enmeshing them.[24]

By around 1950, the Party had organized the "struggle movement" at various levels of development in virtually every province and city in Vietnam. It was strongest in northern Tonkin, along the coast of Annam, and northwest of Saigon. The movement exerted great psychological and social pressure on the entire population in Vietnam—including French civilians and soldiers, colonial troops of African origin, and those Vietnamese who supported the French—to accept the Party's perceptions of "reality," especially its assertion that protracted war would inevitably lead to discouragement and disillusionment of the French Expeditionary Force (FEF) and the collapse of its malevolent designs of re-conquest.

According to Pike, the expansion of the Vietminh, and later the Vietcong infrastructure in the American War, was accomplished through three "action programs." The Binh Van program was directed at the colonial government's officials and soldiers, particularly the Vietnamese, Algerians, and Moroccans who fought in the FEF. The areas under colonial control were flooded with printed propaganda, radio broadcasts, and literally millions of face-to-face clandestine meetings by Vietminh political cadres with those in the enemy camp, or the families of those individuals. Many colonial agencies and military units were penetrated by Vietminh agents who engaged in sabotage and disinformation. The goal: induce defection or at least desertion. Armed propaganda units reinforced these efforts with selective assassinations and threats of terror.

Dich Van was directed not only at ordinary villagers under colonial control, but also at the people of France and the rest of the world following the events in Vietnam. Here newspapers and government-issued communiqués tried to sell the war as a "David versus Goliath" struggle for self-determination and independence. Emissaries were sent abroad to speak on behalf of the Revolution and gain notable allies in the West.

The Dan Van program worked to build the morale and consciousness of the people already under the control of the Vietminh as well as the Vietminh armed forces. Self-criticism meetings and a wide array of cadre-led classes kept alive the flame of revolutionary fervor by drenching the populace with tracts, slogans, demonstrations, and mandatory political education classes. Party members kept a watchful eye on all participants in order to ferret out and correct "deviations" in thought or speech.

The reader will have to judge for himself how much of a factor the political struggle movement played in shaping the course of the two major wars in which Giap commanded the People's Army of Vietnam. It seems certain, however, that Giap thought it critical: The conflict was carried out, he writes,

> by the entire people, a total war. A revolutionary war, because it was carried out on the basis of mobilization and organization of the masses....The people's war generally takes place in conditions where our side enjoys absolute political superiority over an enemy materially stronger than we are...Our military art has determined the following strategic orientation: to promote a war by the entire people, a total and protracted war. We have to wage a long war in which our political superiority will prevail, and we can gradually increase our strength, change the balance of forces between us and the enemy, and ensure victory for our side.[25]

Giap continually sought to exploit a perennial theme of political *dau tranh*: that the Vietnamese people have a unique genius for overcoming adversity in their struggle against foreign domination, that their martial success against China, the Mongols, and the Cham people who occupied much of Cambodia for centuries was achieved not through innovations in military technology or superior numbers but through patience, resilience, and the mobilization of their mystical moral strength and unity of spirit. The Vietnamese Communists, Pike observes, "were the first [people in modern war] to break with the assumption that the principal and primary test of success must be military combat. They realized, dimly at first and then with increasing clarity, that *it might be possible to achieve a change of war venue and determine its outcome away from the battlefield.*"[26]

THE EMERGENCE OF THE PEOPLE'S REPUBLIC OF CHINA

By November 1949, Mao's People's Army had thoroughly vanquished Chiang Kai-shek's Nationalist army and formally established the People's Republic of China (PRC). The emergence of a Communist state in the world's most populous country had immense implications for Cold War politics and the War of Resistance in Vietnam, because the war in Vietnam quickly came to be seen in America and France as a Cold War conflict *as well as* an anticolonial struggle. Before the year was out, the PRC sent a number of senior officers into the Viet Bac to discuss the formation of an extensive military assistance program. Giap, of course, played a central role in shaping the program. In mid-January 1950 China formally recognized the DRV. Other socialist states, including the Soviet Union, soon followed suit. This recognition lent the revolutionary administration a degree of legitimacy it had heretofore lacked. The status of Ho Chi Minh, writes one historian, "changed almost overnight from that of a hunted guerrilla leader into a communist statesman struggling to free his country from an imperial power."[27]

In June 1950 Giap traveled to Nanning, where he reached an agreement establishing training camps and a new all-weather road (meaning it was passable in all but the worst of the monsoon season) network between southern China and northern Vietnam, built by more than 100,000 Chinese nationalist prisoners, to facilitate the transport of troops and heavy weapons into Vietminh base camps.

Even before the PRC had achieved complete victory over the American-supported Nationalists, a steady flow of Giap's regular force noncoms and officers had trekked north to camps in areas of China controlled by the

Communists. There they received intensified political education and instructions. Giap saw to it that they were trained to handle communications equipment and heavy infantry weapons, including recoilless rifles, large-caliber mortars, and machine guns. The PAVN were given tens of thousands of submachine guns and American M-1 semiautomatic rifles—the latter being a first-class modern infantry weapon. Giap knew that for close-in, human-wave assaults, these reliable infantry weapons were essential to success against the FEF. Over the course of the next two years, Chinese weaponry, matériel, and military expertise boosted PAVN's logistical and combat power astronomically.

Giap and theorist Truong Chinh had long been keenly aware of the potential impact of international developments on the war in Vietnam. They were also well aware that the arrival of Communism on the scene in China could have negative as well as positive ramifications. One such consequence might be an effort by the PLA to dominate Vietminh strategy and training, using their massive material support as leverage. In addition, US foreign policy was anchored in the doctrine of containment of Communism; now that China was indeed Communist and was lining up behind the Revolution in Vietnam, American military intervention became very much a live option. Certainly Washington could be counted on to provide vast material support for the French war effort. As we shall see, it did so.

In early February 1950 the Truman administration formally recognized the pro-French government of Bao Dai and allocated $15 million in military aid to that government to conduct the war effort. In fact, Bao Dai's regime had no leverage, and all US aid was dispersed by the French high command. Bao Dai's "government" also served to cover and distort the US role, for it allowed the Americans to claim it was not supporting a colonial war, but a war for freedom against the dark forces of world Communism. The Vietminh, so the American rationale went, were seeking to crush democratic government in Indochina at the behest of the Communist Chinese. Given the dynamics of domestic politics in the United States, the Truman administration had little choice but to come to France's aid in its struggle against Communism in Indochina. Thus, the seeds of another Vietnamese war were planted long before the French demise in the War of Resistance. Soon after Mao's ascent to power, a formal US military advisory group was established in Saigon.

Giap now had two strong incentives to go on the offensive: looming American intervention, and plentiful Chinese help in prosecuting the war. By this point a major re-evaluation of French strategy by Army Chief of Staff General Georges Revers had leaked to the Vietminh, causing a major scandal in Paris, suggesting, as it did, the dexterity of the Vietminh's intelligence agencies in both Vietnam and Paris. It also further polarized French politics into those on the left who wished to negotiate a settlement with Ho in an increasingly costly conflict, and those on the right who clung tenaciously to the belief that France's prestige and national interests were best served by vanquishing its colonial adversaries. The French public's support for the war, always lukewarm, was beginning to disintegrate.

The Revers Report called for the evacuation of the FEF's string of forts along the northern border with China. They were simply too vulnerable to attack and difficult to supply. Revers called for the rapid buildup of the Vietnamese national army to free up the FEF for a new offensive and a graduated shift in French policy from military operations to direct negotiations with the great powers and the Vietminh. The French government waffled, as it so often did in a war it never clearly understood, unsure which way to turn. Giap believed his main forces were ready to strike a major blow against France when the rainy season waned in September 1950, and he prepared accordingly. Not yet forty years of age, observes Logevall, "with prominent cheekbones and deep-set eyes, he had about him a reserved and unassuming air that masked a steely determination...he would become a profoundly important factor in the revolution's success—a largely self-taught military commander who oversaw the forces that took on first the mighty French and then the even mightier Americans. Only Ho himself was more responsible for the ultimate success of the Revolution."[28]

4

THE BORDER OFFENSIVE OF 1950: GIAP'S FIRST VICTORIES

A s the French Indochina War entered its fourth year, foreign policy experts in the East and the West eyed the conflict warily as a potential flashpoint for another world war should the Chinese or the Americans enter the fray directly. With the outbreak of conflict in Korea in June 1950, the first "hot" war of the Cold War, and then the direct intervention of the PLA five months later against UN (primarily US) forces, the United States, slowly but surely, began to see Indochina through the prism of the monolithic struggle between Communism and democracy.

Accordingly, the floodgates of American military aid and advice opened wide—ostensibly to the Vietnamese government of Bao Dai, but in reality to Paris and its expeditionary force. The French, for their part, were beginning to realize that substantial US aid was indispensable if they were to win the war against Giap and the Vietminh. But they found the strings attached to that aid unpalatable, to say the least. Washington exerted increasingly intense pressure for a definitive result: defeat the enemy on the battlefield, or reach a settlement congenial to the West at the negotiating table.

Meanwhile, the American military sought direct access to the FEF's commanders with a view to convincing the command to adapt American strategies and tactics on the ground. From 1950 forward, the United States exercised more and more influence on the direction of the war, but unlike the Chinese-Vietminh relationship, there was sustained ill will and conflict between the Americans and the French, who saw their US allies as naïve interlopers in their war.

As the French and the Americans bickered and much of the new American military matériel throughout 1950 was siphoned off by corrupt colonial functionaries or lay unused in French bases, tons of Chinese advisers flooded into the Viet Bac. As the year progressed, the Vietminh inventory of artillery grew steadily: scores of American 75mm howitzers and a handful of highly effective 105mm guns and antiaircraft weapons were captured from the Chinese Nationalists' stockpiles of deserted military stores. Heavy weapons captured from the Americans in Korea made their way into PAVN artillery units as well. Every bit as important as these modern weapons were PLA-supplied field radios and signal equipment that Giap needed to carry the fight to the enemy on a larger scale. Without them, it would be nearly impossible to effectively coordinate operations involving regiments and divisions.

Giap's PAVN was growing in numbers and power up in the Viet Bac. China supplied each of Giap's divisions with 40,000 porters, greatly enhancing the mobility and range of his regulars. An untold number of military advisory teams made their way to Giap's headquarters to aid in planning and executing large-scale operations as well as training.[1] Between 1950 and the end of the war, it has been estimated that Mao's China provided the Vietminh with 40,000 tons of weapons and military supplies.

In early 1950 Giap's critical opportunity appeared to be at hand. "Now," he wrote, "we are going to pass from the defensive to the offensive by means of a war of movement. In the impending counteroffensive our troops will have to surround the enemy, strike right home to the vital center....It is essential that within a few months, the last bases of colonialist resistance [in northern Tonkin] should be liquidated."[2]

Giap and the other senior leaders of the Vietminh clearly saw that they were on the verge of a critical shift in the nature of the conflict.

After a few preliminary operations to test its mettle before the monsoon season arrived in May, the PAVN would engage in a sustained offensive against an eighty-mile string of remote FEF bases strung out along Route Coloniale 4 (RC4), close to the Chinese border, between Cao Bang in the north and Langson to the south. The FEF had only 10,000 troops between Cao Bang and Langson. Whole Vietminh regiments would be deployed along this ribbon of poorly maintained road. The Vietminh commander in chief hoped he could not only take the bases in lightning-fast mass attacks, but also rip into the FEF's rescue convoys to the forts, for there was no other quick way to get additional boots on the ground but up RC4. His troops were sufficiently trained by this point to attack hard and fast and then disperse into the jungle-covered mountain ridges above the road.

Later on in his career, Giap spoke of this kind of fighting as "mobile war," operations "retaining certain characteristics of guerrilla warfare... involving regular campaigns with greater attacks on fortified positions."[3] The transition to mobile warfare, Giap argued, did not lead to the abandonment of guerrilla fighting. On the contrary,

> there must be close and correct co-ordination between these forms of fighting to be able to step up the Resistance War, wear out and annihilate bigger enemy forces, and win even greater victories. This is another general law in the conduct of [protracted] war.... The conduct of the war must maintain a correct ratio between the fighting forms. At the beginning, we had to stick to guerrilla warfare and extend it [throughout the country]. Passing on to a new stage, as mobile warfare made its appearance, we had to hold firm the co-ordination between the two forms, the chief one being guerrilla warfare; mobile warfare was of lesser importance but was on the upgrade. Then came a new and higher stage, [in which] mobile warfare moved to the main position, at first only on one battlefield—the local counteroffensive came into being—then on an ever wider scope.[4]

In practice, along RC4 Giap would execute his first "local counter-offensive." Meanwhile, he would also begin to deploy steadily increasing numbers of independent regiments inside the Red River Delta, for it was clear to all by this point that the people inside the Delta were the ultimate prize in the War of Resistance. How many units he could deploy there, and how fast he could deploy them, depended on a number of factors: his ability to inflict devastating losses along RC4; the FEF command's reaction to that disaster; French exhaustion in Indochina and at home; improvement of his own lines of communication; and perhaps most important, strengthening his logistical capabilities to conduct big-unit operations far afield from the comparative safety of the Viet Bac.

The French effort by early 1950 seemed mired in torpor. The government was paralyzed by complacency, its senior military leadership riddled with infighting, making the planning of operations and the setting of objectives—exceedingly difficult enterprises in the best of circumstances—all but impossible. After the futility of Operation Lea in 1947, the French abandoned efforts to crush Giap's base of operations and training in the jungles of the Viet Bac despite clear intelligence of impressive growth in Vietminh numbers and combat capabilities.

The FEF had expanded to 150,000 troops by this point. These forces were certainly sufficient to stave off defeat, even to preserve a precarious stalemate. Yet still, Paris and its commander in the field, Marcel Carpentier, persistently underestimated the caliber of Giap's recruiting and training capabilities—and the high motivation and toughness he instilled in his warriors. Carpentier decided to keep the vast majority of the FEF in static garrison positions, guarding the largest bases and towns throughout the three regions of the country. To curry favor in Paris, he refrained from asking for more troops, thereby maintaining the illusion in the minds of French policymakers that so long as the string of frontier "hedgehogs" was kept intact, Giap's forces were safely contained in the Viet Bac, posing little threat to French control over the Delta. It was an assessment tinged with more than a modicum of arrogance.

The complacency of Carpentier is all the more curious given the burgeoning power of revolutionary forces elsewhere in the country. Giap's chief commander in Cochinchina, Nguyen Binh, had thoroughly infiltrated Saigon's governmental apparatus with a vast overlapping network of Vietminh cells, both political and military. The steel-nerved head of the French Sûreté in Saigon, Monsieur Bazin, told a journalist in late 1949 that it was only a matter of time—and not much of it—before he himself would be assassinated. "The whole town is riddled with Viet cells," said Bazin. "They are everywhere. They kill anyone they choose and they make everyone pay taxes.... There are thousands of networks giving their daily orders and carrying out their propaganda, spying and tax gathering almost openly."[5]

Bazin himself was indeed killed a few weeks later by one of the Vietminh's highly trained assassination squads. Terrorism was rampant in Saigon until the end of the summer of 1950, when a shrewd, intelligent Vietnamese secret policeman named Tam, the "Tiger of Cailay," ruthlessly ferreted out the Communist infrastructure in the city. He used a lethal combination of torture, payoffs, and assassinations, effectively employing the Vietminh's own tactics against them.

But Cochinchina was distracting the French from the war's true center of gravity, Tonkin. General Carpentier and his commander in Tonkin, General Marcel Alessandri, had three viable options to challenge Giap's growing power. They could withdraw their overextended forces from the hedgehogs along the Chinese border to positions inside the Delta to challenge the Vietminh's guerrilla operations. They could take a far riskier tack: reinforce the hedgehogs with additional forces drawn from central and southern Vietnam and go after Giap's newly minted divisions before they were fully operational. Or they could invade the Viet Bac and try to crush the PAVN in its main base.

General Alessandri, no friend of Carpentier, believed that Giap and his Chinese advisers had not yet sharpened their claws to a point where they could strike effectively against either the frontier hedgehogs or the strong French defenses around the Delta. In May 1950, he presented to Carpentier a meticulous plan for a massive fifty-battalion attack into the Viet Bac. The FEF would launch columns of five to six battalions from six different points of access, smashing Giap's army right in the heart of the jungle with overwhelming force. French journalist Lucien Bodard describes the plan:

> In the first phase they would seize the approaches and the lines of access, and in the second they would fan out in the mountains and forests in groups of five to six battalions...and drive into the heart of the enemy jungle. The blows were to come from everywhere at once, otherwise the Viets would slip through his fingers like quicksilver....Parachute troops were an important element and so were fighters; but there was to be no artillery—it was essential the men should travel light, that their movement should be rapid, and that everything should be carried out at great speed. It was to be pure fighting, man-to-man combat in the tradition of the columns of the colonial days.[6]

Carpentier turned Alessandri's plan down out of hand. He chose none of the viable options. He decided to leave the understrength garrisons strung out along the Chinese border where they were, maintaining the fiction that they could challenge Vietminh control of northern Tonkin.

GIAP'S FIRST OFFENSIVE

Phase one kicked off in February 1950 with an assault on Pholu, a satellite hedgehog of earth and logs twenty miles east of Lao Cai, surrounded by a lake and an immense forest. Giap's troops stormed the heights surrounding the 150-man garrison there. Stealthily digging a network of camouflaged shelters for their newly acquired bazookas, 120mm mortars, and recoilless rifles supplied by thousands of porters shuffling along jungle paths, the Vietnamese blew the fort to pieces, overran it, and set the place alight.[7]

When two battalions of French paras attempted a rescue mission, they were dropped twenty miles too far to the east. Slashing westward through rough terrain, they were caught by Giap's roving companies and all but annihilated. Only 200 fighters from the two FEF battalions staggered into the main hedgehog at Lao Cai. And they'd managed that by the skin of their teeth: their white smoke distress signal was spotted on the ground by a squadron of French fighters. Six swooped down on the Viet infantry with napalm bombs and machine guns, blunting the attack.

After the victory at Pholu, the Vietminh went on to attack several other satellite bases, including Nghia Do, 30 miles to the southeast of Lao Cai. That hedgehog withstood the initial onslaught, only to be evacuated several days later when the commander recognized that it would not survive another strong assault.

Giap then withdrew his regiments for regrouping and refitting. He had one more test in mind before retiring for the monsoon season. This time he would strike near the border in the northeast. In April, the entire 308th Division smashed into Dong Khe, a satellite hedgehog of the major base at Cao Bang, manned by a single battalion of Foreign Legionnaires. Situated astride RC4, amid mountainous jungle prone to landslides, the road offered the Vietminh a multitude of opportunities to ambush any column sent to rescue Dong Khe. As usual, Giap's preparation was meticulous. It took four battalions to lug heavy mortars and five 75mm cannons into the hills.[8] After a relentless two-day pounding under low cloud cover that prevented French fighters from coming to the aid of their comrades, Vietminh shock troops hurled themselves at the Legionnaires, wiping out most of the battalion.

On the morning of April 28, when the skies cleared, the French Third Colonial Parachute Battalion landed at Dong Khe, and thirty-four aircraft swooped to support the paras. The FEF caught the Vietminh off guard, and a vicious melee followed. In the end, the French prevailed, and 300 PAVN corpses were strewn about the battlefield. Giap learned one vital lesson from the loss: always attack with sufficient antiaircraft weapons in place to keep the infantry from being overwhelmed by reinforcements and air support.

It could be said that the French triumphed at Dong Khe, in the traditional sense that they regained their strongpoint. Yet, as historian Phillip Davidson observed, the 10,000 or so French soldiers who manned the forts along Route Coloniale 4, the men who had seen the skill and determination of the PAVN up close, "knew that when the dry season came in late September, the forts were doomed."[9] A French soldier found a revealing note on the body of a Vietminh political officer. It read:

> Towards September 20 we shall attack once more. We shall be far stronger. Up until now there was only the 308th—by then there will be two or three other divisions ready. We shall take That Khe, then we shall take completely isolated Cao Bang, and then we will move in full force against Langson. That will be very easy, because the Expeditionary Force's morale will have been deeply shaken by our earlier victories.[10]

The generals sitting in Hanoi and Saigon were having none of it. They refused to recognize their extreme vulnerability in the Viet Bac, and failed to evacuate the forts.

After near disaster at Dong Khe, reports began to pile up in Hanoi of Vietminh guerrilla companies all along Route 4 attacking the mile-long convoys bound for the string of hedgehogs between Langson and Cao Bang, bristling as they were with machine guns, armored cars, and truckloads of infantrymen. The FEF built defensive positions wherever ambushes occurred; they dispatched engineers to fix blown bridges and remove booby traps. By summer 1950, whole FEF battalions were going east to sweep through the jungle and limestone peaks that towered over RC4, clearing the path for new columns behind them. But the jungle was just too thick, and the Vietminh too stealthy and numerous, for the sweeps to be effective. The eighty-mile road was drenched in French blood. A grizzled sergeant described one PAVN attack:

> To begin with the Viets paralyzed the convoy. Mines went off behind the armored cars at the head of the column, cutting them off from the trucks. Immediately after that a dozen unattackable machine guns in those limestone cliffs opened up, raking the whole column....Then came a hail of grenades....Regulars went from truck to truck, gathering weapons and the goods that had been left behind; then they set fire to the vehicles. Other regulars attacked the French who were still fighting on the embankments...There were hundreds of single combats, hundreds of pairs of men killing each other. In the middle of all this mess the political commissars very calmly supervised the work in hand, giving orders to the regulars and the coolies—orders that were carried out at once.[11]

As the monsoon season came to a close in early September, a stronger and better-trained Vietminh main force emerged, reinforced with hundreds of communications and artillery officers, and well prepared to wage mobile warfare.

The Chinese and Vietnamese workers had completed a road network leading directly to Giap's key objectives for phase two: he wanted to establish a cordon around Cao Bang and That Khe, then strike once again at Dong Khe and seize it. He reckoned this would force the French to try to consolidate their forces at Cao Bang or That Khe. When they did so, he hoped to ambush any and all convoys moving along RC4.

With an eight-to-one advantage in troops in the area of operations, and behind the veil of the late monsoon mists, the Vietminh launched a powerful artillery barrage against Dong Khe on September 16—Giap's first significant artillery attack in the War of Resistance. The PAVN's big guns, carefully camouflaged amid the cliffs and jungle, blasted away first at the four concrete blockhouses harboring the Legionnaire's artillery. They fell one after the other, killing the crews and destroying the howitzers. Then came wave after wave of infantry, in tight formation. Vicious hand-to-hand combat ensued. Sixty hours after the attack commenced, the fort belonged to the Vietminh. Giap announced on the radio that he had captured ninety-eight prisoners. Weeks later, one French officer and a handful of soldiers stumbled out of the jungle, the only Legionnaires to make their escape. For the French in Hanoi, Saigon, and Paris, it was a shocking loss.

Ironically, on the very day Giap assaulted Dong Khe, General Carpentier announced that Cao Bang would be evacuated with several other nearby minor hedgehogs. He was unwittingly playing his appointed part in his adversary's plan. The evacuation, however, was so poorly conceived and executed that it led first to military disaster, then to widespread panic throughout French Indochina. Indeed, as General Davidson writes, "In a war in which the French consistently drew up unrealistic plans, Carpentier's stands supreme."[12]

Carpentier elected to send a motley force of fewer than 3,000 men, mainly North Africans of dubious fighting ability, from Langson toward Dong Khe, with a view to retaking the base, and linking up with the Cao Bang garrison, which was simultaneously to march down RC4. Then the united French forces would continue south toward the comparative safety of Langson. The commanding officer of the 3,000-man Langson "rescue" column was Colonel Marcel LePage, a sickly artillery officer who was haunted by a sense that his troops were insufficient for their mission and were therefore being sent into a trap. He was entirely correct. LePage headed northwest from Langson along Route 4 on September 16. For his part, the Cao Bang commander, Colonel Pierre Charton, a Legionnaire, called the evacuation plan "madness." Cao Bang itself consisted of fifteen mutually reinforcing outposts, and Giap had old men, women, and children regularly reporting on all of their movements. Its chances of survival were as thin as those of LePage's unit.

LePage's column was beset almost immediately by ambushes, road blocks, and mines as it was heading north toward Dong Khe. The colonel opted to send his artillery and heavy engineering equipment back to Langson in order to speed his drive north. In doing so, however, he made the re-conquest of Dong Khe—an objective Carpentier had inexplicably neglected to mention to LePage as preeminent—impossible.

On September 19 LePage's column straggled into That Khe, a satellite hedgehog of Dong Khe, where it was greeted by the First Foreign Legion Parachute Battalion, a formidable unit composed largely of former German SS fighters. They were under orders to fight at Dong Khe under LePage's command, but the Legionnaires sensed immediately that LePage was way out of his depth.

On September 30 LePage tried to retake Dong Khe. His thinly supported attacks were easily blunted by the PAVN garrison that had taken up residence there. LePage was then ordered to bypass Dong Khe, march southwest into the dense jungle, and then head north along a narrow trail to Nam Nang, on RC4, five miles west of Cao Bang. There he would meet Cao Bang's withdrawing garrison—all 3,000 of them, led by Colonel Charton's 1,600 Foreign Legionnaires. LePage had neither guides nor maps of the terrain to the west of RC4. Several nearby regiments of Vietminh, consisting of men who knew the jungle in the area very well, soon found him. They cut up LePage's column into small groups, and wiped out the largest of these, led by LePage, deep inside Cox Xa gorge, covered on both ridgelines by Vietminh machine gunners.

Now, Colonel Charton, who was meant to be rescued by LePage, tried in vain to rescue the remnants of LePage's unit. Charton's native guides slashed through dense jungle trails toward Cox Xa gorge and LePage's doomed force. By October 7—four days after Charton left Cao Bang— LePage's First Para Legionnaires, his only jungle-savvy unit, broke through the Vietminh lines to connect with Charton's forces. Most of the rest of both French columns—LePage's and Charton's—were captured, killed, or left wandering aimlessly in the bush.

Giap now had all the French forces along RC4 in near panic and disarray. His French counterpart, Carpentier, seemed immobilized and detached from the rush of events. Rather than organize a defense of some sort, he lost his nerve and ordered a retreat of all remaining forces that had stumbled south into the fort at That Khe to evacuate that base and head for the strongest of the French forts on RC4, Langson. On October 10, 1950, the beleaguered FEF forces headed south, along with That Khe's civilians. Giap's regulars, smelling blood and victory, ambushed the column, cutting it up into small groups of desperate, confused soldiers.

In the end, only a few hundred troops stumbled into Langson, deeply shaken by the power and skill of Giap's peasant army. The rest were killed or captured. Among those who fell into the tender hands of the PAVN was Colonel Charton himself. He would later suffer through the rigors of long Communist interrogations, re-education camps, and brainwashing sessions.

Of the French bases along RC4, only Langson remained in French hands. Rather than do the tactically sound thing and organize a powerful mobile defense force to punch up Rte. 1A, unthreatened by Vietminh forces, and reinforce Langson with its immense stores of weapons and equipment, the baffled Carpentier ordered its evacuation on October 17. It was a shameful act, for Giap's troops were days away from closing in on the fort there. The garrison of 4,000, mostly support troops, left in a panic without bothering to destroy its vast stores of weapons and more than one hundred tons of ammunition, much of it for 75mm field howitzers that Giap would put to good use later. The cache included 450 trucks, greatly enhancing Vietminh mobility, which up until then had been on foot and bicycle, 900 machine guns, 450 submachine guns, 8,000 rifles, and vast quantities of food, clothing, and medical supplies. Abandoning Langson long before it was under attack by Vietminh guns, Carpentier confirmed the adage of US Marine General Alexander Vandegrift: "Positions are seldom lost because they have been destroyed, but almost invariably because the leader has decided in his own mind that the position cannot be held."[13]

Carpentier now spoke openly to staffers of looming disaster and even had plans drawn up for the evacuation of all women and children from Hanoi. "When the smoke cleared," writes historian Bernard Fall,

> the French had suffered their greatest colonial defeat since Montcalm had died at Quebec.... By January 1, 1951, the French had lost control of all of North Viet-Nam to the north of the Red River and were now desperately digging to hold on to the key pawn of the whole Indochina war—The Red River delta.[14]

The war, as historian Fredrik Logevall observes, "had entered a new, intensive, deadly phase, as the Cold War not only internationalized the diplomatic nature of the conflict, but militarized it in unprecedented ways."[15] Giap, for his part, celebrated his dramatic victory in the way soldiers all over the world have done for centuries: he joined his comrades in a big party and got himself drunk, reportedly for the first time in his life.

As the new year began, Giap, unopposed in the field, positioned three full divisions around the perimeter of the Red River Delta. His acquisition of tons of military stores and ammunition at Langson no doubt built great confidence among the Vietminh regulars.

In a presentation to the political commissars of the 316th Division after the taking of Langson, Giap stated his vision of the trajectory of the war now that the Revolution controlled all of Tonkin north of the Red River Delta, and many districts within that delta:

> The enemy will pass slowly from the offensive to the defensive. The blitz-krieg will transform itself into a war of long duration. Thus the enemy will be caught in a dilemma: he has to drag out the war in order to win it and does not possess, on the other hand, the psychological and political means to fight a long drawn-out war.[16]

In other words, the conflict appeared to be entering the third stage of protracted war: Giap would seek to liquidate the French military threat before the Americans became directly involved or before French morale could recover from the shock of its series of defeats along Route Coloniale 4. Giap continued:

> Our strategy early in the course of the third stage is that of a general counteroffensive. We shall attack without cease until final victory, until we have swept the enemy forces from Indochina. During the first and second stage, we have gnawed away at the enemy forces; now we must destroy them. All military activities of the third stage must tend to that simple aim—the total destruction of French forces.[17]

5

1951–1953

The defeat of the FEF in the border campaign quite naturally brought the military's Indochina strategy into question in Paris. Either France had to escalate sharply its commitment to defeat the insurgency militarily, or it should reopen negotiations with Ho Chi Minh. French politicians were profoundly ambivalent. Domestic support was clearly crumbling, yet for a variety of reasons, many influential figures in French political and military life believed the honor of France demanded that she prevail against the Communist upstarts. For these men, negotiations were distinctly unpalatable, and in some cases, unthinkable.

The response of the government in Paris to this dilemma was to send additional troops to Vietnam in small increments and authorize an ambitious expansion of the Vietnamese National Army. The FEF would peak at 200,000 men in the War of Resistance, but, given the unforgiving terrain and climate, as well as its mission to defend its own installations and the urban centers, pacify the villages, and conduct offensive operations, the force was fatally undersized. To pay for these initiatives, the French called upon the Americans. Unwilling to countenance the expansion of

Communism in Asia after "losing" China to Mao, and fighting their own war in Korea, the Americans were willing to pay.

France's reluctance to make the hard choices required was masked by the appointment of its most distinguished soldier to replace Carpentier as the commander of the FEF in Indochina. Jean de Lattre de Tassigny had an explosive temper and was regarded by many as a megalomaniac, but his credentials as a combat commander were second to none. His brilliant performance during the first six months of his tenure in Vietnam would foster the illusion that the Vietminh were on the run.

De Lattre insisted on absolute authority in Vietnam. He refused to seek advance approval for his initiatives from Paris, and exercised dual political and military control over all of Indochina. Arriving in Saigon on December 17, 1950, he immediately fired scores of defeatist officers and canceled his predecessor's panicked order to evacuate women and children. He knew his troops would fight harder if civilian lives were at stake. He put thousands of French colonial and Vietnamese civilians to work constructing the "De Lattre Line," 1,200 mutually reinforcing defensive positions around the Red River Delta, with a view to blocking any Vietminh thrusts. The fledgling Vietnamese army, ostensibly an independent force under control of the Vietnamese government but in reality an adjunct force under French command, would man these static posts, thereby freeing up thousands of tough French Legionnaires and paratroopers for offensive operations. Through the sheer force of his personality, General de Lattre restored French morale in Vietnam virtually overnight. Time was of the essence, for he felt sure Giap's forces were about to strike into the Red River Delta. He was right.

Giap had seized the initiative during the border campaign. By December 1950, thanks to unremitting guerrilla warfare, the tentacles of the Vietminh's political infrastructure were extending outward everywhere—even in Cochinchina.

In his analysis of war strategy published early in 1950, "The Military Task in Preparing for the General Counter Offensive," Giap argued that stage three of the war would most likely emerge gradually as French forces were worn down in a series of battles combining increasingly powerful mobile warfare in selective areas with guerrilla operations in the enemy's rear—meaning, of course, all the territory ostensibly under the control of the FEF, at least during the daylight hours. It was not necessary for the revolutionary forces to achieve general military superiority over the adversary before the beginning of the offensive, as Mao had argued. Rather, it was only necessary for the PAVN to achieve temporary superiority in limited locations, leading to a gradual shift in the military balance of forces. Success in the political struggle—the shorthand term for the organizational, psychological, and international dimensions of the conflict—would, as always, remain critically important.[1]

Around December 1950 the Central Committee of the Party approved Giap's campaign plan for a series of assaults against widely divergent points on the perimeter of the Red River Delta. Neither Giap nor other Communist leaders have written much about the planning or execution of the 1951 Red River Delta battles, but in retrospect, it appears that the campaign had several objectives. The most important goal was obvious: to assert the revolution's authority over greater swaths of Tonkin, thereby hastening the decline of French morale in the field. The seizure of Tonkin's major port, Haiphong, was a secondary objective, for the FEF had little hope of sustaining offensive operations in the Viet Bac or Thanh Hoa base area without a steady flow of ship-borne supplies. Giap also hoped to threaten Hanoi, but at this point, it seems doubtful he had any hope of taking the city itself.

On January 13, 1951, two regiments of Giap's 308th Iron Division jumped off from their assembly area in the thickly forested Tam Dao Ridge in assault formation, pressing southward. Within a couple of hours, the Vietminh had overwhelmed a series of small French posts on the rolling hills north of Vinh Yen. The site of a critical road junction leading from the northwestern edge of the Delta to Hanoi, Vinh Yen was a provincial capital held by French Mobile Groups 1 and 3. The two units were separated by a gap of about three miles. Giap's intention was to attack from the north with two regiments of the 308th Division and from the west with the 312th Division, breach their perimeter defenses, either contain or destroy both mobile groups, and then punch through the gap between the two and drive toward Hanoi.

The initial attack succeeded in annihilating a fifty-man FEF fortified outpost in hills north of Vinh Yen. The next morning Mobile Group 3 moved out from its defensive bastion to clear the Vietminh from the hills. It was ambushed, losing a full battalion as it withdrew under close air cover and artillery fire. At the same time, the forward elements of the 312th cracked French defenses northwest of the town, forcing open a gap between Group 3 and Group 1, three miles to the east. All was going to plan, but inexplicably, Giap failed to exploit the gap, opting instead to consolidate his defenses in the hills.

Sensing impending disaster, General de Lattre flew into the city and took command himself on January 14. He ordered a rapid airlift of an entire additional mobile group into the town. The next day, Group 1 took back one of the key northern hill positions. With beefed-up ground and air power, de Lattre pushed the PAVN out of the hills on January 16. The French crisis appeared to have been averted. A few hours later, however, Giap flung the entire 308th Division against the French defensive positions in the hills. Elements of the 312th pressed forward simultaneously from the northwest. In a series of furious and costly human-wave assaults lasting through the night, the Vietminh took back two large hills in the center of the battlefield, but the French beat back attacks on two other hills on the flanks of the PAVN positions despite their being temporarily overrun several times by PAVN assault units.

Giap launched a furious massive assault at dawn on January 17 with virtually every effective company of infantry at his disposal, but by this point in the battle de Lattre had assembled a formidable armada of fighter-bombers, napalm-bearing transports, and well-registered artillery in the area of operations (AO). The combined destructive power of all these supporting arms decimated entire waves of attacking PAVN infantry. Terrified soldiers broke and ran before sheets of liquid fire, as a Vietminh officer recalled:

> All of a sudden a sound can be heard in the sky and strange birds appear, getting larger and larger. Airplanes...all of a sudden, hell opens in front of my eyes. Hell comes in the form of large, egg-shaped containers, dropping from the first plane, followed by other eggs from the second and third plane. Immense sheets of flames, extending over hundreds of meters, it seems, strike terror in the ranks of my soldiers. This is napalm, the fire which falls from the skies...The bomb falls closely behind us and I feel its fiery breath touching my whole body. The men are now fleeing in all directions and I cannot hold them back. There is no way of holding out under this torrent of fire which flows in all directions and burns everything on its passage....In addition, French artillery and mortars now have our range and transform into a fiery tomb what had been, ten minutes ago, a quiet part of the forest.[2]

At noon on January 17, a dispirited Giap ordered a general withdrawal. In his first multi-division engagement, the Vietminh's commander in chief had been trounced by the deft application of the FEF's supporting arms and a virtuoso command performance by General de Lattre. It was at Vinh Yen that Giap began to earn a reputation for callous expenditure of the lives of his own troops. Out of a force of 22,000, 6,000 were killed and 8,000 wounded.

Giap plainly had a great deal to learn about conventional big-unit operations. Nonetheless, we see in the unfolding of the battle signs of promise and nascent capabilities that foreshadowed later successes. Giap had moved two divisions from the Viet Bac to the edge of the Delta without detection. It had taken about two million man-days for the PAVN's porters to position 5,000 tons of ammunition, food, and equipment into place along the line of march. The painstaking efforts Giap had made to develop the army's ability to camouflage the movement of large units, and to pre-position supplies in anticipation of combat were vindicated. These qualities would be hallmarks of PAVN operations for the next twenty-five years. Moreover, the initial scheme of maneuver had worked very well. Unfortunately, Giap had failed to capitalize on his initial success, probably because of failures in his command and control apparatus, which remained limited by the paucity of signal equipment and knowledgeable radio operators.

Chastened by his first defeat, Giap resolved to try another penetration of the De Lattre line. This time he attacked from the northeast at Mao Khe, which lay astride the northern approaches to valuable coal mines and to Haiphong, about twenty miles from the port. At 0400 hours on March 27, the artillery of the 316th laid down a heavy barrage squarely on the FEF positions protecting the mine and its ninety-five defenders. Two regimental-size assaults followed; despite hand-to-hand fighting, the FEF's troops put up a spirited defense, and soon after dawn, fighter-bombers broke up the attack entirely.

Around 0200 hours on March 28, a fresh PAVN regiment swarmed over the village after a heavy artillery preparation. Once again, the fighting turned hand-to-hand, and several French positions fell. Had Giap thrown another of his regiments into the fray, he might very well have overwhelmed the entire FEF force. But he hesitated long enough for accurate FEF artillery to change the momentum of the fight. By early morning, PAVN troops were withdrawing from the town, and the French had another victory. Giap had failed both to anticipate the naval gunfire that blunted the initial assault and to properly coordinate the pace and scope of the regimental attacks.

Having failed in his thrusts from the northwest and the north and paid dearly for it in blood, Giap now attempted a penetration of the southeastern perimeter of the Delta. The Day River campaign was certainly the most imaginatively conceived of the 1951 attacks: the main effort in this three-division operation was carried out by the bulk of the 320th Division, which was to cross from the west side of the Day River to the east, and then turn south to reoccupy the populous Catholic bishopric of Phat Diem, as well as the fertile rice-growing area to the northwest. If the initial attacks succeeded, PAVN units might press as far east as Thai Binh, thirty miles from the coast.

The terrain in the area of operations was well suited for attack, as the western bank of the Day River in this area rose above the French positions on its eastern side. Here the terrain was studded with limestone cliffs, jungle, vegetation, and many caves that offered Giap's troops excellent cover from the inevitable French artillery and mortar bombardments. In addition, two PAVN regiments supported the attack from their positions deep inside the Delta, which they had successfully infiltrated months before the operation. Those regiments would engage in guerrilla operations, blocking and harassing any FEF reinforcements attempting to push westward toward the main PAVN attack into the Delta. Meanwhile, elements of the 308th and 304th would mount diversionary attacks northwest of Phat Diem, at Phy Ly and Ninh Binh.

The initial PAVN attacks by the 308th against Ninh Binh on May 29 caught the FEF and de Lattre completely by surprise, as Giap's troops swarmed over a series of outposts protecting the town. De Lattre's only son, Bernard, was killed in a desperate defensive action at a small fort overlooking Ninh Binh proper. When the French attempted to blunt the attack with a *dinassaut*—a heavily armed amphibious force of about a dozen small craft with artillery, mortars, and a company or two of marines—PAVN bazookas on both sides of the Day River ripped into the flotilla, sinking several craft, and damaging others. De Lattre then rushed several mobile groups and para battalions to the battle zone to avert disaster.

Sustained and brutal combat to the east of the Day River persisted through June 4. That night, the battle reached its apex when the Vietminh gained and lost a critical piece of terrain called Yen Cu Ha. By the morning of June 5, Giap's attack began to wane. His troops came under increasingly intense air and artillery fire in the flat rice paddies on the east side of the river. Near Phat Diem, the Catholic bishopric militia, staunchly anti-Communist, joined the fighting on the side of the FEF, slowing down the Vietminh advance. When the French *dinassaut* cut the Vietminh supply lines across the Day River, ammunition and food grew short.

Giap realized by the end of the first week of June that continuing to fight would be an exercise in futility. By the time the PAVN withdrew into the hills west of the Day River, it had suffered around 10,000 casualties. Another 1,000 main force troops were captured before they could retreat to the west. Overconfidence after the stunning success of the border campaign and impatience to vanquish France before American military assistance enhanced the FEF's military capabilities unquestionably factored into the failures of the 1951 offensive drives. But an equally important factor was the disposition of the attacking and defending forces. All three of the attacks were launched along "exterior lines," meaning Giap's forces were attacking from outside the horseshoe-shaped area of the Delta, defended by fixed French positions. In order for the 1951 operations to succeed, the main attacks needed to be well supported by secondary attacks elsewhere against the De Lattre line in order to prevent French forces inside the horseshoe from reinforcing their comrades positioned against the main Vietminh attacks. Giap's strategy of striking with virtually all his forces from a single direction in all three operations meant that the French could concentrate overwhelming force against Giap's offensive drives.[3]

Taken together, the defeats of 1951 demonstrate that Giap had misread the strategic situation of the war at this point in time. Although the documentary record is thin on this issue, it appears that only the strong support of Uncle Ho, with his immense personal prestige, persuaded the Central Committee of the Party not to sack Vo Nguyen Giap. Such losses in the French or US armies certainly would have led to the relief of the commander.

Giap remained in command of the army. It wouldn't be the last time that reverses on the battlefield would lead an influential clique to question the wisdom of retaining the army's commander in chief, most notably in the early years of the American War, when the Le Duan–Nguyen Chi Thanh clique called for his ouster for lack of aggressiveness.

In the wake of the 1951 losses, the Central Committee decided to revert to stage two of protracted war conflict with a reduced level of combat, while nonetheless preparing diligently for the inevitable return to the conventional operations associated with stage three. With the exception of one failed attack against a French fortress at Na San in November 1952, the PAVN would avoid conventional attacks against strongly defended positions until the Dien Bien Phu campaign in spring 1954.

Mobile warfare operations carried out by the regular PAVN divisions against remote, vulnerable targets, supplemented by guerrilla operations carried out by regional forces to disperse French forces and disrupt their communications lines, dominated the fighting in 1952 and 1953. Giap anticipated that the tempo of operations over the next two years (1952–1953) would increase gradually. Time would be his greatest weapon. Time to build and improve the PAVN; time to disperse and wear down the French through mobile operations.

The promising areas for PAVN campaigns after 1951 were not in or around the Red River Delta, but in the rugged northwest region, home of the Thai mountain people, in the highlands of western Annam, and in lightly defended northern Laos—places far from the FEF's airfields clustered around Hanoi. Here the terrain would mitigate the FEF's superior firepower and road mobility.

The defeats of 1951 lent Giap a new sense of urgency in solving his army's deficiencies. Chinese training and material support would help to resolve most of them within the next two years. The general staff was reorganized along Chinese Communist lines into five discrete sections: personnel, intelligence, communications, planning, and operations. The Central Political Bureau of the army became one of three separate departments, joining the general staff and the supply service. Aside from providing officers in regular units from company to division levels, the Political Bureau refined indoctrination training techniques and expanded the number of internal publications to bring the word of the Revolution forward.

Not long after the failed 1951 offensive, the first "heavy" division—the 351st—reached operational strength, with two regiments of Chinese-supplied artillery, including some US 105mm howitzers captured in Korea, and one regiment of combat engineers. It was around this time, too, that antiaircraft sections, many manned initially by Chinese troops, were imbedded into the infantry divisions. Giap placed very high priority on developing the PAVN's antiaircraft defenses over the next year to compensate for his lack of air power. In the remaining campaigns of the war, the army's capacity to inflict punishment on FEF fighter-bombers and transports proved an essential element in its success.

HOA BINH

As usual, neither adversary attempted to mount big-unit operations in the monsoon season. But by November 1951 General de Lattre was ready to cap his string of defensive victories with a full-blown offensive strike into Vietminh territory. If he could seize and hold a target of clear strategic value to the Vietminh, the doubting Thomases in Paris and Washington might well be moved to furnish him with the reinforcements and hardware he needed to inflict a fatal blow. A dramatic victory might even re-ignite public enthusiasm in France itself. De Lattre chose as the target of his operation the city of Hoa Binh, then under the administrative control of the Vietminh.

Situated some twenty-five miles southwest of the De Lattre Line, the city stood astride the major road junction between the Viet Bac and the Vietminh's rice basket south of the Delta in Thanh Hoa.

Seizing Hoa Binh proved easy. On November 14, three battalions of paratroopers descended on the town, brushed aside token Vietminh regional forces, and occupied it within a few hours. Holding Hoa Binh, which was deep in Vietminh territory, however, would prove far more difficult. It had an airstrip, but it was dominated by two forested hills. The main challenge facing de Lattre lay in controlling the two avenues of approach to the town: the Black River ran directly north to Trung Ha, a supply point about forty miles away. The river banks were covered in thick jungle—excellent cover for any force attempting to cut the supply line. Route Coloniale 6, a thin ribbon of road in very bad repair, ran northeast toward Xuan Mai on the edge of the De Lattre line. It was flanked throughout by thick underbrush.

De Lattre deployed a massive force of fifteen infantry battalions, well supported by armor, artillery, and amphibious assets, to clear the river and the road. In a burst of frenetic activity, ten strong points were established on RC6 by combat engineers, and then manned by a seasoned force of Legionnaires and African infantrymen; meanwhile, French marines in *dinassauts* guarded supply convoys ferrying down the Black River to Hoa Binh's garrison. On both banks, the engineers constructed a string of forts and smaller outposts under the watchful eye of French fighter pilots. In late November the ailing de Lattre returned to Paris—he had cancer—and General Raoul Salan assumed command of the entire FEF as well as the impending battle of Hoa Binh, which the French press described rather dramatically as "a pistol pointed at the heart of the enemy."[4]

While Salan's force braced for a pincer counterattack against the town, Giap bided his time. He had no intention of conducting yet another conventional assault along exterior lines to recapture the town. Giap planned instead to attack Salan's lines of communication, cutting them off through a series of slashing attacks against the many French strong points on both the river and the road, and then encircle the town and its FEF garrison.

The operation got under way when Giap sent three PAVN divisions from the Viet Bac toward Hoa Binh. Moving undetected through the jungle at night, the 312th deployed its battalions along the west bank of the Black River, while the 304th and 308th crept into positions south and east of Hoa Binh along RC6.

Because so many of the French units occupied defensive positions along the river and road approaches, Giap ruled out the possibility that Salan would mount a strong attack out of Hoa Binh proper against his encircling forces. To prevent French mobile forces in the Red River Delta from responding to the encirclement of Hoa Binh, Giap ordered elements of the 320th to infiltrate the Delta from the south to conduct diversionary operations. The 316th did the same from the north.

The battle of Hoa Binh (November 14, 1951, to February 23, 1952) commenced with a forty-minute artillery barrage against an anchoring strong point of the Black River defense line at Tu-Vu, followed by a ferocious attack by three PAVN regiments. Within two hours human wave attacks from several directions turned the post, manned by two companies of tough Moroccans supported by five tanks and mortars, into smoking ruins. By then, the defenders were on the verge of running out of ammunition. Bernard Fall recounts the end at Tu Vu in *Street without Joy*:

> At 0300, five battalions threw themselves against the 200-odd men of Tu-Vu. The tanks of the armored platoon, guns depressed to minimum elevation, fired into the screaming human clusters crawling over the parapets into the position, their heavy treads crushing heads, limbs, and bodies by the dozen as they slowly moved like chained elephants into the little open space left in the post. But soon they, too, were submerged by

the seemingly never ending human waves, with scores of hands clawing at their turret hatches trying to pry them open; stuffing incendiary hand grenades into their cannon, firing tommy gun bursts into their driving slits; finally destroying them with pointblank bazooka bursts which lit up their hulls with the sizzling white-hot metal. The sweetish smell of searing flesh rose in the air. All five tank crews died to the last man, roasted alive in their vehicles.... As the morning came, heavy silence reigned over Tu-Vu, and Moroccan patrols slipped... back into the post. They found it deserted of enemy soldiers and stripped of all weapons.[5]

Some 400 PAVN dead were left on the battlefield at Tu Vu—a costly victory. Similar carnage attended many of the other Vietminh assaults around Hoa Binh throughout December. Yet, as would be the case time and time again, Giap's battalions licked their wounds and returned rapidly to the battle line, displaying a resilience their opponents found as astonishing as it was dispiriting. By mid-January 1952, Hoa Binh took on the coloration of a rescue operation for the French. The five FEF battalions inside Hoa Binh were running low on supplies and demoralized by shelling from the hills above the airfield. On January 8 the entire 308th Division had attacked a series of outposts along RC6. Most of the attacks were launched at extremely close range and quickly devolved into hand-to-hand combat as the Vietminh managed partial penetrations, only to be repulsed after hours of furious fighting with heavy casualties on both sides. The French often prevailed, but by January 20, both of Hoa Binh's supply lines had been cut. Meanwhile, the operations of Giap's 320th and 316th inside the Delta had succeeded in wresting control over scores of villages from the colonial government. The ignominious French withdrawal from Hoa Binh in mid-February required a massive logistical effort; thousands of French soldiers fell to Vietminh artillery and ambushes as they marched down RC6.

Giap wrote a few years after the war that Hoa Binh was "typical of the coordination between guerrilla warfare and mobile warfare" that he viewed as essential to the successful prosecution of protracted war.[6] And indeed, Hoa Binh was exactly that, for it combined a highly effective operation combining strong ambushes by platoons and companies of FEF columns and regimental attacks against enemy strong points—classic mobile warfare—with guerrilla operations far afield to tie up potential reinforcements and fuel the process of *pourissement,* or rotting away, of French control over the population.

THE FALL 1952–WINTER 1953 CAMPAIGN

Between March and September 1952, guerilla operations were the order of the day. People's war called for long stretches of small-unit operations, and this was such a period. As the monsoon season of 1952 waned in September, the Vietminh army was poised to engage in a mobile warfare campaign that would expose the FEF's political and military vulnerabilities as dramatically as it revealed Giap's growing strategic maturity. The spring and summer had been put to good use refitting the PAVN's infantry divisions with tons of modern small arms and artillery from China. PLA advisory teams developed a more systematic training regimen for combined operations at the divisional level, while the drawbacks of relying heavily on porters were studied and at least partially resolved by the introduction of several hundred trucks acquired from the Soviet Union.

In the second week of October 1952, three PAVN divisions marched along a forty-mile front toward the Nghia Lo Ridge between the Red and Black Rivers. Here the French had established a string of lightly garrisoned outposts anchored by one strongly defended fortress in the town of Nghia Lo. In September 1951, the single French regiment there had handily repulsed Giap's first effort to penetrate Tai country. Now he would try again, but this time with a force that was considerably larger, and more seasoned. The attack proved a shocking surprise to General Salan and the rest of the FEF's senior leadership.

The forts along the ridge were too remote for the French to employ effective air support. Giap had every expectation of overrunning them rapidly and pressing on with his three divisions along a southwesterly axis to attack a much stronger line of French strong points on the western bank of the Black River. Those fortresses ran from Lai Chau in the northwest to Moc Chau in the southeast. Even if this thrust was blunted, Giap reckoned he could gain invaluable intelligence on France's capacity to defend the Red River Delta and a remote region in the hinterlands of Tonkin simultaneously.

PAVN divisions traveled at night, marching independently, making their way undetected to the first line of outposts on the Nghia Lo Ridge. The first hammer blow struck on October 15, when a regiment of the 312th encircled a lone company at Gia Hoi, ten miles west of Nghia Lo. Salan read the 312th's attack at Gia Hoi as a diversion. Accordingly, he dispatched a single elite para battalion to a neighboring post to the northwest at Tu Ve on October 16 to conduct a rescue operation. The paras fought their way through to Gia Hoi and evacuated the besieged defenders in a harried with-drawal back toward the tenuous security of Tu Ve.

At 1700 hours on October 17, the Iron Division struck Nghia Lo with overwhelming force. A 120mm mortar attack prefaced three rapid regimen-tal assaults. The French garrison was completely overrun. When French planes reached Nghia Lo at dawn, it had been reduced to smoking ruin, and a long column of FEF prisoners was spotted, flanked by two columns of PAVN troops. The collapse of Nghia Lo and the loss of 700 French troops there, writes Edgar O'Ballance, "was like the breaching of a sea dyke."[7] The string of small posts between Lao Cai and Yen Bay were either evacuated, with troops fleeing toward the Black River strong points, or overwhelmed as the PAVN pressed down on them from the northeast.

As the FEF's Sixth Paras at Tu Ve attempted to cover the withdrawal at a critical mountain pass just west of the base on October 20, Giap's troops attacked, catching these elite and seasoned fighters in a trap as they were strung out in a column between the pass and a hill line. The unit fought for its life, losing half its complement in the process. A veteran French lieuten-ant who survived the harrowing combat recalled that the density of auto-matic weapons fire during the battle was greater than any he had heard before. Another officer, a POW who passed by the battlefield around Tu Ve several days later, reported that it "looked like something out of Dante's Inferno or one of the paintings of Goya. The wounded were still lying there just like on the first day, intermingled with men who had died several days ago and who were beginning to rot. They were lying there unattended, in the tropical sun, being eaten alive by the rats and the vultures."[8]

LORRAINE AND THE LAOS CAMPAIGNS

While Giap was punching into Tai country in the mountainous northwest, Salan was putting the finishing touches on Operation Lorraine, an ambitious two-pincer thrust toward the Viet Bac from the northwest edge of the De Lattre Line, up Route Coloniale 2. Salan's primary objective was to lure several Vietminh divisions then fully engaged in the campaign in the northwest back toward the low-lying plains around Phu Doan and Yen Bay where the PAVN had several important supply depots. Salan reckoned that Giap could ill afford to lose the depots if he intended—as Salan felt sure he did—to launch a major thrust into the Delta before the rainy season began in May 1953.

Lorraine was truly a massive effort. Some 30,000 FEF troops thrust out of the Red River Delta at the end of October, supported by the lion's share of FEF airpower and even some *dinassaut* flotillas for river operations. Like so many FEF offensive operations, Lorraine got off to a promising start. By November 7, Salan's two pincers converged at Phu Doan and, meeting only light resistance, seized 500 square miles of Vietminh-controlled real estate, threatening the supply depots.

Giap refused to take the bait. He would keep his force in the northwest to keep up the pressure in an area of operations where the French were vulnerable. His understanding of Salan's dilemma of holding on to territory in the Delta while conducting hinterland offensives was clearly maturing. By this point in the war, the Vietminh's network of clandestine agents was well placed in the French rear to obtain excellent intelligence on all of Salan's operations in advance. The Vietminh's commander believed that Lorraine would sputter out before it could reach his major supply depots at Yen Bay and Thai Nguyen. He was exactly right.

The French were able to capture hefty quantities of weapons and ammunition in hidden stores around Phu Doan, but the Vietminh had by that point transported most of its weapons and stores out of reach of the leading French units. Salan opted to bypass Yen Bay; his communication lines were growing dangerously thin. After reaching as far north as Phu Yen on November 13, he ordered a withdrawal. Meanwhile, Giap had detached two seasoned PAVN regiments from their parent divisions and deployed them in the Lorraine area of operations. Joined by substantial guerrilla forces along the route of withdrawal, they harassed the French with roadblocks and sniper fire as they struggled to return to the Delta. The French public affairs spokesman put a positive gloss on Lorraine, but it had plainly been a failure all around.

As Lorraine foundered, Giap pressed on confidently against the Black River strong points from Lai Chau in the northwest to Moc Chau in the south. If he could break through the line, he could penetrate into northern Laos, thereby exerting enormous pressure on Salan to airlift a large force from behind the De Lattre Line to defend the Laotian capitals of Vientiane and Luang Prabang. The capture of either of those cities or, indeed, of substantial portions of Laotian territory would be a political disaster for the government in Paris. Around November 20 the 316th overwhelmed the garrison at Moc Chau.

Meanwhile, the 308th pressed in on the heavily fortified base at Na San airstrip. Salan saw Na San as a vital anchor for the defense of Laos. Determined to hold the base at all costs, he airdropped a number of battalions of troops into the area of operations. By the time Giap attacked, at least ten battalions of FEF troops defended the base. Giap had reckoned that the base was manned by half that number. Uncharacteristically, Vietminh intelligence failed to detect the FEF's rapid buildup of forces there. The 308th lost at least 3,000 men in a series of one- and two-regimental attacks between November 23 and December 1, 1952.

Salan saw Na San as a vindication of the concept of fighting from a *base aeroterrestre*—a well-defended combat base in Vietminh territory without road links, supplied entirely by air. After Giap's initial regimental attack on November 23, Na San had been rapidly reinforced with 300 tons of barbed wire, a hundred vehicles, and tons of extra ammunition. As such, the battle went far to instill confidence in the French high command that the Na San scenario could be repeated elsewhere on a larger scale, perhaps bringing about a decisive defeat if Giap opted to fight a pitched battle somewhere else in the northwest.

Giap saw the Na San engagement quite differently. After withdrawing from the battlefield, he regrouped and bypassed the French strongpoint before plunging into Laos. Once there, the army swept through a handful of small FEF outposts, gaining valuable intelligence for Giap's planned 1953 spring offensive drive deep into the Laotian countryside.

Soon after the withdrawal from Na San, an American journalist with Communist sympathies named Joseph Starobin was taken to Giap's headquarters, a bamboo shed with a roof of thatched palm leaves. "We are leaving them there [at Na San]," said the PAVN commander in chief. " Let them use their supplies to hold it. [Na San] illustrates the French dilemma. Either they try to extend their strong-points once again, with their depleted manpower, in which case they spread themselves thin, or else they move out of their strong-points, which frees territory and population to us."[9]

Na San can be read as an early example of Giap's startling ability to "lose" an engagement—in the traditional Western sense of suffering heavy losses in a failed attempt to achieve a given objective—and yet implant in the minds of his adversaries illusions that would ultimately result in a shift in the overall "balance of forces" in the Communists' favor. Such was the case with Na San. Indeed, it could be said that the loss at Na San set the stage for Dien Bien Phu, the climactic pitched battle of the war that stands among the great disasters in the long history of French warfare.

The Vietminh campaign in the northwest from the fall of 1952 through the winter of 1953 offered a dramatic demonstration of Giap's ability to maneuver several divisions deep in the jungle without revealing his ultimate campaign objectives. Seasoned PAVN troops displayed the skills that were their hallmarks for the next twenty years of conflict: the ability to mask their movements in the daytime by continually altering their camouflage to fit the terrain on the march, and their mastery of moving stealthily in the dark of night. As Giap told Starobin, "In the battle of Na San we had to move deep into valleys. We had to cross 30 streams, some of them 250 yards wide, and make our way over high mountains. The French officers whom we captured told us later they did not see how we could have done it. They did not understand how our forces could appear at Na San hundreds of kilometers from our bases."[10]

At Na San, FEF defenders also witnessed Giap's terrifying assault tactics, as PAVN sappers, commandos with special training in explosives and lightning fast raids, sprinted through minefields and flung themselves directly into the barbed wire perimeter so their comrades could penetrate defensive positions more quickly by running over their corpses. What unnerved the French infantry was the Vietminh units' ability to sustain frightful casualties, only to rebound and attack again after a day or two of refitting and regrouping. No Western army in modern memory has sustained such a level of casualties so often in so many places.

Undaunted by the setback at Na San, Giap continued to press southwest into northern Laos with elements of three divisions. After bypassing Na San, the PAVN overran a string of thinly garrisoned French outposts on the Laotian border and headed in the direction of Sam Neua, a provincial capital in northern Laos. Within a month, though, Giap's failure to conscript loyal porters in the Tai country—the Tais were largely pro-French—caused his drive to lose steam. He drew all three of his divisions, the 308th, the 312th, and the 316th, back into northwestern Vietnam, where they rested for further action in the spring of 1953.

1953 OFFENSIVES

In early January 1953, Giap opened up yet another offensive, this time deploying two regiments in the highlands of central Annam to threaten the strategically vital towns of An Khe and Pleiku, as well as Route 1, the main north-south route along the central coast. These attacks were designed to force the French to further disperse an FEF force already stretched tight as a bow and wear down the Mobile Groups who carried out the FEF offensive operations. They succeeded in both objectives. Several FEF mobile groups were dispatched from the Delta to counter the PAVN drive in the waist of the country. Inconclusive fighting continued through February. But according to the doctrine of protracted war, battlefield stalemates always favored the revolutionary forces. Such was the case in central Annam.

By early 1953 the PAVN were operating with a level of skill and boldness that would have been unthinkable in the early days of the war. Moreover, the critical base areas where PAVN troops deployed in between operations— the Viet Bac, the southern Tonkin base area around Thanh Hoa, and a large swath of coastline between Nha Trang and Danang in the middle of the country—were growing daily thanks not so much to regular PAVN regiments engaged in mobile warfare, but to independent PAVN companies and battalions engaged in guerrilla warfare in the enemy's rear. As the mobile warfare campaigns in the northwest and Laos forced the FEF out of the areas of French control, the guerrillas went to work, securing one village and district after another.

There was a kind of synergy between the fighting methods of guerrilla, mobile, and ultimately pitched battles. This was the very essence of the Giapian strategy for protracted war. His forces were clearly now strong enough to have another go at the De Lattre Line. Most sources have it that this was his initial intention. Not only were his divisions of regulars highly motivated and at peak strength, but he had also developed a robust antiaircraft capability, sure to inflict severe damage on an overstretched FEF air force supporting ground operations. Moreover, his regional and local forces were successfully countering FEF pacification operations in the Red River Delta, using the old "oil slick" strategy of clearing and holding one sector at a time; but the "holders," largely Vietnamese army troops, were poorly trained and motivated. Generally, operations in the Delta were "like sweeping aside water with a brush; [the water] came rushing back when the [FEF] forces moved on."[11]

After the Central Highlands fighting came to an end, Giap consulted General Wei Guoqing, his chief PLA military adviser. Chinese advice had become increasingly important to Giap and his staff because Vietminh mobile operations now involved multiple divisions on the same front and coordination of those "big unit" campaigns with guerrilla warfare elsewhere. The PAVN was still short of its specialists in communications, antiaircraft, engineers, and artillery. The PLA filled the gap. Wei Guoqing argued persuasively in March 1953 for Giap not to make his main effort in the Red River Delta, but to press deep into Laos—far deeper than his initial foray in December 1952—where French strongpoints could be isolated and defeated in detail. In northern Laos the FEF could muster only limited air support due to the 200-mile distance between the area of operations and its Hanoi airfields.

In early April, the PAVN units that had been in Tai country drove southwest from their bases around Moc Chau in the north and Dien Bien Phu, a deep valley seventy miles northwest of Na San that had been easily secured by the 148th Independent Regiment the previous year. In a remarkably well-coordinated drive, Giap's forces, three divisions abreast, bottled up the large garrison at Na San with one regiment of the 308th, while the other three regiments bypassed the city, penetrated easily into Laos, and threatened Louang Prabang, forcing the French to mount a frenzied airlift to prevent the Laotian capital from falling. Meanwhile, the 316th Division moved out of Moc Chau on the eastern flank of the attack heading for Sam Neua. Salan wanted to reinforce the three battalion force there, but the air strip proved too short. Confusion and dismay were beginning to permeate FEF headquarters. Salan had fallen into an ominous pattern of responding passively to Communist initiatives. He ordered the three Sam Neua battalions to retreat by foot to a large French camp in the Plain of Jars, about sixty miles to the southwest. The 316th caught up to the rear of the FEF force as it withdrew. On April 15, all three battalions were destroyed in a series of slashing attacks on the column.

Three weeks after initiating the drive, the French were in disarray. The PAVN had complete freedom of movement in northern Laos. Political commissars were busy mobilizing a Laotian Communist guerrilla infrastructure. Only the limitations of Giap's logistical system and the looming monsoon rains prevented the army from pressing on to seize Vientiane and Louang Phrabang.

Salan had been completely outgeneraled. He was increasingly frustrated by the gaping lacunae between Paris's stated policy objectives and the means it was willing to provide to obtain them. The series of crises precipitated by Giap's Laotian offensive had drained the Delta of maneuver forces, and the Vietminh regional and guerrilla units had taken advantage of their deployment, liberating a great many villages from government control. Giap had fought "a war of movement on true protracted warfare principles," Edgar O'Ballance observes,

> and the watching Mao Zedong must have benevolently applauded at such a well-executed campaign. Formations of divisional size had calmly marched into Laos, bypassing serious opposition. Giap had succeeded in drawing off French reinforcements far, far from the Red River Delta, and forced General Salan to employ his entire fleet of transport aircraft to supply them. The whole... operation was an object lesson in mobility that had kept the French guessing right until the last minute.[12]

The Americans, for their part, were increasingly skeptical of France's half-hearted prosecution of the war. Until the invasion of Laos in April 1953, President Dwight D. Eisenhower had believed that the French would ultimately prevail—albeit with a great deal of American advice and expertise. Now Eisenhower feared the worst, evoking a variant of the domino theory that would later form the primary justification for the American War. "If Laos were lost," he told the National Security Council, the West "would likely lose the rest of Southeast Asia and Indonesia. The gateway to India, Burma and Thailand would be open."[13] Admiral Arthur Radford, chairman of the US Joint Chiefs of Staff, spoke for American policymakers in claiming that "Salan was overcautious and defense-minded." He was fighting the war with a World War I "barbed-wire" strategy.[14] President Eisenhower and his staunchly anti-Communist secretary of state, John Foster Dulles, placed considerable pressure on Paris to grant the US military advisory group in Saigon more power, and most importantly, to promise the Associated States of Indochina real independence as a way of energizing their commitment to the fight against the Vietminh.

For the French, real independence remained unthinkable; at the very least, Paris envisaged the conflict ending in negotiations and partition of the country into a French state in the south and a Vietminh state in Tonkin. Giap's strategy was making progress in a sphere removed from the combat of the battlefield. It was causing dissension and disagreement among his chief adversaries.

Time was running out for the French in Indochina. France's political willpower was faltering and could not be sustained without a resounding victory on the battlefield, and soon. Could a new commander, General Henri Navarre, a distinguished staff officer with a special interest in military intelligence and avoidance of the press, take the initiative away from Giap and save the day? That was the critical question in Paris. Within a year, the answer would be clear.

6

DIEN BIEN PHU, AND VICTORY

The fortunes of the Revolution looked very bright indeed in spring 1953, as Giap's last campaign had succeeded admirably in dispersing the FEF widely throughout Vietnam and Laos, sapping the strength of its mobile units, and wearing down public support for the war in France. As a military commander and strategist, Giap had shown audacity and flexibility, as well as the acute sense of timing that figures so prominently in Vietnamese military thought. Since the battle of Hoa Binh, in fact, the Vietminh commander in chief had demonstrated a striking ability to control the momentum and direction of the War of Resistance. For two years he had stymied the FEF with a lethal blend of tireless mobilization, small-unit guerrilla combat, and mobile warfare campaigns. In the northwest, as well as in the Red River Delta, Giap had shown a knack for deciding when and where to strike—and equally important—when and where to pull his punches and wait out the French.

As Giap and the rest of the Central Committee planned the campaign for winter 1953 through spring 1954, they had little incentive to revise the core strategy that had paid such handsome dividends. The French were on the horns of a dilemma. As Giap wrote about the situation at the conclusion of the spring 1953 campaign season:

> The enemy found himself face to face with a contradiction: Without scattering his forces it was impossible for him to occupy the invaded territory; in scattering his forces he puts himself in difficulties. His scattered units would fall easy prey to our troops, his mobile forces would be more and more reduced and the shortage of troops would be all the more acute. On the other hand if he concentrated his forces to move from the defensive position [to an offensive one], the occupation forces would be weakened and it would be difficult for him to hold the invaded territory. Now, if the enemy gives up the occupied territory, the very aim of the war of re-conquest is defeated.[1]

The critical issue was to determine where to launch the major offensive and how best to support it with more limited operations—guerrilla actions, secondary offensives, and, of course, political and diplomatic agitation. No matter which theater was selected for the major offensive in the fall of 1953, Giap hoped to keep his regular forces in the Viet Bac and the northwest out of major combat until well after the first rains subsided in September.

Success in the upcoming campaign required improvement and further expansion of the PAVN. Yet more heavy weapons from the Chinese had to be integrated; complex command and control issues involved in multi-division operations had to be worked out through trial and error in classrooms and training grounds. Giap now had around 300,000 well-trained soldiers between the regulars and the regional forces, and at least 200,000 local militia to support the regulars and provide intelligence. In the Delta the Armed Propaganda units and political operatives worked assiduously, conducting an increasingly effective subversion campaign against the Vietnam National Army and the villagers who were still under control of the government.

Giap had more highly motivated recruits than his training camps could handle. Most importantly, Giap had time on his side. It was no exaggeration to say that the Vietminh could prevail in the conflict simply by continuing to engage in a series of inconclusive battles and campaigns. The French were under increasing pressure to reverse the revolution's gains of the past two years before the public and politicians lost the will to carry on with the "dirty war." Giap enjoyed the advantages of operating within a unified and totalitarian political system. Only the Central Committee could call an end to the war before it had achieved its ends, and this seemed inconceivable in 1953, just as it would in 1963. Communist propaganda could mask defeats in specific engagements from the population. Indeed, there were no acknowledged defeats at all—at least no defeats in the public record.

THE FRENCH

We turn now to French prospects and plans. General Henri Navarre had never served a day in Indochina before assuming command of all French forces there in May 1953. He claimed no particular expertise in matters of Communist war strategy or doctrine, and we have little evidence that he gained much during the year he spent there. Indeed, in retrospect it appears that he left Indochina somewhat more baffled than he had been upon his arrival.

Navarre was not particularly well liked by his FEF comrades, for he cultivated an air of mystery and detachment. Nonetheless, after a tour of French installations throughout Vietnam, he arrived at an astute diagnosis of what ailed the FEF effort. Even elite mobile units seemed in the grips of a defensive mentality. The De Lattre Line had 1,200 outposts ringing the Red River Delta, where five French divisions were deployed, yet the Vietminh had been able to infiltrate 60,000 troops into the Delta and extend its control over half of its 7,000 villages. The Vietminh were highly motivated, fought to a common plan, lived a spartan existence, and were growing stronger every day. FEF operations under Salan had worked toward no common objective, and, as noted by American combat photographer David D. Duncan, the French fought a "languid" war on "banker's hours."[2] What could be done to remedy the situation? Navarre had a plan, and a good one, considering the conditions on the ground and the tendentious politics swirling around the war effort in Paris. Well aware that he needed more troops, Navarre requested an increase from 165,000 to 217,000 by early 1954. From the summer of 1953 through the autumn of 1954, Navarre proposed to focus on pacification operations that would sweep Communist guerrillas and the shadow government from the Delta. In the northwest, he proposed to remain on the defensive, seeking only to disrupt and harass Vietminh forces. With funding from the United States, Navarre planned to accelerate the expansion and training of the Vietnamese National Army.

The Navarre plan, however, did call for one major offensive in the upcoming 1954 campaign season. He called it Operation Atlante, and it was to be a powerful drive against Giap's forces in Interzone V, along the highly populous coast between Danang and Nha Trang. The PAVN already had twelve regular battalions and substantial regional units there, and more troops were trickling in every day. Atlante's objective was to decimate those forces and close the door on further penetration by revolutionary forces.

In phase two of the Navarre plan, projected to last from late 1954 through early 1956, a considerably larger and more powerful FEF would punch deep into the Vietminh's main bases in northern Tonkin, and perhaps around the PAVN's southern stronghold in the Thanh Hoa area, placing France in an advantageous military position before concluding the conflict through negotiations.

As of June 1953, Navarre had perhaps 190,000 French Union troops in the FEF, but 100,000 were tied down in static defense. The training of the Vietnamese National Army was ominously behind schedule. Its operational units suffered from a high desertion rate and an incompetent officer corps. Navarre's options, though, were constrained by the reluctance of politicians in Paris to provide badly needed equipment and adequate reinforcements, and by a lack of support for the war effort at home. He had asked for 12 additional infantry battalions and 3,000 additional officers and noncoms. Paris promised to meet his request, but because of the pressure from France's NATO allies of having to supply troops for the defense of Europe, Nararre received only 8 new battalions and 500 officers.

To his credit, Navarre realized that the FEF needed an injection of confidence to snap it out of its torpor during the summer monsoon season before the big campaign season got under way. Nararre came up with the goods in admirable style by launching a dramatic attack on a Communist supply base at Langson in late July. As the French force closed in on Langson, Giap ordered his security force at the depot to disperse into the jungle rather than resist, leaving 500 tons of Vietminh weapons and supplies for the French to capture. He could afford the loss.

A month later, the French mounted a brilliant deception operation, evacuating more than five battalions of troops and most of their heavy weapons from the remote fortress at Na San right under the noses of the PAVN. So much for the preliminary summer attacks.

PAVN PLANS FOR THE NORTHWEST

Meanwhile, the senior leadership of the Vietminh devoted much time in the summer to determining when and where to launch their fall offensive. Initially, it appears they gave much consideration to attacking the French in the Delta, as the Laotian attacks during the past year had drawn considerable numbers of enemy units to the remote northwestern hinterlands. But it was not to be. In October 1953 Ho, Giap, and Truong Chinh, the major strategists of Vietnamese protracted war, met with other senior leaders around a small table in a bamboo house in Thai Nguyen Province to decide where to launch the major offensive. A consensus emerged after considerable debate. The offensive would be in the northwest.

Without question, their decision reflected the advice of the Chinese Central Committee and its military advisers. The Chinese were against attacking the Red River Delta on the grounds that the French, while weakened there, were still too strong. The northwest was far more promising because the French forces there were widely scattered. Nowhere was a full division deployed. Yet credit for the strategic decision to fight in the northwest must be shared by the Chinese and Vietnamese, as it evolved out of a series of conferences.[3]

It was at the October meeting that Truong Chinh voiced the rationale for the decision:

> The enemy's dispositions [in the northwest] are relatively week and exposed, but they cannot abandon these areas, and this is especially true for the mountain jungle region. If we launch an attack in the Northwest region we will certainly draw in enemy forces and force the enemy's strategic mobile force to disperse to defend against our attack.... The enemy may only be able to bring in supplies and reinforcements by air. If we can overcome the problems with logistics and supplies, our forces will have many advantages fighting up there and we will be capable of attaining and maintaining military superiority throughout the entire campaign, or at least in a certain sector of the campaign area. In that way we may be able to win a great victory.[4]

Truong Chinh was saying, in essence, that stage three of the people's war was finally in the offing. Yet the plan was tempered with the recognition that even if a great victory in the northwest were achieved, it was unlikely to lead to a complete victory. Almost certainly, the war would continue even with a victory in the northwest, perhaps for several years.[5]

As Giap gradually built up strength in the northwest and kept an eye on French movements throughout Vietnam, he identified several potential targets for the northwest drive. It might be directed at Lai Chau, the last island of French military power in the region. It might take the form of another invasion of Laos, followed by the sacking of Luang Prabang, the royal capital, and the installment of a Communist Pathet Lao regime there. Or perhaps the major Vietminh attack would fall directly on French forces, should the High Command mount its own drive deep into the Tai country. Finally, Giap could close in on a strategic valley in the heart of Tai Montagnard country called Dien Bien Phu. The Tais had believed for centuries that whoever controlled the valley held the key to the entire northwest and the gateway to Laos.

Both Giap and the French High Command were well aware of the strategic value of Dien Bien Phu. Giap has described the valley as "the biggest and richest of the four plains in the hilly region close to the Vietnam-Laos frontier . . . In the theater of operations [i.e., the northwest] and upper Laos, Dien Bien Phu is a strategic location of the first importance."[6]

Ten miles from the Laotian border, the heart-shaped valley eleven miles long and six miles wide—roughly 180 Manhattan blocks north to south, and from the East River to the Hudson—was surrounded by rolling hills and mountains up to 6,000 feet, covered with thick foliage. The Tai farmed fruits and rice there, and it was a major marketing center for opium, a highly profitable commodity. Most importantly, the village stood at a road nexus for three routes amid trackless terrain: China to the north, Laos to the south, and a Vietminh supply depot at Tran Giao to the northeast.

A small French garrison had been deployed in Dien Bien Phu during the Indochina War until November 1952, when General Salan ordered its withdrawal as the PAVN 316th Division closed in on the valley. But two months later, Salan made clear his intention to take it back, as its reoccupation was "the first step for regaining control of the Tai country, and for the elimination of the Viet-Minh in the area west of the Black River."[7]

The FEF's first major operation of the 1953–1954 campaign commenced on October 14, when six French mobile groups attacked the 320th Division of the PAVN in a pincer movement south of the Red River Delta with a view to surrounding the division and seizing a big supply depot. Giap's division took heavy casualties but managed to transport the most critical supplies out of the area and then slipped out of the noose. Navarre had hoped Giap would order one or more of his divisions from the northwest to reinforce the 320th, but he resisted the temptation to do so. Instead, in early November he dispatched the 316th Division from Thanh Hoa in the direction of Lai Chau in order to strengthen his position in the northwest. It would take the division about a month to arrive at its destination.

Then, on November 20, much to Giap's surprise, three battalions of crack French paratroopers drifted downward into Dien Bien Phu. Quickly reinforced by several additional infantry battalions, engineers, and a limited number of field guns, the French began construction of a new *base aeroterrestre*. "Operation Castor" had begun in earnest.

Why Navarre decided to retake Dien Bien Phu and why he opted to remain there, despite mounting evidence that he was not so much setting a trap as falling into one, remains highly controversial. In fact, his rationale at any given time for launching the operation and staying put tended to vary and was often out of sync with that of the base's commander, Colonel Christian de Castries, and his immediate superior, General René Cogny, commander of all forces in Tonkin.

As the situation developed between December and the spring of 1954, Navarre justified the deployment of a division of troops to the valley by turns as a way of drawing off Giap's divisions far from the Red River Delta, which he envisioned as the main theater of operations; as a hub for offensive operations to take back all of Tai country from the Vietminh; and ultimately as a lure, tempting Giap into a siege operation in which French supporting arms and infantry could destroy PAVN regiments en masse as they assembled for a major assault.

As the French quickly built up the initial force in late November with three additional battalions and heavy weapons, and began construction of a large camp, Giap, though unsure of Navarre's intention, nonetheless told his commanders that an operation at or around Dien Bien Phu could work in their favor. Navarre's decision was congenial to Giap's broad campaign plan, which was a good start. Perhaps he could maneuver Navarre into some type of critical engagement where his own forces might fight under advantageous conditions, despite his lack of air power and overall inferiority in artillery.

Accordingly, Giap ordered the single regiment in the area to withdraw into the hills to monitor and harass the French in the valley. He waited for a few days to see what his adversary's next move might be. When French press reports and local intelligence at the end of November suggested strongly that Navarre planned a major campaign to oust the Vietminh from Tai country, or to establish another Na San on a grand scale, Giap responded definitively: he sent the two infantry divisions along with the 351st Heavy Division to march toward Dien Bien Phu.

French communications intelligence intercepted PAVN radio traffic in the first day or two of December, at which point Navarre ordered General Cogny "to accept battle in the northwest" and to center his defense "on the air-land base of Dien Bien Phu, which must be held at all costs."[8] Cogny then ordered the garrison at Dien Bien Phu to be reinforced yet again. By the end of January, the garrison would be further expanded to 10,000 men in twelve battalions—the lion's share of all the mobile reserves at Cogny's disposal. He also ordered an immediate withdrawal of the 2,100-man garrison at Lai Chau to Dien Bien Phu, as Giap's 316th Division was clearly en route to that hedgehog and might reach it within four or five days.

Of course, a major battle was not called for in Navarre's original plan for spring 1954, but like his Vietnamese counterpart, the French commander sensed that he had a golden opportunity. He felt sure Giap could not sustain two or three divisions in so remote an area, in such difficult terrain, given the limitations of his logistical system. Even if he were able to do so, Navarre reckoned that he could destroy those divisions with air power and artillery.

Ironically, Navarre's senior commanders in Tonkin argued vehemently against mounting Operation Castor at all. They did not think the FEF had the necessary assets to either build a resilient fortified base or supply a full division at that base exclusively by air. Logistical calculations by the air commander were particularly troubling. Even if he had all air transport assets in Indochina at his disposal, he could not come even close to meeting the daily needs of 10,000 men in a combat situation.

Despite these dire assessments, Navarre held fast, even after the French government contradicted its earlier directive, informing him that his first priority should be the preservation of the expeditionary force, not the protection of Laos. Navarre defended his decision by comparing Dien Bien Phu with the battle for the airhead at Na San, where the FEF had blunted several attacks by two PAVN regiments in late 1952. A much larger base with far more firepower, he reasoned, could do the same. The artillery commander at Dien Bien Phu reinforced this misconception when he assured Navarre that he could silence any artillery Giap could bring to bear with counter-battery fire within a few hours after their opening barrage. Again, Navarre's senior commanders dissented from this sunny assessment. Many felt that the differences between Na San and Dien Bien Phu outweighed the similarities. First of all, Dien Bien Phu was roughly ten times larger. Air supply was far more tenuous, and Giap's force far, far larger and more capable at Dien Bien Phu than it had been at Na San.

Three days after Navarre ordered the base held at all costs, Giap presented a plan for the largest battle of the war. The evidence suggests that he had learned of Navarre's decision, though the verdict is still out on this question. In any case, by December 6, 1953, Giap had decided to fight the set-piece battle he had studiously avoided since the 1951 defeats. It would require the deployment of four to five infantry divisions and virtually all of the artillery, engineers, and antiaircraft assets in the PAVN inventory. All told, 42,000 troops, 14,000 civilian porters at the front alone, and well over 100,000 from all over northern Vietnam were needed to transport matériel and heavy weapons from as far away as 500 miles in Cao Bang province and southern China. All-weather roads would have to be built and maintained. Three hundred tons of ammunition would be required at the front before commencing the attack, and the campaign could be expected to last forty-five days. He would enclose the base in a ring of steel and then close in.

The Politburo approved the plan on the same day Giap proposed it. Ho Chi Minh's final remark that day to Vo Nguyen Giap reflected his enduring faith and confidence in his close lieutenant: "I give you complete authority to make all decisions. If victory is certain, then you are to attack. If victory is not certain, then you must resolutely refrain from attacking."[9] Years later, Giap explained the thinking behind his decision to do battle in the valley in *People's War People's Army*:

> However, the importance of Dien Bien Phu [as a strategic position of the first rank] could not be regarded as the decisive factor in our decision to attack it. In the relation of forces at that time, could we destroy the fortified entrenched camp...? Could we be certain of victory in attacking

it? Our decision had to depend on this consideration alone....Dien Bien Phu was a strongly fortified entrenched camp. On the other hand, it was set up in a mountainous region, on ground which was advantageous to us, and decidedly disadvantageous to the enemy. Dien Bien Phu was, moreover, a completely isolated position, far away from all the enemy's bases. The only means of supplying Dien Bien Phu was by air. These circumstances could easily deprive the enemy of all initiative and force him on to the defensive if attacked....On our side, we had picked units of the regular army which we could concentrate to achieve supremacy in power. We could overcome all difficulties in solving the necessary tactical problems; we had, in addition, an immense rear, and the problem of supplying the front with food and ammunition, though very difficult, was not insolvable. Thus we had conditions for retaining the initiative in the operations....It was on the basis of this analysis of the enemy's and our own strong and weak points that we solved the question as to whether we should attack Dien Bien Phu or not. We decided to *wipe out at all costs the whole enemy force*...after having created favourable conditions for this battle by launching numerous offensives on various battlefields and by intensifying preparations on the Dien Bien Phu battlefield.[10]

THE CAMPAIGN BEGINS

The first major engagement of the campaign began not at Dien Bien Phu itself, but at Lai Chau, fifty-five miles north of the big base. With four divisions converging on Lai Chau, Cogny had to evacuate its garrison or face annihilation. On December 9, the French force there mounted out, moving south into the jungle en route to Dien Bien Phu. Leading elements of the 316th ran straight into the column from Lai Chau, and "like hungry wolves attacking the stragglers of a caribou herd," shredded it in a series of well-executed ambushes.[11] Only 185 of the 2,100 troops in the withdrawing column managed to stagger into Dien Bien Phu more than a week after their harrowing ordeal in the jungle began.

Meanwhile, three battalions from inside the perimeter of the fortress of Dien Bien Phu had been sent out to rescue the Lai Chau survivors. This elite force of paratroopers ran into a wall of PAVN steel, and had to withdraw with heavy casualties. The commander of that force, Lieutenant Colonel Pierre Langlais (who would later become the de facto commander of all the besieged troops inside Dien Bien Phu when their original commander, Colonel de Castries, fell into a dysfunctional depression), noted "the incredible ability of the enemy to camouflage his gun positions and camps so as to render them invisible to aerial observation and ground reconnaissance."[12]

The lead element of the rest of the 316th Division entered the base at Lai Chau on December 12, having marched at the extraordinary pace of twenty miles a day, and thirty during the night, when it no longer had to worry about air strikes. By early January 1954 the Vietminh had flooded the valley with infantry. In fact the FEF's patrols were taking heavy casualties—by January 15, about 150 soldiers had been killed and 600 wounded. When several FEF patrols attempted reconnaissance in force missions just a few hundred meters beyond the perimeter of the base, they were forced to withdraw under withering fire. All hopes of breaking out from the slowly tightening siege ring around the base with mobile offensive forces were fading fast.

By this point French troops were working with engineers under intense pressure to finish building hundreds of bunkers, communication trenches, and blockhouses within the largest and most complex combat base in all of French Indochina (see map on page xviii). The main center of resistance (MCR) consisted of a cluster of four major strongpoints on both the east and west sides of the Nam Yum River: Dominique, Elaine, Claudine, and Huguette. Colonel Castries's main headquarters and the key supply depots were positioned in and around the center of these five strongpoints. An airstrip stretched out from the center of the base in a northwesterly direction into the northern sector of Huguette.

Ringing the MCR were the satellite strongpoints (going clockwise) of Gabrielle, Beatrice, Isabelle, and Anne Marie, meant to shield the MCR from assaults by Giap's infantry. For the most part, the many defensive positions within the strongpoints—firing positions and blockhouses—had interlocking and mutually supporting fields of fire. Two-thirds of the French artillery was inside the MCR; one-third was at the independent strongpoint Isabelle, four miles to the south of the MCR. Isabelle's big guns could support the defense of the MCR, but not that of Beatrice or Gabrielle, leaving those two strongpoints somewhat vulnerable to mass infantry attacks.

Taken together, the main centers of resistance and the satellite strongpoints constituted a formidable target for any attacker, but it suffered several deficiencies. The fortifications in most places were vulnerable to destruction by 105mm howitzers. Not a single pound of concrete had been used in construction. The water table was such that several strongpoints could be expected to flood by April 15. As Giap remarked at the time to his commanders, "if the battle goes into the rainy season, we are on the slopes and can dig drainage ditches while the enemy on the plain will be deep in mud."[13] The FEF artillery was inexplicably exposed to fire from the hills. Equally inexplicably, the perimeter of the base was far too extensive to be defended effectively by only 10,000 troops.

There were ominous signs around the base in mid-January that the attack was imminent. The Vietminh were seemingly ubiquitous in the hills and even on the valley plain. Every day, skirmishes broke out close to the perimeter. The Vietminh shelled the base from the hills, albeit sporadically. The French prepared their positions and reviewed their firing plans with a newfound sense of urgency.

So, too, did the Vietminh. Giap made the weeklong trek to his forward command post, a cave under fifteen feet of solid rock covered by jungle, nine miles north of Dien Bien Phu, arriving on January 12.[14] His commanders were informed around January 15 that a massive assault was slated for January 25. Yet, as the date approached, the commander in chief was not at all sure that the decision to attack in late January was a good one, nor was he certain that the planned method of attack was correct. The critical question of *how* to conduct the attack had been the subject of debate for several weeks, and was still open to question as late as January 14 when Giap's senior commanders joined the chief Chinese adviser, Wei Guoqing, to discuss the two options that had been under consideration. Wei argued for a Korean-style massive attack by several divisions from the north and northwest. Their immediate objective: overrun the satellite strongpoints immediately and punch through the formidable defenses of the MCR, inflict crippling losses in the opening attack, and seize most of the western half of the MCR and the northern end of the airstrip, thereby preventing reinforcements from landing and dooming what was left of the garrison to certain annihilation. The shorthand description of this method was "swift attack, swift victory." It promised a short campaign, thereby relieving great pressure on the logistical system.

Giap feared that such an approach was too risky. What if the initial attack was repulsed and the PAVN suffered devastating losses among its assault units, trained to a razor's edge? His replacements had not been trained to a standard anywhere near as high as his first-line troops. If the first attacks failed, he might not have the strength left to continue the attack at all, and the French would have a resounding victory.

As he pondered the situation on the ground and the level of pre-paredness of his own forces, his worries only grew deeper. The alternative approach was referred to by the Vietnamese as the "steady attack, steady advance" method, with more limited attacks by regiments against indi-vidual strongpoints over a period of weeks. After seizing the satellites with overwhelming force in the opening days of the campaign, the Vietminh would encircle the entire MCR and punch in the French perimeter gradu-ally by attacking in great force against one sector, while pinning down FEF reinforcements with secondary attacks elsewhere. The Vietminh artillery commander during the campaign summed up the difference between the methods nicely: it was a choice between eating an orange by using a knife to cut it to pieces, or taking one's time and peeling the fruit by hand.[15]

On January 14, Giap reluctantly gave in. The Vietminh would mount one massive attack by two or three entire divisions, commencing on January 25.

However, second thoughts lingered. On January 24, Giap weighed the considerable supply and morale difficulties he was sure to encounter with a prolonged delay against the possibility that the massive human wave attack would fail. As he agonized over the decision, a crucial development arose. A Vietminh soldier was captured and revealed that the opening assault was slated for 1700 hours on January 25. Vietminh radio monitors picked up French transmissions indicating that they had the critical information. Giap set a new date of 1700 hours on the 26th.

After another night of restless sleep and angst, Giap finally came to a firm decision. The French had built up the strength of their positions steadily. His own artillery was not yet fully in place, and he questioned the training of his gunners. The big question was, could he be reasonably confident of victory? In the end, his answer was "no." And so he made the crucial decision to postpone the opening salvos for more than a full month and developed a battle plan that he felt sure would accomplish the objec-tive. He described that plan clearly and concretely:

If we attack in stages, we will reinforce our positions with each stage. We will keep the initiative, attacking when we want, where we want. But we will attack only when we are ready, and we will only occupy the positions we have taken when necessary. We will exploit the enemy's essential dif-ficulty—its supply lines. The longer the battle lasts, the more wounded he will have. Supplying the garrison will grow more difficult....Our troops have never attacked more than two battalions. This time we will proceed sector by sector. We must prepare for a relatively long campaign. We should not fear the enemy air force or artillery as long as we maintain secrecy and camouflage. During the transfer of our artillery pieces, we were able to hide for twenty days tens of thousands of men on a stretch of road within enemy artillery range....The enemy is surrounded on the ground, and if its air supply is hampered, it will encounter insurmountable difficulties...the morale of this army of mercenaries will collapse. We will also suffer losses. Battles are won with blood and sacrifice. But if we attempt a rapid attack to avoid further losses we will end up with greater losses.[16]

To reduce the fort as a whole, Giap planned to attack the satellite outposts in the opening phase and then, in phase two, mount a series of assaults by entire regiments directed against one quadrant of the fortress's MCR under cover of artillery. (Typically against one or two contiguous strongpoints.) These would be quickly followed by a similar series of attacks against a different quadrant, thereby causing the French to shift their limited reserve forces (virtually all stationed within the MCR) from one quadrant to another.[17] Attacks on *individual positions* within strongpoints—for instance Elaine 1 or 2, or Dominique 6 or 7—would come in waves against a narrow and changing front against a position in the east, then in the north, and so forth, always under the cover of artillery and mortars.

After serious damage had been inflicted on the MCR and French supplies depleted, the assault troops would be pulled back for rest and refitting, and to extend the trench network, tightening the noose of steel around the MCR. Giap would then unleash a sustained series of attacks by full divisions from several different directions until all resistance was crushed.

SECONDARY OPERATIONS

On January 20, General Navarre launched Operation Atlante, the centerpiece of his 1953–1954 campaign, at least as he had planned it the previous summer. Atlante was a massive and unwieldy drive into Vietminh Interzone V, the rice-rich coastal area between Nha Trang and Danang that contained 2.5 million people and perhaps 30,000 PAVN and regional troops.

In launching this attack, Navarre hoped to force Giap to send at least one division from the northwest to the coast of central Vietnam, relieving pressure on the French fortress in the valley of Dien Bien Phu.

Atlante called for an amphibious landing about fifty miles north of Nha Trang and, eventually, ground assaults toward the heart of Interzone V from the north, the south, and the Kontum area in the western Central Highlands. Navarre hoped to clear the zone, destroy the Communist forces or force their removal, and re-establish control of the population. He had hoped "to subordinate to [Atlante] the conduct of the whole Indochina campaign during the first semester of 1954," but the impending battle at Dien Bien Phu invalidated that notion.[18]

In the initial drive to the north in late January, Giap's forces effectively harassed and blocked elements of the FEF's fifteen battalions, many of them part of the largely untried Vietnamese National Army, forcing them to sputter and fall apart. Under the pressure of PAVN the Vietnamese units began to disintegrate, in some cases deserting en masse.

Atlante was a failure on a major scale. It made substantial reinforcement of Dien Bien Phu, then shaping up into a set-piece battle of unprecedented proportion, impossible, and placed great strain on already inadequate FEF air assets. The FEF had only seventy-five transport planes, and by January 1954 this small fleet was the only means of supply for several remote garrisons, of which Dien Bien Phu was by far the largest. Atlante wore down vehicles and equipment that might have been used much more profitably elsewhere. (By this point in the war, PAVN units were often better armed and supplied than the FEF.) Lackluster performance in Atlante had another unfortunate effect. It heightened American skepticism about France's prosecution of the war, which, in turn, churned up seething resentment of the Americans in the French command.

Less than a week after Atlante commenced, Giap countered with several secondary attacks that he hoped would further disperse French mobile forces and place additional strains on the FEF's air force. The 803rd Independent Regiment debouched from the mountains in the western Central Highlands, swept over the defenses of Dak To, and seized that town on February 2. Turning south, the 803rd threatened Kontum. Navarre countered by airlifting several mobile groups to its defense. When the 803rd, joined by regional units, surrounded the French forces, Navarre evacuated them, again by air. Heavy fighting then erupted around Pleiku. The French quickly dispatched Mobile Group 100 to Pleiku, and barely held on to this strategically important town, but Mobile Group 100 lost an entire company in an ambush before the Vietminh withdrew into the mountains.

A few days earlier, on January 27, Giap had ordered the 316th, then bivouacked at Lai Chau, to drive into Laos. En route, the division joined Pathet Lao Communist troops in wiping out a French battalion that was defending the hedgehog at Muong Khoa. The 316th then pressed deep into Laos, within twenty miles of Luang Prabang. Once again, Giap forced Navarre to airlift his mobile reserves to protect the approaches to the city.

Everywhere, Giap seemed to be taking the initiative, forcing Navarre to deploy his mobile ground forces and paratroopers to locales that were far afield from the main battlefield at Dien Bien Phu. After demonstrating conclusively that the FEF at Dien Bien Phu weren't able to accomplish the very task that had initially spurred their deployment—the defense of Laos—Giap decided to order the 316th to withdraw from Laos and march back to its positions in the hills as the reserve force for the attack at Dien Bien Phu. Giap most likely decided to order this withdrawal because of a development far from the battlefield: he had just learned that the great powers had formally agreed to hold a conference in Geneva in late April, with the fate of Indochina on the docket. The impending battle at Dien Bien Phu was sure to have a crucial effect on negotiations one way or another. It was imperative to maximize his chances of defeating the French in the valley.

By the time the 316th marched into the hills around the valley in early March, Giap had all but completed one of the most impressive feats in the history of military logistics. It had taken three months to position the equivalent of five divisions, both combat and support troops, in and around the valley. Since early December they had traveled down winding roads, sometimes in trucks, but mostly on foot, through trackless jungles, swamps, and mountains.

Giap's senior supply officers, along with Chinese and Vietnamese engineers, planned and supervised a vast and efficient logistical network, improving several hundred miles of roads for use by 800 2.5-ton Soviet-built trucks, some hauling artillery pieces shipped from China, from as far away as Cao Bang in the Viet Bac. New roads and reinforced bridges, some of them a few inches under water, were built from scratch. Supplying and maintaining the combat troops took stupendous effort. It took a full week to bring bulk supplies from China to the main PAVN supply base at Tran Giao, thirty-seven miles northeast of Dien Bien Phu. Many of the roads had to be constructed from scratch for the operation. An all-weather road linked the supply base and the valley.

Well over 100,000 coolies and construction workers made indispensable contributions to the vast logistical effort. A host of road maintenance crews, the latter consisting in part of thousands of women stationed at encampments along the route, used wooden shovels, picks, and straw baskets to repair damage inflicted by French air power on the supply routes every day. The flow of Vietminh supplies was hampered by continual air interdiction, but never halted. Late in the battle, PAVN troops were placed on severely limited rice rations, but neither the assault troops nor the artillery batteries suffered serious ammunition shortages over the course of seven weeks of combat. The support effort became a national crusade, built around the slogan, "Everything for the Front!" It was hardly an exaggeration. Virtually the entire regular army was deployed at Dien Bien Phu. The defeat of that army in the looming battle might very well set back the revolutionary cause for a decade or more.

Whole volunteer bicycle companies of volunteers marched as far as 200 miles, just to begin serving at the front. Bikes were reconfigured with steel rims, and forks were replaced with iron rods. Hard bamboo sticks extended from the handlebars. Teams of five men were assigned to one bike, which could haul up to 400 pounds of rice across mountains, streams, and jungle tracks. Writer Ted Morgan recounts the story of Dinh Vin Ty, a bicycle porter from Hanoi: "At the Ban Phe Pass, the slope was so steep it took six men to push a single bike. One man held the handlebars. Two men ahead of the bike pulled it by a rope. Three men pushed from behind. That day, after hauling fifteen bikes up to the pass, Dinh collapsed from exhaustion."[19]

Inside the valley, Chinese engineers supervised the digging of a trench network that could facilitate the rapid movement of infantry units into assault jump-off points with little chance of being attacked by French supporting arms. Many trenches were within one hundred yards of French strongpoint perimeters.

On the eve of the initial attack of March 13, Giap had accomplished the seemingly impossible. He had five divisions in and around the valley, and well over 150 heavy guns in the hills that were so well dug in and camouflaged that the enemy would have great difficulty knocking out many of them with either an air attack or artillery.

Most of the lethal 105mm guns had been moved by truck to Na Nham, some six miles from the rim of the valley. Moving more than 150 heavy guns into positions on the edge of the valley proved to be a feat of human endurance rarely rivaled in modern war. The most challenging guns, of course, were the American 105mm howitzers, which had to be transported all of a piece. They could not be broken down like the 75mm field guns. The 105s had to be hauled to their emplacements by teams of men using block and tackles and oxen on a trail cut through the foothills of several low-lying mountains. It took a team of more than one hundred men a full week to move a single 105 into the forward slope of the hills east and north of the combat base.

From the time of Giap's cancellation of the January 25 attack, French forces were compelled to remain inside their perimeters or face dire consequences. At the end of January, a regimental-size force of paras and Legionnaires attempted to take Hill 683, 2,000 yards from the northernmost strongpoint at Dien Bien Phu. Here, for the first time, French forces encountered well-fortified Communist positions in combat. The advancing patrols saw nothing until they were suddenly fired on almost directly from under their feet. The Vietminh had built bunkers directly into the ground and underbrush; their firing slits, hardly wider than a mail slot, barely revealed themselves.

In February, a platoon attempting to locate Vietminh artillery stumbled against a well-concealed bunker system. Most of the soldiers in the platoon were killed in a matter of minutes, and the Vietminh captured a large-scale map of the entire base with artillery batteries clearly marked. Now the Communists' artillery could fix its targets with exceptional precision.

THE BATTLE: PHASE 1

The initial assault came exactly where the French expected—against Beatrice, the northeastern satellite strongpoint—and, although it was defended by a battalion of Legionnaires, the most difficult to defend. Around noon on March 13 the French attempted to clear the PAVN assault troops from their trenches 200 meters from Beatrice's perimeter, and the Vietminh opened up with a heavy artillery barrage. At 1700 hours, March 13, six battalions of the 312th Division left their trenches and attacked along three axes with bugles blowing. Like many Vietminh assaults, this one was covered by the partial darkness of early evening under a new moon, which afforded the attackers just enough light to see their targets. The Legionnaires put up a spirited defense despite the death of their commander at 1830 hours, fifteen minutes after he had called in artillery fire almost on top of his own position. The Vietminh took Beatrice around midnight, following several hours of intense hand-to-hand fighting. Fewer than 200 of the 700 Legionnaires manning Beatrice straggled back to the comparative safety of neighboring strongpoints. The 312th suffered some 600 men killed and 1,000 wounded.

On the morning of March 14, a French counterattack against Beatrice was blunted and turned back by powerful PAVN artillery. The charred landscape was strewn with corpses and the wounded of both armies, many of whom were moaning and near death. Giap asked for a four-hour truce to collect the dead and wounded. Castries assented. It was the first and last such truce in a brutal fifty-six-day siege. That night, Gabrielle, the satellite strongpoint with two defensive lines, manned by a tough Algerian battalion, fell to two regiments of the elite 308th Iron Division after a ferocious series of attacks and counterattacks.

The initial PAVN attacks into the northwestern and northeastern slopes of Gabrielle, which occurred at 2000 hours on March 14, made slow progress before stalling after two hours. The Vietminh artillery ceased at 0230 hours on March 15, and the assault troops dug in and regrouped. At 0330 hours, they resumed the assault. At 0400 hours, a PAVN artillery shell landed amid the French command group, severely wounding the commander, his replacement, and his staff. The forces on Gabrielle could no longer wage a coordinated defense on their own.

De Castries then ordered Lt. Colonel Pierre Langlais, who commanded the entire defense of the MCR, to launch a tank-infantry counterattack on Gabrielle. Langlais assembled a tank squadron and a company of Legionnaires, along with an FEF para battalion that was exhausted from a harrowing jump into the base the previous day, to counterattack. The Legionnaires and tankers made impressive progress at first, but the para battalion lost its nerve under Vietminh artillery fire, and the counterattack broke down into a chaotic withdrawal of all French forces in and around Gabrielle at 0800 hours on March 16.

Gabrielle cost Giap at least 1,000 men killed and 2,000 wounded with French casualties about 1,000 in all, making the fight for this strongpoint among the bloodiest of the battle. But the French could hardly hope to survive long sustaining such frightful casualties, while the Vietminh could do so handily. Gabrielle's loss, wrote Bernard Fall, "had a disastrous effect on the morale of the [French] garrison."[20]

With the fall of Gabrielle, the general pattern of combat at Dien Bien Phu began to emerge. Overwhelmingly superior numbers of PAVN assault troops would attack French defensive positions and overrun them; the French would counterattack with limited success and at frightening cost. Individual positions within strongpoints would change hands. Then the Vietminh would regroup and counterattack, sometimes immediately, sometimes several days later. Finally the French strongpoint would fall, usually for good.

Anne Marie, the last of the three satellite strongpoints forming a semi-circle north of the main center of resistance, fell early on the morning of March 17, but in a decidedly atypical fashion. Anne Marie was manned by a battalion of Tais, who performed well in mobile operations in their mountainous homeland but were wholly unsuited to defensive fighting. Giap's political cadres had been working an effective propaganda campaign against the Tais for weeks, urging them to abandon a fight that was not theirs in the first place, and promising them good treatment if they put down their arms. The hideously destructive combat of the previous few days completely spooked them. On the night of March 17, they deserted their positions en masse. The French officers and the few Tais who remained had no choice but to withdraw into Huguette, where they became part of that strongpoint's garrison for the duration. The first phase of the battle was over. It had been costly for both sides, but things had gone very much as Giap had planned.

THE LULL

Phase one was followed by a lull that lasted from March 18 until March 30. PAVN troops took up picks and shovels under the direction of Chinese engineers and further developed a massive network of trenches and tunnels, coming in some places as close as fifty yards to the French defensive positions. Digging methodically day and night, often under makeshift covers of beams, wood platforms, and earth, they approached the perimeter, wrote one American correspondent who visited the camp, "like the tentacles of some determined, earth-bound devilfish."[21] By this point, Vietminh guns in the hills had rendered the airstrip too dangerous for landing reinforcements in any number. The last flights evacuating the wounded departed on March 26. About fifty Communist Chinese gun crews manning lethal 37mm antiaircraft guns ringed the French camp, and even aerial resupply had become extremely hazardous for flight crews. The garrison required 150 tons of supplies a day to fight, but poor weather and Giap's antiaircraft crews ensured that on many days less than half that amount could be delivered. Thus, the garrison found itself operating under increasingly severe shortages of ammunition, food, and even drinking water.

The lull in the fighting was not uneventful. The French struggled to halt the constriction of the creeping network of trenches with napalm and local ground attacks, but they lacked the air and artillery assets to do more than inflict peripheral damage on the trench network. The Vietminh were able to dig more than 100 kilometers of tunnels before the end of the month. One by one, the gaps in the cordon around the MCR were closed off. A well-coordinated French tank-infantry raid on March 28 caught Vietnamese antiaircraft crews west of the MCR by surprise, knocking out seventeen antiaircraft weapons and killing perhaps 300 PAVN soldiers in the process.

PHASE TWO

Giap renewed the attack at 1700 on March 30, when the 312th and the 316th jumped off from their trenches to seize five key hills within strongpoints Dominique and Elaine, the eastern half of the MCR. Phase two had begun. Two hills within Dominique fell almost immediately as an Algerian battalion broke under the terrifying weight of an accurate artillery bombardment followed by waves of screaming infantry. The 312th assault battalions were on the verge of taking a third hill, putting them in a position to outflank the FEF troops defending the main headquarters bunker. Had they done so, the French defense of the entire fortress might well have collapsed. Disaster was averted at the last minute when a battery of French artillery on a neighboring hill lowered its muzzles and fired directly into the assault waves, cutting down hundreds of Vietminh in the vanguard waves and forcing later waves to break into disorderly retreat. In the end, the hill held.

Meanwhile, the 316th smothered all the French positions on one hill in less than an hour; by midnight they had taken half of another. As the fighting died down early on the morning of March 31, the French hold on Dien Bien Phu was extremely perilous. A powerful FEF counterattack at 1330 hours retook two of the three hills, but to hold this hard-won ground, fresh troops would need to replace the exhausted assault units and dig in fast. Langlais, however, had no fresh troops to spare. He had no choice but to withdraw from both hills rather than risk the annihilation of the troops who had taken the hills in the first place. As if this weren't demoralizing enough, the FEF's artillery ammunition was almost exhausted. The dispiriting withdrawal from the eastern hills exposed yet another French blunder in the battle's preparation phase: no counterattack maneuvers had been worked out in advance, and the three battalions reserved for counterattacks were stretched too thin to fulfill their role in a protracted siege.

Over the next two days, supplies were stretched thin as inadequate reinforcements and resupplies floated down out of the sky, and murderous PAVN antiaircraft fire forced transports ferrying a battalion of fresh reinforcements to turn back toward Hanoi. Early in the morning of April 2, Giap launched a successful secondary attack from positions northwest of the MCR against a hill protecting the northern end of the airstrip. A counterattack supported by three tanks forced the Vietminh to withdraw, but the defensive positions had been destroyed and, again, the French abandoned the hill.

The grueling pattern of attack and counterattack continued as Vietminh regiments ripped into beleaguered French companies, many of which were reduced to as few as seventy or eighty effectives. The Vietminh made little additional progress in the eastern hills after April 2. Had they done so, the battle almost surely would have ended within a matter of several days. Only herculean French efforts kept the eastern hills sector from complete collapse.

After April 5 the intensity of the fighting slackened somewhat as Giap adapted a more deliberate approach. Sapping and digging followed by short, fierce engagements by small units for limited gains were the order of the day. Between April 10 and 12, after the battlefield had taken on the macabre atmosphere of World War I trench warfare, a desperate battle swirled around what Giap referred to as "the most important of all" the eastern hills, Elaine 1.[22] A hastily assembled two-company assault French force broke down into independent assault squads and fire teams and scurried up the hill, bypassing the outer defenses held by PAVN troops who were momentarily dazed by artillery fire. Sharp hand-to-hand fighting followed. This time the French prevailed. Two relatively fresh FEF companies quickly replaced the assault troops in the defensive positions just in time to face a PAVN regimental counterattack. Miraculously, the French held despite additional counterattacks by two PAVN battalions on the evening of April 12. The French clung tenaciously to Elaine 1 until early May.

Meanwhile, the Vietminh made slow but steady progress against Huguette's positions in the northwest. These gains paved the way for PAVN artillery and direct-fire heavy weapons to move in so close to the MCR that the crews could zero in on crucial targets—the already-diminished artillery batteries, the supply dumps, and even helicopters attempting to evacuate the wounded—with deadly accuracy. Giap's 308th Division was able to gain control over much of the northern end of the airstrip in a punishing series of assaults around April 12, when the main axis of attack shifted from the east to the northwest, only to return once again to the eastern hills.

Fears of asphyxiation gripped the entire FEF garrison by mid-month. It was clear to every FEF soldier left alive that the flow of supplies and replacements would continue to dwindle. In the last week of April came another lull, as Giap rested his battered assault units and brought them up to full strength in preparation for the last assault phase. The French were now compressed inside a circular perimeter only a mile in diameter. Giap summarized developments in the battle during the lull and the second phase of attacks as follows:

> Our offensive on the eastern hills of the central sector [the MCR] had obtained important successes, but had failed to reach all the assigned objectives.... We have therefore decided to continue to execute the tasks foreseen for the second phase of our offensive: To advance our attack and encirclement lines, improve our positions and occupy new ones; progressively tighten further our stranglehold so as to completely intercept reinforcements and supplies... utilizing trenches which have been driven forward until they touch the enemy lines, the tactic of gnawing away at the enemy piecemeal.[23]

By April 13, one reliable source puts Giap's total casualties at Dien Bien Phu around 19,000 men, including 6,000 killed. Another three weeks of fighting remained. Not surprisingly, morale began to flag in the Vietminh infantry divisions. Troops refused to leave their trenches, and political officers were reduced to forcing them out at gunpoint. Giap's response to the rise of morale problems was predictable and effective. He instituted an intense, all-encompassing program of indoctrination and "remolding" courses to correct "negative rightist thoughts" and to heighten "revolutionary enthusiasm." As Giap explained,

> To maintain and develop... [the] determination to fight and win was a whole process of unremitting and patient political and ideological education and struggle, tireless and patient efforts in political work on the front line....In accordance with the instructions of the Political Bureau, we opened in the heart of the battlefield an intensive and extensive struggle against rightist passivity, and for the heightening of revolutionary enthusiasm and the spirit of strict discipline with a view to insuring the total victory of the campaign.[24]

As we have noted earlier, Giap always conceived of military activity in a broad political context. The sacrifices of fighting a positional battle on the scale of Dien Bien Phu were justified in Giap's mind by his conviction that a victory there was sure to have a salubrious effect on the looming deliberations at Geneva, as well as on the morale of the revolution's supporters throughout all Vietnam.

THE FINAL PHASE

The final phase of attacks commenced at 1700 hours on May 1, when powerful elements of three divisions—the 312th, the 316th in the east, and the 308th in the west—jumped out of their trenches in a massive assault on the battered shambles of the MCR. Elaine 1, the critical eastern hill strongpoint, fell, this time for good; so did Dominique 3, despite heroic resistance by paras and Legionnaires. At 2005, General Cogny in Hanoi received a telling cable from the main CP in the headquarters bunker at Dien Bien Phu: "No more reserves left. Fatigue and wear and tear on the units terrible. Supplies and ammunition insufficient. Quite difficult to resist one more such push by the Communists, at least not without bringing in one brand-new battalion of excellent quantity."[25] Yet the terrible fighting went on.

The delegations of the main powers and the participants prepared their final briefs on Indochina for the Geneva summit in the first week of May.

During this time, it rained almost constantly in the valley, intensifying the suffering as Vietminh regiments attacked swamped, partially collapsed fighting positions held by battered companies frightfully reduced by combat, exhaustion, and sickness. On Elaine 2, the French held on. More than 1,500 corpses between the two armies were strewn about the hill in grotesque poses. At 2300 hours on May 6, Giap's sappers set off a 3,000-pound charge of TNT directly under the hill, killing most of the two companies manning the defenses and blowing its bunkers and blockhouses to smoldering ruins. At 1500 hours on May 7, Giap ordered simultaneous division-size attacks on what was left of the MCR. At 1730 hours, Captain Ta Quang Luat and his assault team burst into Castries's command bunker and took him prisoner. Within minutes, the Vietminh flag fluttered above the corrugated steel roof of the bunker. It was all over at last.

WHY GIAP PREVAILED

In seeking to explain the outcome of Dien Bien Phu, virtually all Western historians focus their attention on French gaffes and misconceptions. This is understandable, because the French mistakes were as egregious as they were numerous. What sort of battle did France hope to fight at Dien Bien Phu, and to what end? In truth, the French senior command's answers to these questions were ambiguous and inconsistent from the planning stages until the garrison was locked into a desperate siege against an enemy force far larger and more capable than French intelligence had predicted.

Yet Western historians of the battle seldom point out that the French blunders wouldn't have resulted in disaster if the People's Army had lacked superior strategic and tactical leadership, and a well-trained, highly motivated fighting force supported by a logistical system nothing short of miraculous. Giap had brilliantly exploited French weaknesses, both political and military. He had indeed "trapped the trapper" by moving substantial forces in late November 1953 toward the front, convincing Navarre to stand and fight at Dien Bien Phu despite the objections of his senior commanders.

It was Giap's organizational genius, more than anything, that was responsible for sustaining the assault troops in battle. He had supervised the construction of a vast logistical "tail" of the operation in exceedingly rough terrain, hundreds of miles from his army's home bases and training camps in northern Tonkin and near Thanh Hoa south of the Red River

Delta. So, too, Giap correctly assessed the weaknesses of the enemy disposition. At the last minute, he rejected a method of attack that had considerably more risk than the method he ultimately adopted. In adopting the plan, Giap showed his faith and confidence in his entire army from the privates in the assault waves and supply units to the divisional commanders. When morale flagged, he turned to his tried-and-true method for rejuvenating fighting spirit: intensive reiteration of the key themes of the revolutionary doctrine, coupled with draconian incentives—threats of execution, imprisonment, and humiliation to those who refused to press on in the most trying circumstances. It was a harsh, even brutal system, but it got the job done.

In the end, it could be said that many French errors and misjudgments at Dien Bien Phu stemmed from Navarre's egregious underestimation of his adversary, while a critical ingredient in Giap's success was his correct assessment of his enemy's strengths, as well as its weaknesses.

Fighting in Vietnam continued for several months after the battle, but it amounted to very little in the grand scheme of things. Giap's victory at Dien Bien Phu sealed the fate of the French in Indochina, ensuring the demise of French empire there. According to historian Bernard Fall, it also "signaled in an unequivocal manner the coming age of the Vietnam People's Army."[26]

RAMIFICATIONS

Less than a week after the start of the siege, the French had appealed to the Eisenhower administration to use massive airpower to intervene at Dien Bien Phu. But the Americans found themselves on the horns of a profound dilemma. Eisenhower was deeply troubled by the Cold War ramifications of a French exit from Southeast Asia, but he was nonetheless dead set against unilateral American intervention, for it would taint the United States with the stigma of supporting French colonialism and might provoke the Chinese to intervene directly in the conflict.

Eisenhower had engaged in intense discussion with his advisers as to whether or not to intervene. Various rescue plans had been put forward by the Joint Chiefs of Staff and top civilian advisers, including one scenario involving the use of nuclear weapons. In the end, Eisenhower refused to mount any operation to save the day without the participation of a coalition of forces. The British were adamant in their refusal, and so the discussions ceased.

Ironically, it was during the Dien Bien Phu intervention discussions that Eisenhower first put forward publically the rationale for the American commitment to a "free" Vietnam. His White House successors would invoke that rationale for expanding the American commitment to South Vietnam for the next fourteen years. Eisenhower remarked in a press conference that "You have broader considerations that might follow what you would call the 'falling domino' principle. You have a row of dominos set up, you knock over the first one, and what will happen to the last one is the certainty it will go over very quickly. So you could have the beginning of a disintegration that would have the most profound consequences."[27] So it was that Dien Bien Phu formed a fateful bridge between the end of the French war in Indochina and the beginning of the American War.

Flush from victory at Dien Bien Phu, the Vietminh delegation at Geneva had high hopes for a negotiated settlement. The accords that resulted—a signed cease-fire and an unsigned declaration—were a partial victory for the Vietnamese Communists, whose interests were circumscribed by their own allies, China and the Soviet Union, as well as by the reactions of the United States. For complex reasons of international policy, neither Communist power wished to unduly antagonize the United States or France, and they put strong pressure on the DRV delegation to accept terms far short of what they expected given the strength of their military position on the ground.

The terms themselves were couched in vague enough language to allow for varied interpretation, and for an uncertain future for the Communist revolutionaries. The country was divided temporarily at the 17th parallel into two zones: Ho's Democratic Republic of Vietnam in the north and a pro-Western state, initially under Bao Dai in the south. French military forces would be regrouped to the south and Vietminh forces to the north within 300 days. Free movement of the population between the zones would be allowed for the same length of time. An unsigned declaration called for a "free general election" in July 1956 to unite the country under one government, but the partition and election formula was cloudy. While the declaration established a cease-fire, it left the political future of Vietnam essentially undecided. Neither the United States nor the government of what would soon be known as The Republic of Vietnam (South Vietnam) signed the documents.

Although Washington officially "took note" of the agreements and agreed to refrain from using force to disturb them, Secretary of State John Foster Dulles made it clear that the United States was deeply unhappy with the arrangements and that the Eisenhower administration would take actions, diplomatic and otherwise, to shape the political landscape of Indochina to fit its own interests. Within a few months the National Security Council in Washington called for the use of "all available means" to undermine the Communist government in Hanoi, and to "make every possible effort…to maintain a friendly noncommunist government in South Vietnam and to prevent a Communist victory through all-Vietnam elections."[28]

By the end of the year, a CIA team under Colonel Edward Lansdale implemented a clandestine program of harassment of the DRV. The American crusade in Vietnam had begun in earnest. George Herring, a pioneering historian of America's war in Vietnam, summarizes the Eisenhower administration's policy in Southeast Asia nicely:

> The Eisenhower administration in 1954 and after firmly committed itself to the fragile government of Ngo Dinh Diem [head of state in South Vietnam from 1955 to 1963], eased the French out of Vietnam, and used its resources unsparingly to construct in southern Vietnam a viable, non-communist nation that would stand as "the cornerstone of the Free World in Southeast Asia."…Had it looked all over the world, the United States could not have chosen a less promising place for an experiment in nation-building.…In southern Vietnam, chaos reigned. The colonial economy depended entirely on exports of rice and rubber to finance essential imports. It had been devastated by nearly fourteen years of war and was held together by enormous French military expenditures that would soon cease.…Diem's government lacked experienced civil servants. Tainted by long association with France, it had no base of support in the countryside or among non-communist nationalists in Saigon.[29]

7

THE LONG STRUGGLE IN THE SOUTH BEGINS: 1954–1965

The American War, as the conflict in South Vietnam from 1954 to 1975 is called by the Vietnamese today, had an unusually protracted and complicated gestation period. The origins of the conflict between the United States, its Vietnamese allies, and the forces of the Communist Revolution lie in the unyielding commitment of both Hanoi and Washington to establishing a society in their own image in South Vietnam. Hanoi refused to recognize the legitimacy of the US-sponsored Republic of Vietnam, or Government of Vietnam (GVN). That entity was the successor to the State of Vietnam, formed in 1949 by the French. The Democratic Republic of Vietnam (DRV), widely known as "North Vietnam," supported the successor movement to the Vietminh in the south. Without a formal sobriquet until 1960, this movement was called the Vietcong insurgency in the West; after 1960 it was christened the National Liberation Front (NLF) although

Americans continued to use the term "Vietcong" to denote the Communists in South Vietnam.

Throughout the American War, Hanoi claimed the NLF functioned independently as the true voice of the people of South Vietnam. In fact, neither the Republic of Vietnam nor the NLF was a truly independent entity. The Republic was a child of the United States, just as the NLF owed its survival to the DRV.

After 1958, the military forces of the NLF, the People's Liberated Armed Force (PLAF), were formally integrated into the PAVN chain of command. The armed forces of the Republic of Vietnam were never formally integrated into the US chain of command, but for all intents and purposes, they did America's bidding in Vietnam until US combat forces arrived in strength in 1965. After that, they operated in support of American forces and in effect took their orders from the US military command.

Neither the Americans nor the Communists in Hanoi intended to engage each other directly in a major war after France's defeat. Indeed, between 1954 and early 1965, Hanoi and Washington went to extraordinary lengths to achieve their core objectives *without* deploying large numbers of forces from their own regular armies. Both sides made strenuous attempts to halt the march toward full-scale war through political maneuvering, diplomacy, and military assistance to their proxies on the ground in the south. They failed to do so for a variety of complex reasons.

Between 1954 and 1965, the United States and the DRV would pursue strikingly similar strategies of incremental military escalation, in which one side and then the other stepped up military and economic support for its proxy in the South. Most historians today believe that President Lyndon Johnson's reluctant decision to deploy US ground forces in early 1965 was triggered by the imminent collapse of South Vietnam. By that juncture, Hanoi's post-1954 strategy of breaking down the authority of the GVN had paid great dividends in the countryside. Whole districts had fallen under the control of the Revolution. Moreover, Communist regulars, now fighting at battalion level as members of the PLAF, were embarrassing Saigon's army in the field. Defeat followed defeat.

NGO DINH DIEM

After the 1954 Geneva conference, the United States firmly committed itself to constructing and defending a pro-Western state in the south as a bulwark against Communist expansion in Asia. When a young senator from Massachusetts remarked that "Vietnam represents the cornerstone of the Free World in Southeast Asia, the keystone in the arch, the finger in the dike....It is our offspring, we cannot abandon it, we cannot ignore its needs..."[1] he was neatly summarizing the rationale for President Eisenhower's Vietnam policy. When John F. Kennedy became president in 1961, he made it clear that the United States was in Vietnam to stay until the insurgency there was defeated, even as it became clear that this objective could not be achieved without sustaining far greater costs than the American foreign policy establishment in the mid-1950s had envisaged.

Kennedy's successor, Lyndon Johnson, was, if anything, more firmly committed to seeing the war through to a successful conclusion than Kennedy had been. He viewed success in Vietnam as vital to maintaining American prestige and influence on the international stage. Like his predecessors, he ascribed to the domino theory and saw the fall of South Vietnam to the Communists as a disaster on a major scale. No American president had lost a war. If LBJ faltered in Vietnam, his dream of achieving greatness as a champion of civil rights and the Great Society at home would go up in smoke.

The United States put its money where its mouth was. Between 1954 and 1961 alone, it poured $1 billion of military and economic aid into the Republic of Vietnam. Although South Vietnam had neither stability nor a social structure compatible with Western ideas, Washington set about energetically attempting to create a democratic nation sustained by Western values and institutions. The uncanny ability of Hanoi to hang tough despite its considerable limitations in military and economic assets only heighted Johnson's commitment to vanquish Communism in South Vietnam by any means necessary, save nuclear war or invasion of the DRV.

So it was that the struggle in Vietnam took on the vestments of an American crusade. It was at one and the same time referred to as a test case of the American commitment to defending freedom in a dangerous world, and a noble experiment in nation building.

After a short period of grave questioning and doubt over his capabilities, the United States installed a mysteriously aloof former colonial official named Ngo Dinh Diem as head of state in South Vietnam in 1955. He remained so until late 1963, when his intractability and repression of political dissent led to his assassination by a coterie of South Vietnamese generals, with Kennedy's tacit consent. As the leader of a fledgling republic,

Diem was well out of his depth, but at the time of his rise to power, there seemed to be no better alternative. The most inspiring anti-Communist nationalists had been killed in Giap's purge of 1946 or had been tainted by collaboration with the French.

A devout Catholic steeped in Confucianism, Diem was astutely described by the veteran American correspondent Stanley Karnow as "a mixture of monk and mandarin" imbued "with a sense of his own infallibility...Diem expected obedience...Above all he could not comprehend the magnitude of the political, social and economic revolution being promoted by his communist foes."[2]

Diem was an ardent patriot and anti-Communist, but he was utterly lacking in charisma or the organizational-managerial skill that Ho and Giap possessed in such abundance. Diem had no blueprint to transform Vietnam from a war-ravaged society stunted by a long history of colonialism into a prosperous modern state. Yet to the surprise of his many detractors, he was able to maintain control over its fledgling army and defeat a 1955 coup attempt by the Binh Xuyen—a kind of crime syndicate of warlords—a feat that prompted the Eisenhower administration to refrain from engineering his removal from office at the last minute.

Soon after taking over the reins of power, Diem launched a "Denounce the Communists" campaign against the 15,000-man clandestine infrastructure the Vietminh had left behind in the countryside. Communist sources claim that some 2,000 cadres were executed by Diem's secret police and another 25,000 sympathizers imprisoned.[3] Diem's strong-arm tactics hurt the Communists badly, leading to the breakdown of much of the infrastructure in a number of strategic areas, and to something of a crisis among the senior cadres operating in the South. His success in decimating the Communists prompted the Eisenhower administration to launch a major pro-Diem propaganda campaign aimed at the American public as well as the Vietnamese people. But the anti-Communist program, brutal and indiscriminating as it was, also alienated South Vietnam's political class and its intelligentsia. Hanoi challenged the American propaganda campaign with one of its own. Its efforts along these lines surely deepened opposition to the authoritarian government in Saigon, but they had little impact on public opinion in the United States, where Vietnam remained a back-page story until the mid-1960s.

Despite the Eisenhower and Kennedy administrations' extensive support during his eight-year tenure, Diem resisted increasingly strident

American pleas to institute social and political reforms. In the cities, corruption and nepotism ruled, feeding on kickbacks to government administrators from vast quantities of American aid. Diem came to rely almost exclusively for political advice on his brother Ngo Dinh Nhu, an opium-smoking megalomaniac in charge of the secret police. In the villages, corrupt and poorly trained administrators replaced the traditional elected councils of respected elders as arbiters of law and order. Government funds earmarked for educational and medical improvement programs were siphoned off into the pockets of officials. And Diem's support in the countryside, never robust, dropped off precipitously. American aid created an artificial sense of prosperity, but only among those with connections to Diem and his close circle of family advisers and senior military officers. Hundreds of tons of consumer goods flooded into Saigon, Danang, and other cities, and a small army of American military and civilian advisers and administrators arrived to build up South Vietnam's army, infrastructure, and social institutions.

But this massive influx of American wealth and know-how, observes historian George Herring, clearly "fostered dependency rather than laying the foundation for a genuine independence."[4] In fiscal year 1957, the United States paid all costs associated with South Vietnamese defense, 70 percent of its government expenditures, and 90 percent of its imports. Nonetheless, an endless flow of reports and articles from American journalists, military advisers, and the US embassy in Saigon extolling progress in South Vietnam made their way to senior decision makers in Washington, and to the American public, reinforcing the impression that the American crusade against Communism was a glowing success. So began the chronic American penchant for interpreting events in Vietnam not as they were, but as the United States wished them to be.

As a new decade came into view, ominous signs for the United States and Saigon were on the horizon in the South. In January 1959, Giap and Ho had decided to begin to shift Communist strategy in South Vietnam from widespread political subversion to a combination of armed and political struggle. The effects of Hanoi's more aggressive policies immediately made themselves felt in the countryside. Guerrilla attacks by well-trained squads and platoons intensified. A highly intimidating assassination program aimed not only at government officials but at health workers and teachers—anyone who could build up trust and loyalty between the people and the government in Saigon—ate away at the vitals of Saigon's effort to control the population. Communist guerrillas stepped up their base-building areas deep in the Cau Mau Peninsula in the Mekong Delta, north-west of Saigon, and in the jungles of the Central Highlands (more about these developments follows later in this chapter).

The Army of the Republic of Vietnam (ARVN) seemed incompetent and lethargic in responding. In part this was the fault of the Americans. The US Military Advisory Group later expanded to become Military Assistance Command, Vietnam (MACV) trained the ARVN to fight in conventional mobile operations with air and artillery support. But the army didn't possess sufficient material assets to engage in such operations, nor did it have sufficiently trained personnel. Meanwhile, little emphasis was placed on counterinsurgency tactics appropriate for dealing with Communist guerrillas. But far more significant factors in the army's lethargy and incompetence were the yawning gap between the French-educated officer corps and the peasant-class enlisted men they looked down upon with disdain.

For their part, the peasant soldiers were given no clear reason to fight the Communists. The Saigon regime inspired no loyalty. Little wonder the ARVN was beset by a lack of fighting spirit. Diem's response to American pleas for concerted reform of his armed forces was exactly the same as his response to requests to undertake reforms in the political arena. He promised changes in return for additional aid and support. Typically, Washington obliged and Diem made no reforms whatsoever. A shockingly high percentage of the new aid package would make its way into Saigon's thriving black market, controlled by senior ARVN officers.

Thus, an ominous dynamic emerged in which Diem was able to resist American pressure for concrete reforms while he succeeded in building up his personal power at the expense of his people. The United States had little leverage, as it needed his cooperation in halting the spread of Communism—at least in theory—to avoid the appearance of being yet another colonial power bent on the conquest of Vietnam for its own selfish ends. By 1960, the Americans had invested too much in Diem to refuse his demands. Thus, as one American official in Vietnam at the time put it, Diem "was a puppet who pulled his own strings."[5]

HANOI'S STRATEGY

Hanoi's initial strategy in the postwar period was to employ limited political struggle against Diem and his American backers while it focused on building up the North's military and economic strength. As late as April 1956, Giap and the rest of the Politburo were reasonably confident that Diem's regime would collapse of its own weight. Those Communist cadres who had remained in the South after Geneva were instructed by Hanoi to eschew armed violence in favor of engaging in political work such as protests, marches, political consciousness-raising classes, and adversarial journalism in order to challenge Diem's initiatives and degrade his authority in the eyes of the populace of the South. Party salvation associations in the South were officially disbanded after Geneva and reconfigured as legal organizations containing a wide variety of nationalists, but surreptitiously controlled by the Communist Party.

Giap and the rest of the Politburo initially hoped that Diem would abide by the Geneva accords and seek peaceful unification through elections. Even after Diem steadfastly refused to enter into talks because of alleged North Vietnamese ceasefire violations, Hanoi clung to the naïve hope that elections would nonetheless bring the revolutionary forces to power in the South. Ho's closing speech at the ninth plenum of the Central Committee in April 1956 reaffirmed the pursuit of peaceful unification and the primacy of developing the DRV rather than stepping up armed struggle in the South with combat forces from the North:

> [W]e must always raise high the flag of peace, but we must at the same time also raise high our defenses and our vigilance....If you want to build a good house, you must build a truly solid FOUNDATION...North Vietnam is the FOUNDATION, the ROOTS of the struggle to complete the liberation of our people and the unification of our nation. Therefore everything we do in the north is aimed at strengthening our forces in the North and the South.[6]

By 1957 Southern cadres and sympathizers grew increasingly frustrated and militant in the face of Diem's harsh repressive measures. Vigorously supported by senior Politburo member Le Duan, Hanoi came under intense pressure from the Party's leadership in the South to challenge the Government of the Republic of Vietnam (GVN) by violent means. Communist histories of the period invariably cite Le Duan's August 1956 "Tenants of the Revolution in the South" as a landmark document, calling on the Party as a whole to recognize that "the road to advance the revolution in South Vietnam was the road of revolutionary violence."[7] A few months later, the Party's Committee for the South affirmed that while it was not yet time to resort to general guerrilla warfare, the Party's military apparatus in the South was sufficiently well developed to launch Armed Propaganda Units (APUs) in the countryside and form self-defense units at the hamlet and village level. The APUs had been put together by General Giap in the waning days of World War II as the initial military formations of the People's Army. The task of the APUs in the South was described in the Politburo's resolution of December 1956. They were to expose

> the true face of the enemy to the people. They will encourage hatred, develop revolutionary organizations among the masses, suppress enemy thugs and intelligence agents, win support of enemy troops and governmental personnel to support our mass struggle movements....These units will be dispersed into cells and squads for purposes of living, traveling, and operations, but they must be organized into platoons with a command section to administer the unit, carry out political operations and train the unit's troops.[8]

In 1957 and 1958, the APUs pressed forward aggressively, organizing self-defense units and laying the groundwork for the first companies of light infantry troops that would operate under the Committee for the South, which, in turn, took its orders from the Central Committee in Hanoi. Several hundred local and district GVN officials were neutralized in a limited assassination program carried out by the APUs. As Diem stepped up his efforts to counter Communist initiatives, the Party responded by formally approving the resumption of armed struggle in the South in January 1959. A midlevel southern cadre who rejoined the revolutionary movement in 1956 described the shift in activities that characterized the movement in the South:

> From 1956 to 1959 we lacked the right conditions [for armed struggle]: on the one hand, there were successive government troop operations; on the other hand, we cadres lacked means. Our small number of cadres have to live secretly in remote zones....We were like fish out of water....Toward the end of 1959 and the beginning of 1960, we received orders to enlarge the field of our activities to attack military posts, to arouse the conscience of the people, to make ourselves known publically. Two comrades and I, with the help of three volunteers from the militia to help us as spies, successfully attacked the village militia [of the GVN] and seized one sten

gun and five rifles. In February 1960, profiting from this success, we penetrated the village and made contact with P-----, who joined us with a typewriter. We, the fish, were now in the water.[9]

In January 1959 the fifteenth plenum of the Politburo announced a subtle but nonetheless seminal shift in strategy by declaring for the first time that "it is possible that the popular uprising of South Vietnam may become a protracted armed struggle between ourselves [meaning the DRV, as opposed to the Communist infrastructure already struggling in South Vietnam, led by the Central Office for South Vietnam, or COSVN] and the enemy. Our party must plan for this possibility and make adequate and vigorous preparations for any eventuality."[10]

It was Hanoi's formal recognition that the Revolution could only prevail if the DRV shifted its current allocation of resources from consolidating its 1954 victory in the North to liberation of the South. The tacit understanding was that it was time for Hanoi to assume complete responsibility for directing the struggle in the South.[11]

Developments soon after the plenum strongly suggest that Hanoi expected military struggle to assume a greater level of importance in the struggle than it had up to that point. The General Military Party Committee (GMPC), chaired by Vo Nguyen Giap, laid out a broad program to expand PAVN's role in the South by reinforcing the southern cadre's efforts to build up base areas in remote areas where the population was already under Party control.

In May 1959, the GMPC established a two-battalion unit called Military Transportation Group 559. The new unit took responsibility for developing the transportation and communication network leading from North Vietnam into Laos and then into western South Vietnam. This marvel of logistical planning and effort soon became known to the Americans as the Ho Chi Minh Trail. By year's end, work on new roads leading south had begun, and 500 PAVN soldiers, mostly company-level commanders and sapper trainers, headed down the trail and were dispersed among newly formed APUs and guerrilla companies. Most of these early PAVN infiltrators were deployed in Interzone V.[12]

The trail slowly developed from a series of foot trails and unpaved roads into a complex transportation network on both the western and eastern sides of the Annamite Mountains, replete with repair crews, supply depots, barracks, PAVN security troops, and even an oil pipeline. Despite a massive

American interdiction campaign, the trail remained the revolution's lifeline in the South. As the war progressed, the numbers of troops and tons of war matériel steadily increased. The interdiction campaign was one of several major American initiatives that failed outright.

Throughout 1959 the entire 338th PAVN Division in North Vietnam, composed largely of Southern re-groupees, was broken down into training groups and tasked with preparing several thousand southern civilian recruits who had moved to the North after 1954 to return to the South to serve in full-time battalions. Between 1959 and 1961, the politico-military structure in the South, buttressed by the organizational and insurgency skills of PAVN troops dispersed into local units, made very impressive gains, wresting control over entire districts in the Central Highlands, the Plain of Reeds, and the forests north of Saigon near the Cambodian border. The assassination program took an increasingly heavy toll on the GVN apparatus. In 1959, 1,200 GVN officials were eliminated; in 1961, some 4,000 died at the hands of Communist assassination teams.

The National Liberation Front for South Vietnam (NLF) was formally established on December 20, 1960, along with its constituent committees for provinces and districts throughout the South. According to the official PAVN history, "these organizations served to gather together all the forces of the front and served as our revolutionary governmental administration. Military Command Sections were established at the region, province, district and village levels to aid the Party at these levels" in command, recruiting, and receipt of supplies.[13]

In early 1961, the senior leadership formally adapted the protracted war strategy Giap, Ho, and Truong Chinh had refined during the War of Resistance to fight the "special war" waged largely by the South Vietnamese, a steadily increasing number of American advisers on the ground, and American pilots and air power. The coming war would almost certainly be more complicated and arduous than the War of Resistance. It could not be expected to unfold straightforwardly, according to Mao's three-stage model. Giap envisaged different "fighting forms" in each of South Vietnam's three strategic regions. The Central Highlands would serve as the "Viet Bac" of the American War. Hence it was essential to expand the Ho Chi Minh Trail deep into the mountainous jungle there. Here the PLAF would train its main force regulars. The lowlands or plains near the coast were the key contested area, for here in the populous rural areas the revolutionary forces would struggle to wrest control of the villages from the South Vietnamese government. In the cities, clandestine political work would dominate, supplemented with assassinations and terrorist tactics.[14]

Again, three types of armed forces were required in the South to meet the looming challenge: main-force PLAF units *(bo dai chu luc)*; local or regional forces *(bo doi dia phuong)*; and militia units of two types—lightly armed guerrillas *(dan quan du kich)* and village self-defense forces *(dan quant tu ve)*. The General Military Party Committee's directive in January 1961, made public only in the 1990s, makes it clear that, as the commander in chief of the People's Army of Vietnam, Giap exerted overarching command of the People's Liberation Armed Forces, although the planning of individual campaigns, operations, and the training of PLAF units fell under the direct responsibility of the Central Office for South Vietnam (COSVN).

GIAP'S RESPONSIBILITIES

And what of Giap's activities during this period, beyond shaping broad strategy along with his compatriots Ho Chi Minh, Truong Chinh, and, increasingly, Le Duan? Giap, as the leading member of the General Military Party Committee and the minister of defense, developed and supervised the first five-year plan (1955–1959) for expansion of the army. By the end of 1956, revamping the PAVN's tables of organization had been completed. The seven-division force (six infantry, one artillery, and engineers) that had prevailed against the French was expanded to fourteen infantry, four artillery-antiaircraft, and several independent regiments and battalions of engineer, signal, and transport troops. Small naval and air force structures were put in place, though at this stage the training of jet pilots was still on the drawing board, and the navy consisted largely of lightly armed patrol boats similar to American PT boats. Technical training schools, repair facilities, and large troop installations to accommodate the newly minted divisions were constructed, and new staff agencies at all echelons were put in place. By 1958, small arms had been standardized with new shipments of SKS rifles and Kalashnikov assault rifles from China and the Soviet Union.

The implementation of universal military service in April 1960 and the looming threat of facing off against American ground troops led to an intensification of combat training and expansion of the reserve forces of 750,000 newly minted soldiers between the ages of 18 and 25, led by a hard core of 30,000 Vietminh veterans. Of that force, 130,000 were kept under tight control and trained to a high enough standard for instant activation in the regular forces. Between 1955 and 1957, all units in the army were trained from the squad up to the battalion level for combat in regular terrain, and selected units completed training for jungle and night combat operations. Combined arms training at the regimental and divisional levels commenced in May 1957.

Since the early days of the revolutionary struggle, Giap had seen political education as the lifeblood of the army's success in battle. The potential challenges of conflict with the Americans demanded that the army institute even more systematic and intensive political education programs than it had done in the war with France. The objective of this training, wrote one historian of the American War, "was to engage the total consciousness of each soldier," thereby making his own future and that of the Revolution one in the same.[15] Ever realistic about the trials and sacrifices that fighting a protracted war against the United States would demand, Giap "repeatedly stated that motivation and morale was always 'the decisive factor' in combat, and strengthening it became the objective of the Party's entire military organization."[16]

QUESTIONS OF AUTHORITY AND CONTROL

Communist historians today freely admit what they categorically denied throughout the war: that the entire Communist movement in the South took its orders from Hanoi. Its various regional and provincial headquarters took orders from the Politburo of the Vietnam Workers' Party (the formal name of the Communist Party), and the People's Liberation Armed Forces was, in effect, a branch of the People's Army of Vietnam, headed by Giap. During the war Hanoi claimed—vehemently—that the Southern insurgents operated independently. This was dissembling. In fact, the claim was a central tenet of Hanoi's propaganda campaign designed to win sympathy for the Revolution internationally, as well as to suggest that the United States, not Hanoi, was the aggressor who was in flagrant violation of the Geneva accords. (In fact, both sides violated the terms of the Geneva agreement many times.)

So, too, the consensus among American historians today is that the Republic of Vietnam was never a truly independent nation calling on America to support its own struggle for survival against "external aggression from the

North." It was, in reality, a creation of the United States. Its struggle against Giap and the Communists was spearheaded by American aid and would surely have collapsed had it not been for direct American intervention.

This is not to say that either Hanoi's or Washington's proxies on the ground—that is, the NLF or the government of Vietnam in Saigon—had no room to maneuver independently. Directives from Hanoi and Washington were challenged by these entities, albeit to radically different degrees. As the war progressed from bad to worse, the relationship between the United States and the South Vietnamese was increasingly beset by mistrust and rancor. By 1968, Washington and Saigon often seemed to work at cross purposes. By 1970, it could reasonably be argued that Washington and Saigon were no longer truly allies at all.

Hanoi's relationship to the NLF was occasionally tense, and heated debates regarding strategic priorities were common, particularly in the desperate days for the southern insurgents, before political *dau tranh* gave way to armed *dau tranh* as the decisive pincer of Communist strategy in the early 1960s. For the most part, however, the Communists in the South fully accepted the Politburo's war strategy and worked in a disciplined and cooperative fashion to achieve a goal that was as clear as it was shared.

What's more, the distinction between the southern and northern Communists, which the Americans were at such pains to make during the conflict, was rather a gray one in need of qualification. Several southerners served on the Politburo in Hanoi during the war. Le Duan was a southerner. Having served as the head of the Committee for the South, the governing body for Communist activities south of the seventeenth parallel in the 1940s, he rose to be the first among equals on the Politburo after Ho Chi Minh died in 1969, surpassing Giap in power and influence. Tens of thousands of southerners traveled to the north to serve in Giap's PAVN after Diem began his anti-Communist purge in the mid-1950s. William Duiker, that meticulous historian of Vietnamese Communism, says it best: "The insurgency was a genuine revolt based in the South, but it was organized and directed from the North."[17]

THE ROAD TO WAR IN THE EARLY 1960S

By the fall of 1961, internal political strife, government indifference to the social and economic problems of the populace, and the rise of the insurgency combined to produce what Kennedy administration adviser General

Maxwell Taylor called "a deep and pervasive crisis of confidence and a serious loss of morale."[18] In light of Taylor's report, Kennedy authorized another substantial infusion of military and economic aid to the Government of the Republic of Vietnam. Several thousand more military advisers were sent to Vietnam, bringing the total to 11,300 in December 1961 from a mere 900 a year earlier. The Vietnamese air force was supplied with three hundred planes. Two squadrons of Marine Corps helicopters (with their Marine pilots) sailed for Vietnam from the United States to beef up ARVN mobile operations.

With American funding Diem instituted the strategic hamlet program, a misguided effort in which peasants from different villages were rounded up and forced to live inside fortified encampments. In theory at least, new medical dispensaries and schools inside the encampments were designed to gain the loyalty of the populace and keep the Vietcong "fish" out of the "sea" of people. Like virtually every Saigon initiative, the hamlet program was wonderful on paper and a nightmare in reality. The program was administered by poorly trained administrators, immediately infiltrated by NLF sympathizers, and, thanks to graft, underfunded. It failed miserably. The inept GVN defense forces in the hamlets were no match for seasoned Vietcong guerrillas units. Hundreds of strategic hamlets were attacked and destroyed within a few months after their creation.

During 1962, the Politburo in Hanoi rebuffed requests by the Central Office for South Vietnam to intensify the conflict and move to full-scale war, confirming its intention to defeat Diem and the Americans with a strategy of protracted war, and calling for an "intensification of political and military struggle to defeat the enemy gradually, to gain advantage step by step, to progress toward final victory."[19] The Politburo did, however, instruct Giap to prepare contingency plans for the deployment of entire PAVN units to the South for the first time. The influx of PAVN infiltrators to the South ramped up markedly. They joined PLAF guerrilla and main-force units as platoon and company commanders, specialists, and instructors. According to the PAVN official history, between 1959 and the end of 1963, more than 40,000 regular PAVN soldiers traveled down the Ho Chi Minh Trail—far more than US intelligence at the time had estimated. The number of main-force PLAF troops jumped impressively from 15,000 in December 1960 to 70,000 three years later. The PAVN infiltrators—not the revolution's indigenous sympathizers in the South—formed the core of the growing body of PLAF main-force units and virtually all of the military specialists.

By 1963, PLAF battalions were regularly chewing up ARVN units, despite the latter's being kitted out with the latest US weapons, including armored personnel carriers and fighter bombers. PLAF forces also methodically expanded their base complexes and training grounds in the Central Highlands, northwest of Saigon near the border with Laos and Cambodia, and in the Cau Mau peninsula of the Mekong Delta. Smaller base areas cropped up elsewhere, especially in eastern Interzone V.

For the GVN, things went from bad to worse in the summer of 1963, as Diem's repression of the Buddhist majority prompted widespread protests by monks, students, and political opponents of the regime. When Ngo Dinh Nhu's police force fired on protesters with live ammunition, it provoked riots in Saigon and Hue. Shocking photographs of the self-immolation of a Buddhist monk in protest against Diem's repression of Buddhists and other groups prompted a worldwide outcry, gaining the movement much sympathy around the world, including in the United States.

With the entire country on the verge of exploding into chaos and anarchy, Diem and his brother Nhu refused to make conciliatory gestures. Instead they responded with even more brutally repressive measures. Intrigue had long been the favored sport of the senior ARVN generals. When a coterie of generals surreptitiously approached US ambassador Henry Cabot Lodge about launching a coup, President Kennedy gave them his tacit consent on the assumption that the diminutive head of state would not be killed but stripped of power and ushered out of the country. The generals' assassins chased down Diem and his brother as they took refuge in a Catholic church and killed them on November 2, 1963.

The coup confirmed Hanoi's critique of Diem's regime in Saigon, but his downfall was in no sense a cause for celebration in Hanoi; precisely the opposite. Popular hatred for Diem in the South had generated a great deal of sympathy for the NLF, lending credence in Hanoi to the idea that a "revolutionary situation" was in the making, possibly setting the stage for a "general uprising" against the GVN and the Americans by the people in the South, led by the NLF. Some in Hanoi felt that the deepening friction between Diem and the United States might lead the South Vietnamese leader to begin to distance himself from America, perhaps even seek direct negotiations with the NLF.[20] But these hopes were soon dashed when it became clear that the new military junta in Saigon was enjoying a honeymoon in the wake of Diem's demise. An imminent uprising leading to the collapse of the government in Saigon was clearly out of the question, as the South

Vietnamese people were overjoyed by Diem's fall, and his replacements enjoyed something of a honeymoon. (In fact, the honeymoon proved to be short-lived, and the new junta, mired in corruption and intrigue, itself fell in yet another coup in early 1964.)

Three weeks after the Diem killings, John F. Kennedy fell to an assassin's bullet, and Lyndon Johnson assumed the presidency. Hopes in Hanoi that the new American president might change course and pursue negotiations rather than military escalation were quickly dashed when Johnson retained Kennedy's foreign policy team and announced his intention to carry on with Kennedy's initiatives. He promised that under his watch, the Communists would be defeated in Vietnam. Aggression, he remarked on several occasions, could not be tolerated. American resolve would not, could not, falter in the pursuit of freedom.

In December 1963, the Central Committee met for a stormy session in Hanoi to reconsider strategy for the South in light of recent developments. There was a clear consensus, as one official resolution put it, that

> now [that] we are stronger than the enemy politically, we must continue to strengthen our political forces. However, we are still weaker than the enemy militarily. Therefore *the key point at the present time is to make outstanding effort to rapidly strengthen our military forces in order to create a basic change in the balance of forces between the enemy and us in South Vietnam....* If we do not defeat the enemy's military forces, we cannot overthrow his domination and bring the revolution to victory. To destroy the enemy's military forces we should use armed struggle. *For this reason, armed struggle plays a direct and decisive role.*[21]

But should entire PAVN units be sent south for the first time? How much aid should the North allocate to the struggle in South Vietnam? We do not know the details of the debate, but the bulk of the evidence suggests that Giap pressed for restraint, for continuing to devote the lion's share of resources then available to build up military power in the North, while continuing to aid the southerners with additional shipments of weapons and individual PAVN troops, but not entire infantry units. Such a dramatic escalation, Giap probably reasoned, might very well result in an American decision to do the same. And that was to be avoided at all costs. At least for the time being.

The argument for sending entire PAVN units south as soon as possible was spearheaded by Le Duan and his protégé, Nguyen Chi Thanh, the only other senior general in the PAVN. Both men had more extensive contacts with the NLF military and political leaders than did Giap, and in effect, they became spokesmen for the southerners' concerns during this critical period before full-scale war. Thanh, in fact, is generally thought to have consistently argued throughout the next several years for more aggressive military action and the deployment of more PAVN units in the South than Giap.

In late 1963, Giap's view apparently prevailed. The resolution to emerge from the December 1963 conference confirmed his view that the upcoming war would almost certainly move from guerrilla actions at the battalion level or lower to mobile warfare involving entire divisions—a progression Giap had often described in his writings since the early 1950s. He also advocated political action aimed at a target far from the battlefield: American popular opinion. Again, his view was reflected in the official resolution: "We must also win the sympathy and support of the people of the nationalist and imperialist countries (the U.S., France and England)....Along with the intensification of our armed and political struggles in South Viet-Nam, we must step up our diplomatic struggles for the purpose of isolating warmongers, gaining the sympathy of antiwar groups in the U.S. and taking full advantage of the dissensions among the imperialists to gain the sympathy and support of the various countries which follow a peaceful and neutral policy."[22]

Early in 1964 a conference of the CPMC and the Ministry of Defense considered the buildup of forces in the South, and laid out some tactical and doctrinal guidelines for the upcoming conflict. Operations were to be of three types: (1) Maneuver operations planned and executed by main force units. These involved closing in on strong enemy units as they were deployed in the field. (2) Attacks on enemy bases by a combination of main force and regional forces. (3) Guerrilla operations by all three types of forces, including independent companies detached from their main-force parent unit. The conference also called for intensive focus on close combat, night operations, and "continuous combat," meaning operations where Communist forces would engage and withdraw in good order, only to attack and withdraw again somewhere else.[23] Interestingly, US ground forces' training at this time emphasized none of these types of operations.

As the United States and North Vietnam crept step by step toward direct military confrontation, Giap had already developed a remarkably prescient critique of his American adversaries and their dilemma. In *The South Vietnam People Will Win* (1964), he exhibited a particularly shrewd appreciation of the United States' strengths and weaknesses as it waged its "special war" in the early 1960s, well before the deployment of American ground forces. "Militarily speaking," wrote the commander in chief of PAVN in 1964,

> ...their army is superior to ours in effectiveness, modern weapons, and mobility. All their temporary strong points must be studied carefully, especially when solving questions regarding operations and campaigns. However, it is certain that all these strong points cannot make up for their most basic weak points in morale and politics, which are inherent in an enemy of the people, in a counter-revolutionary army. But in the south of our country, these weak points are all the more serious owing to the weakness of the southern reactionary forces [i.e., the ARVN]....In a revolutionary war, the people's political superiority will be translated into a material force capable of turning the tables on the enemy, overcoming all difficulties and handicaps to defeat...an enemy who is at first several times stronger.[24]

Giap understood very early in the game what the major players in America's strategy failed to grasp until 1968—that a South Vietnamese government and society sustained by American power was by definition mired in "contradictions," the Marxist-Leninist term for internal tensions and problems that render a regime dysfunctional, at odds with itself. Again writing in 1964, Giap pointed to "two fundamental contradictions: *one* between our southern people and the aggressive imperialists [the Americans] and their henchmen; *the other* is the contradiction between the peasants, and feudal landlordism."[25] The regime's strategic hamlet program, designed to provide security and freedom, in fact amounted to little more than a "huge system of prisons."[26] Without the support of the people, it was bound to fail. By 1965, it had done so.

So, too, America's relationship with its "ally" in Saigon was marred by contradiction and dysfunction. Hindsight confirms the wisdom of Giap's claim that the "internal contradictions between the U.S. imperialists and their henchmen grew so sharp that in late 1963 and early in 1964, the U.S. imperialists had to stage two coups d'état aimed at switching horses in midstream and salvaging the situation."[27] Of course, neither of the coups could have happened without American complicity, a fact that went far to confirm that the United States was indeed a neocolonial power. The Americans, Giap continued, claim the Republic of Vietnam is an independent and sovereign state "because they want to overshadow the fundamental contradictions between our people and the aggressive imperialists, and to create conditions for the puppet administration hidden behind the false pattern of nation and sovereignty to deceive the masses and win over them."[28]

Throughout 1964, the forces of the Revolution made startling progress. By year's end total troop strength in the South reached approximately 170,000, including 50 main-force battalions. Senior American officials looked on with dismay as ARVN forces were outclassed by PLAF units of inferior size and mobility. ARVN casualties jumped from 1,000 a month early in the year to 3,000 in December. Even when the Communists took heavy casualties from ARVN supporting arms, ARVN infantry invariably lacked the aggressiveness to close in on its enemy with fire and maneuver tactics. Most PLAF casualties were inflicted by artillery and airpower, not in direct combat with ARVN infantrymen. American advisers also noted the resilience of the PLAF units. Even after sustaining heavy casualties, they were able to bounce back quickly and launch new attacks, often in locations distant from the initial engagements, and at times and places of their own choosing.

In December 1964, while the Johnson administration engaged in tortuous debate over how to respond to the looming crisis in South Vietnam, the PLAF launched powerful attacks throughout Vietnam. Forty miles south of Saigon the largest Communist operation of the war to date unfolded around the "secure" village of Binh Gia. Two reinforced battalions of PLAF troops took on seven ARVN battalions. In a series of carefully planned lightning attacks, the Communists isolated and then shredded several South Vietnamese units, ambushed forces sent in for relief, and then quickly retired in good order to hidden base areas where the ARVN forces dared not follow.

On January 2, 1965, the PLAF reemerged near Binh Gia and ambushed two companies of elite ARVN rangers supported by tanks, inflicting very heavy casualties. All told, 200 ARVN troops died around Bing Gia, along with five US advisers. In a comment that would be echoed hundreds of times by other American professional soldiers, a US officer on the scene at Binh Gia remarked, "The Vietcong fought magnificently, as well as any infantry anywhere. But the big question for me is how its troops, a thousand or more of them, could wander around the countryside so close to Saigon without being detected. That tells [us] something about this war. You can only beat the other guy if you isolate him from the population."[29]

Meanwhile, Johnson's senior advisers were split on the issue of what the United States should do. Walt Rostow urged the president to send in combat troops immediately to show Hanoi that the United States was "prepared to face down any form of escalation."[30] George Ball feared that direct American intervention would "set in train a series of events leading, at the end of the road, to the direct intervention of China and nuclear war."[31] Ball wisely believed that, in the long run, the United States couldn't substitute its own presence for an effective South Vietnamese government. Maxwell Taylor, who served as ambassador to South Vietnam from 1964 to 1965, also believed that the key to defeating the insurgency ultimately lay in the emergence of a stable government in Saigon. Without it, American aid was only a "spinning wheel unable to transmit impulsion" to the ARVN's struggle in the field. But Taylor quickly added, "It is impossible to foresee a stable and effective government under any name in anything like the near future.... We sense the mounting feeling of war weariness and hopelessness that pervade South Vietnam...there is chronic discouragement."[32]

Despite the penumbra of skepticism about Vietnam in Washington, the American crusade had its own curious momentum. Too much had been invested by late 1964 to give up the ship. Already, thousands of federal bureaucrats and experts from scores of different non-governmental organizations (NGOs) were busy at work upgrading Vietnam's underdeveloped infrastructure, economy, and government, but the massive effort was fraught with interagency quarreling and lacked coordination. Relationships between "can do" American officials and wary South Vietnamese were already strained by misunderstanding and mistrust. For the time being Johnson waffled. He would not seek a political settlement through negotiation, nor would he seek to inflict a devastating military defeat on the insurgency.

By early 1964, the administration had formed a contingency plan for obtaining a congressional resolution to take direct action in the event of North Vietnamese "provocation." It was tacitly understood, rather cynically, that such a "provocation" could be announced whenever it suited Johnson's convenience. A graduated response to the provocation was envisaged, beginning with air attacks against North Vietnam, and progressing, if need be, to the deployment of American ground forces. In early August the administration found its pretext for direct attacks against Hanoi when North Vietnamese patrol boats fired torpedoes at US destroyers, the North Vietnamese captains believing, not unreasonably, that the destroyers were part of a South Vietnamese commando raid then taking place on the coast in the vicinity of the American vessels. Johnson immediately ordered US fighters to attack targets inside North Vietnam.

A few days later, on August 7, 1964, after deceptively presenting the incident as an unprovoked attack, Johnson obtained from Congress the Tonkin Gulf Resolution granting him wide authority "to take all necessary measures" to defend US forces in Southeast Asia. The resolution served as the legal basis for the deployment of American forces in Vietnam for the rest of the war. Johnson was heard to remark that the resolution gave him an open checkbook to take action. "It's like my grandmother's nightshirt," Johnson quipped. "It covers everything."[33]

Giap and the rest of the senior leadership in Hanoi responded with alacrity to the attack, reading it correctly as a signal of American intention to shift the conflict in South Vietnam from a "special war" waged by the South Vietnamese with American support to a "limited war" fought directly by the American military forces. In September, several PAVN regiments already trained for operations in South Vietnam began their trek down the Ho Chi Minh Trail. Senior General Nguyen Chi Thanh was sent south to COSVN to take command of operations on behalf of Giap and the rest of the Politburo.

In early February 1965, a daring PLAF raid on a helicopter base at Pleiku resulted in eight American deaths and more than one hundred servicemen wounded. Johnson ordered another retaliatory air strike, prompting yet more Communist attacks. In early March Johnson initiated Operation Rolling Thunder, a program of gradually intensifying air attacks against North Vietnam that was designed to halt the flow of supplies and troops into the South. On March 8, 1965, two battalions of US Marines landed on a tranquil beach in Danang. The first American ground troops had arrived, ostensibly only to protect the giant airbase near the city; but within days, the Marines were engaged in offensive combat against PLAF forces. The United States was at war against Communist forces in South Vietnam.

As the Marines landed, the Communists braced themselves for what was by far the greatest challenge to the realization of their dream: war against the military forces of the United States of America. It was, to say the least, a sobering prospect, this business of taking on a superpower, a nation with almost unlimited military assets. Yet Giap and his colleagues on the Central Committee faced the challenge without fear, even with a kind of steely confidence. Their commitment to success had never been stronger. Defeat was not an option. Despite the deepening American commitment to South Vietnam, they could look back with pride on political and military developments in the south since 1954. Hundreds of millions of dollars, sophisticated weapons and military equipment, special forces advisers—none of it had strengthened the legitimacy or effectiveness of the South Vietnamese government. In 1962, Vice President Johnson had spoken of Ngo Dinh Diem as "the Churchill of the decade."[34] But as events proved, Diem was no more a Churchill than were any of the handful of officers who formed the military junta that replaced him in power. No question about it, the Americans operated in Vietnam under serious political vulnerabilities despite their military power. No question, too, thus far in the game, despite the comparative weakness of its hand, Hanoi had played its cards far better than its Western adversary had.

The challenge for Giap—the challenge for Hanoi—was now to find a way to exploit their adversaries' political vulnerabilities while making the enormous sacrifices of doing battle with the most formidable military force in world history.

8

PEOPLE'S WAR AGAINST THE UNITED STATES: THE ESCALATION PHASE: 1965–1967

As the National Liberation Front (NLF) for South Vietnam appeared to be on the verge of winning the "special war" against the wobbly Army of the Republic of Vietnam (ARVN) in late 1964 and early 1965, the men in the White House and the Pentagon were in crisis mode, working assiduously to develop a coherent strategy for an Americanized war. By June 1965, after weighing the comparative merits of adopting counterinsurgency or conventional warfare doctrine to shape strategy, Washington opted for the latter, all the while paying lip service to incorporating elements of the former. Vietnam would be fought according to a "search and destroy" strategy as outlined by General William Westmoreland. That strategy would be implemented as follows. Highly mobile US ground forces, supported by air power and artillery, would "find, fix, and destroy" the main-force Communist units, eventually inflicting casualties in sufficient numbers to prevent Hanoi from replenishing and rebuilding its divisions in the south through infiltration of fresh North Vietnamese units or individual replacements for the People's Liberation Armed Forces (PLAF). Westmoreland anticipated that this critical "crossover point" would take perhaps eighteen months to reach. Thus, the primary goal of Westmoreland's strategy was not to seize and hold the villages, but to destroy the Communists' military capabilities in the South. In military parlance, Westmoreland was to pursue a strategy of "attrition." Only after destroying Giap's main-force units would US and ARVN forces seek to crush once and for all the Communists' political infrastructure in the villages and the small guerrilla units that protected that infrastructure.

The campaign plan called for US ground troops to blunt the insurgency's momentum in three key strategic areas by year's end, as those forces expanded to 175,000 troops. A Marine division would be deployed in the five northern provinces, designated as I Corps tactical zone—one of four such zones in South Vietnam, running north to south. The Marines were tasked with protecting the DMZ, and establishing three large coastal enclaves at Danang, Phu Bai, and Chu Lai on the highly populous coast. Here they would engage in search-and-destroy operations in the tactical zone where Communist forces were strongest.

The US army would assume the defense of the Central Highlands, where People's Army of Vietnam General Nguyen Chi Thanh had already begun to mass troops in preparation for an offensive thrust to the east along Route 19 from Pleiku all the way to Qui Nhon on the coast, with a view to cutting South Vietnam in half. To the north and west of Saigon, additional US Army divisions would be deployed in the vicinity of large, well-fortified liberated zones, where PLAF forces were already so strong that many ARVN commanders dared not venture for fear of annihilation.

Stage two of the operational plan consisted of a series of highly mobile "search and destroy" offensives. As Westmoreland saw it, the success of the American ground war was largely contingent on isolating the battlefield, for only then could he hope to destroy Giap's forces in sufficient numbers. That meant choking off the steadily increasing flow of troops and matériel flowing down the Ho Chi Minh Trail, and, to a lesser extent, the influx of weapons and supplies from the Sihanouk Trail in Cambodia and coastal shipping from North Vietnamese ports to the south.

Westmoreland planned to use a rejuvenated and expanded ARVN in static defense duties of installations and in pacification operations to gain and maintain control over the villages that then formed part of the NLF infrastructure and its varied types of guerrilla forces. The ARVN would work with US military civic action teams as well as NGOs on rural development projects, ranging from medical dispensaries to improved agricultural production programs, schools, and economic reform at the local level. For the American strategy to succeed, the air force and the navy had to break down North Vietnam's war-making ability—its oil storage, factories, military bases, and communication lines—via Operation Rolling Thunder.

GIAP'S STRATEGIC VIEW OF THE AMERICAN WAR

Even before Westmoreland's strategy had been formally approved by Johnson, the PAVN commander in chief in Hanoi had worked out a rough blueprint for how he would fight against the Americans, the South Vietnamese, and their allies, including South Korea, Thailand, and Australia. Most probably, Giap surmised the war would steadily escalate in intensity over several years and then plateau. By that point, perhaps three or four years after the beginning of the conflict, US casualties and the indecisiveness of the fighting would lead first to US disillusionment and then to gradual disengagement. Protracted warfare—people's war—had succeeded against the French. Giap firmly believed it could succeed as well against the Americans, but not without even greater effort and sacrifice on the part of his comrades in the North and the South than the French war had required. The level of combat and the military balance of forces were sure to be protean, and to vary from one region of South Vietnam to another.

In Giap's public writings and speeches in the early and mid-1960s, we detect the same defiant confidence in Hanoi's ability to defeat the Americans that he had exhibited toward the French, even granting the frightful cost such a victory would entail. Ultimately, the PAVN would need the capability to initiate larger-scale campaigns of greater duration and complexity than had been in the case in the War of Resistance, and to protect itself from a military machine whose lethality far exceeded that of France in the 1950s. Pronouncements of great battlefield victories aside, Giap knew full well that the capacity to *survive* sustained combat against the Americans was far more important than defeating them in big-unit battles. A more efficient and elaborate logistical system had to be constructed to feed the battlefield and frustrate American efforts to break that system down. North Vietnam's entire population had to be efficiently mobilized in the war effort as producers of matériel, as defenders of the homeland, and as participants in a vast and disciplined propaganda apparatus.

As the Politburo weighed its options in early 1965, Giap argued strenuously for caution rather than haste in attempting to challenge the buildup of American ground forces. At least in the first phase of the conflict, it was far more important to expand and intensify PLAF small-unit guerrilla operations and to build up the political infrastructure than to rush insufficiently trained PAVN regular units into the South. As Giap wrote in *The Military Art of People's War* (1964), "according to our military theory in order to ensure victory for the people's war when we are stronger politically than the enemy and the enemy is stronger materially, it is necessary to promote an extensive *guerrilla war* which will develop gradually into a *regular war* combined with a guerrilla war. Regular and guerrilla war are closely combined, stimulate each other, deplete and annihilate enemy forces, and bring final victory."[1]

Yes, regular forces and mobile warfare would ultimately take up a prominent role, but in 1965 and 1966, guerrilla operations and political struggle had to take precedence. Vietnam was a poor agricultural country. The Revolution could not do everything at once. The war would be lost, and fast, unless the North's production and military establishment was extensively strengthened and protected from destruction. That would take time, and plenty of it. It was vital, at least at first, to exploit the political forces of the masses as shaped by the Party, rather than to challenge the US military head on. As always, the main objective of the political struggle was "to mobilize and organize the people, to guide them in the struggle against the enemy in all ways, and at the same time closely to coordinate with the military struggle and to help it win the greatest victories for the resistance."[2]

And then there was a crucial factor to be addressed far from the battlefields of South Vietnam: obtaining firm commitments from China and the Soviet Union to keep up the massive flow of modern weapons required and to assist Hanoi in fomenting intensive propaganda efforts aimed at convincing American and world opinion of the injustice and immorality of the United States' "neocolonial" campaign against a poor Asian nation.

In the North, an air defense system had to be built with the steadily growing assistance of the Soviet Union's weapons and its expertise. Without such a system, it would be impossible to prevent the outright destruction of North Vietnam's war-making assets by the US Air Force and Navy. The creation of this system alone would prove to be a massive undertaking, ultimately requiring the efforts of hundreds of thousands of specialists, soldiers, and civilians to construct and repair bridges, roads, and fuel lines.

As the size and scope of the war escalated, Giap anticipated using his main-force units more frequently, preferably at the time and place of his choosing. Geography would dictate the location of those operations to a large degree. The area around the DMZ, where short lines of communication would permit his divisions to be readily resupplied from North Vietnam's panhandle, seemed a promising locale. The Central Highlands also held great promise because it afforded the PAVN the sanctuaries of the mountains and of bases in Cambodia.

STRATEGIC DEBATES AND EARLY OPERATIONS

The senior leadership in Hanoi was by no means of one mind about how to conduct the first phase of a war of escalation against the greatest military power in the world. We know little of the details of these senior-level debates. What evidence we have suggests strongly that Giap, Ho, and Truong Chinh appear to have been the leading figures of the "North-first" school strategy outlined above, while Le Duan and Nguyen Chi Thanh spearheaded the "South-first" school. What did this mean in practice? Le Duan and Thanh, both southerners with extensive experience in the South since the 1950s, strenuously disagreed with Giap's priorities, arguing for rapid infiltration of regular PAVN units in 1965 and big-unit operations in order to crush Saigon and seize power before the Americans had built up enough combat power to stanch the Communist onslaught.[3] Scholar Robert Brigham has aptly described Thanh's approach as Clausewitzian in its tight focus on rapid annihilation of the enemy's armed forces. "Thanh advocated a land-based offensive strategy by large units as the only way to defeat the Americans.... Thanh claimed southern cadres would make up in spirit what they lacked in material goods."[4]

Apparently the Politburo initially rejected Giap's approach in favor of Thanh's. Thanh had been sent south in mid-1964 and given direct command over both military and political operations in all of South Vietnam save the northernmost fourteen provinces, which remained under the direct control of Giap as commander in chief of the PAVN. It appears that by mid-1965, a Politburo increasingly dominated by Le Duan as Ho Chi Minh's health declined ordered Thanh to direct operations in the South, while Giap was tasked with the responsibility of building up and modernizing the army, establishing a fledgling air force and navy, creating embarkation and special training areas, and organizing the expansion of the Ho Chi Minh Trail.

General Thanh's offensive main-force operations throughout 1965 and early 1966 continued to be highly effective against ARVN troops. With some 47,000 main-force PLAF troops organized into about 60 battalions, he was able to seize several provincial capitals, including Song Be, just 70 miles north of Saigon, and hold them temporarily. But it was a different story in the early battles with the Americans. In August 1965, the PLAF First Regiment engaged Americans in the vicinity of the Communists' fortified hamlet complex about ten miles south of Chu Lai. Thanh's regiment was in the process of planning an attack on the Marine air base there. The Third Marine Regiment conducted an amphibious assault to the south of the base, while two of its battalions landed by helicopter to the west. In five days of sustained combat, the Marines destroyed at least one PLAF battalion entirely, and killed 600 Communist troops while losing 45 Marines killed and 200 wounded.

In November, a PLAF ambush of a US Army battalion northwest of Saigon was transformed by heavy American fire support into a rout: 200 PLAF bodies littered the field while the US battalion suffered 20 fatalities in battle. A month earlier, Thanh had prepared almost an entire division of PAVN troops in and around the Ia Drang Valley, excellent terrain for moving troops and supplies from Cambodia into a major supply depot in the Central Highlands. It seems likely that Thanh planned a drive eastward to the coast, thereby cutting South Vietnam in half. If such an operation had been successful, it might very well have caused panic in Saigon and a fatal collapse of ARVN morale.

The Americans discovered large concentrations of PAVN troops in the Ia Drang Valley in early November. There they launched a devastating attack, evading the PAVN concentrations by deploying elements of the innovative First Cavalry Division, whose 400-plus helicopters were used to maneuver entire battalions of infantry around the battlefield. A ferocious battle ensued in the valley, as one US battalion landed in the midst of the PAVN's Sixty-sixth Regiment and was almost overrun in a bitter, close-in fight including hand-to-hand combat. Quick reinforcements, as well as B-52 tactical airstrikes, inflicted devastating casualties on the PAVN troops, who were forced to retreat into Cambodia or into the jungle surrounding the valley. Estimated losses for the PAVN were 2,000 men killed or wounded; Hanoi's plan to split South Vietnam in the Central Highlands had been foiled.

But a day after the main battle ended came an engagement that foreshadowed many others to follow over the next few years: about 600 PAVN troops caught the 400-man Second Battalion of the Seventh Cavalry in a perfectly executed ambush as they marched in a column away from the battlefield toward a landing zone. More than 150 US soldiers were killed. The PAVN battalion commander ordered his troops to close in tight on the American column, grabbing the Americans "by the belt."[5] But it should be noted that the success of the revolutionary forces at Ia Drang was in a large, guerrilla-style ambush, not a major multi-battalion battle.

Big-unit engagements in the dry season of 1966 (January to May) appear to have had unhappy results for Communist forces, especially those in Binh Dinh Province on the coast in II Corps, where PAVN units held their ground for as long as four days against a powerful American infantry force. Giap's unit sustained horrendous casualties in the process. In another operation in the strongly defended Iron Triangle PLAF base area northwest of Saigon, American units inflicted heavy casualties on revolutionary forces, in addition to uncovering vast quantities of weapons and explosives. This pattern of ground combat—the inability to defeat US forces in battalion and larger-size operations, and the ability to get the better of US forces frequently in small-unit actions—persisted for the first three years of the American conflict.

It was against this background that Thanh was recalled to Hanoi in the spring of 1966 to defend his strategy. According to scholars William Duiker and Patrick McGarvey, Giap was the most prominent critic of Thanh's performance as a commander. A secret August 1966 CIA memorandum goes far in confirming their assertion.[6] In Hanoi during the spring of 1966, wrote the CIA analyst, there was "considerable opposition to the way the war was being fought" in Hanoi, and Giap was the leading advocate of shifting over to a protracted war, with its greater emphasis on small-unit guerrilla action to disrupt pacification operations, provide solid intelligence on major US operations in advance of their execution, and extend the clandestine NLF infrastructure into areas currently under GVN control.

Giap clearly felt that by the end of the 1965–1966 campaign season in May 1966, the South's underground political infrastructure and its guerrilla forces were insufficiently developed to sustain the momentum of a growing war. In the great tradition of protracted warfare, Giap wanted to reallocate military resources to small unit attacks of a battalion or less. The American troops fighting the guerrillas fought under disadvantages. They were unaccustomed to tropical heat, jungle combat, and, more generally, fighting guerillas who were indistinguishable from the civilian population. They did not know the local terrain. The most striking evidence of this shift in strategy is in basic engagement statistics: Small-unit actions grew exponentially from 612 in 1965, to 894 in 1966, to 2,422 in 1967. Big-unit attacks went in the other direction: from 73, to 44, to 54 during the same time period.

By late 1966, the shift to political and guerrilla struggle from big-unit actions appeared to be producing good results in the villages, frustrating the US-Saigon pacification programs. In a confidential memo to President Johnson at the end of 1966, Secretary of Defense Robert McNamara wrote,

> Pacification has if anything gone backward. As compared with two, or four, years ago, enemy full-time regional forces and part-time guerrilla forces are larger; attacks, terrorism and sabotage have increased in scope and intensity; more railroads are closed and highways cut; the rice crop...is smaller; we control little, if any more of the population [than before]....In essence, we find ourselves no better [off], and if anything, worse off.[7]

While Thanh waged war in the South, incurring frightful losses, Giap integrated Soviet and Chinese artillery, armor, and communications specialists into his army's divisions in the North. He supervised the construction of a vast array of new training camps, the writing of new military doctrines, and the curricula for specialist schools.

The development of military power in the North would have mattered little if that power, in the form of modern PAVN regiments and divisions, had not been able to penetrate the South. It is in this context that Giap's work on the Ho Chi Minh Trail in the mid-1960s can be seen as one of his most important accomplishments. It was a stunning organizational effort. With the help of Soviet and Chinese engineers and hundreds of thousands of Vietnamese workers, many of them women, the trail became, in the words of historian Richard Stevens, "a massive labyrinth of hundreds of paths, roads, rivers, streams, caves and underground tunnels."[8] Despite numerous US/ARVN ground operations to cut the trail in Laos, and gradually more intensive and sophisticated air interdiction attacks, the flow of PAVN units and supplies increased steadily from 1965 through 1970, when an estimated 8,000 PAVNs and 10,000 tons of supplies arrived in South Vietnam *each month*.[9]

Indeed, the trail, and the battles that swirled all around it, formed the fulcrum of the entire war. "Forged by man in the face of a hostile, unexplored nature," writes historian John Prados, "the Trail became a true lifeline."[10] According to postwar accounts published by Hanoi long after the end of the war, the trail consisted of 12,000 miles of road—five main roads, twenty-nine branch roads, and hundreds of cutoffs and passes. About one million soldiers made the trip from the North in the course of the fighting. Perhaps 50,000 PAVN troops were deployed to defend the Revolution's main supply line by 1968. Maintenance crews and bomb-disposal specialists defused 56,750 unexploded bombs and took 1,196 prisoners in the process. "By any standard of human endeavor," writes Prados, "what happened on the Ho Chi Minh Trail must rank high among the works of men and women."[11]

As Giap's forces grew stronger in the North, signs of chaos and contradictions within what Giap called "the enemy camp" slowly but surely began to surface. He had predicted as much. The Saigon regime and its army began to lose what little respect they enjoyed among the populace of South Vietnam as the Americans assumed the burden of the fighting and the leadership of the conflict. South Vietnamese political culture, always factious and governed by byzantine familial and feudal relationships, was destabilized rather than strengthened by massive American intervention. Huge quantities of American consumer goods and development funds earmarked for rural development programs were siphoned off by the urban elite that dominated the ARVN officer corps and the GVN administration. These same officers and officials refused to investigate corruption because they were its prime beneficiaries. The South Vietnamese charged with executing pacification programs in the nation's various provinces and districts, writes historian Marc Jason Gilbert,

> were college educated urbanites who often exhibited the worst characteristics of Vietnamese feudal elitism when addressing their overwhelmingly poor, illiterate, and rural rank and file soldiers and the masses of farmers from which the latter were recruited. The distribution of military, police, provincial and district assignments according to political and financial criteria of familial or feudal obligation not only impeded the government effort to defeat the Viet Cong [the PLAF] but also...condoned counterproductive behavior, from the taking of bribes to petty harassment for personal gain. These inequities turned the government's officials into living propaganda for the Viet Cong.[12]

THE DMZ WAR

In July 1966 Hanoi initiated a bloody campaign in a theater where Giap's main forces were fully equipped with modern Soviet and Chinese heavy weapons, including tanks: the DMZ. Several PAVN regiments infiltrated Quang Tri and Thua Thien Provinces, South Vietnam's northernmost provinces. Here PAVN forces enjoyed the advantages of sanctuary and superior numbers against the United States Marines. The 324B PAVN Division fought a series of intense, bitter engagements from July through October, when the Marines finally drove them back into North Vietnam with heavy casualties, but the 324B was quickly rebuilt for even more extensive combat against a string of Marine strongpoints built across the DMZ from Khe Sanh, a few miles east of the Laotian border to Gio Linh near the eastern coast.

Beginning in February 1967 the PAVN conducted several World War I–style conventional sieges against such Marine bases as Con Thien, forcing Westmoreland to divert more and more of his limited maneuver battalions from the three military corps to the south of I Corps to the embattled Marines near the DMZ. The campaign in I Corps against the Marines fell outside of Thanh's area of command. Here it appears Giap planned operations and commanded PAVN forces directly. In April the American Marines beat back sustained assaults against hill positions protecting their base at Khe Sanh. Both sides took extremely heavy casualties. MACV began to suspect Giap was planning either another Dien Bien Phu against that base, or perhaps a full-blown invasion of South Vietnam's northernmost provinces with a view to seizing several provinces all of a piece. Accordingly, Westmoreland ordered a reluctant Marine command to build a continuous line of strongpoints, mine fields, and sensors just below the DMZ across the entire width of South Vietnam, the "McNamara Line," to discourage major PAVN offensives and cut down on infiltration. General Lewis Walt, commander of the Marines, objected strenuously to the plan. Walt had long favored the "ink blot" or "oilslick" strategy of gradually expanding enclaves rather than a search-and-destroy strategy, or a static defense of the entire DMZ.

As it happened, the McNamara Line project soon proved an exercise in futility and was abandoned well before completion. It failed to halt infiltration across the DMZ. Several company-size Marine patrols protecting the construction workers were badly mauled by superior PAVN forces, and the Marines and Seabees building the fortifications were often forced to work under punishing PAVN artillery bombardment.

THE IRON TRIANGLE AND THE HIGHLANDS BATTLES

While the Marines were battling regular PAVN units, the US Army launched its largest operations to date against the NLF stronghold north and northwest of Saigon—in the Iron Triangle and War Zone D. In Operation Cedar Falls (January 1967), 30,000 US and ARVN troops swept into the Iron Triangle. US forces uncovered several large supply depots and tunnel complexes. Where these were found, the civilian population was removed en masse, and Agent Orange was sprayed all across the area of operations to destroy the forests, thereby denying the Communists cover should they attempt to return. Cedar Falls was declared a victory by Westmoreland. Most historians (wisely) disagree. In fact, Giap had ordered the vast majority of the Communist forces there to retreat to Cambodia. The elusive PLAF units that remained sustained only light casualties. Within a few months, the PLAF had returned to the Iron Triangle and rebuilt its base of operations to threaten Saigon. The results were essentially the same in Operation

Junction City, mounted later in 1967 against the Communist forces in War Zone C.

In November 1967, two months after a public opinion poll showed that for the first time more Americans opposed the war than supported it, Giap launched another offensive in the Central Highlands. Again he drew off US forces from fighting the PLAF units operating in the populous coastal areas, where the fight for hearts and minds was being waged, and lost, by the United States. Giap's troops isolated and nearly succeeded in annihilating the American garrison at Dak To. In an effort to open the main road to Dak To, the Americans had to root out well-dug-in PAVN units on Hill 875 in a battle that became a kind of symbol of the futility of Westmoreland's strategy among American grunts and, of course, an increasingly skeptical American public.

For several days the PAVN units held out against repeated ground assaults. After intensive air strikes, including a costly bombardment of American infantry units by the US air force—friendly fire was a chronic problem for the United States in Vietnam—the two PAVN regiments defending the hill slipped away at night into sanctuaries in Cambodia. Almost 300 American soldiers died for a piece of ground that was for all intents and purposes strategically irrelevant.[13] The two PAVN regiments engaged in combat were found to be refitted and engaged in operations in the Highlands several months later. These sorts of engagements hardly buttressed lagging support for the war among the American people. Indeed, they seemed to deepen the feeling of exhaustion, even despair, over the war. But their effect on Hanoi, on the Communist-controlled population, was negligible. In fact, information about lost engagements and horrific casualties was suppressed from the population and, officially at least, within the PAVN.

PAVN TACTICS AND CULTURE

While US Army and Marine units unquestionably inflicted very heavy casualties on the increasing numbers of regular force units in 1966 and 1967 and almost always defeated Giap's forces in combat in mobile operations, the PAVN's "hit, run, hide" style of operation frustrated Westmoreland's search-and-destroy strategy, limiting its effectiveness and preventing the destruction of entire Communist units that was its core aim.

As Giap initiated mobile and conventional warfare in selective the-
aters, the guerrilla war remained by far the dominant form of combat in
the war in general. Throughout the entire period of escalation, thousands
of small-unit actions by guerrilla units, both companies and platoons,
proved enormously frustrating to American infantrymen. Guerrilla tactics are largely timeless, and we have discussed them at length earlier in
the book. Suffice it to say here that PLAF guerrillas across South Vietnam,
like their Vietminh predecessors, were masters of the tactical doctrine that
has been nicely summarized as "four fast, one slow." What this came down
to in thousands of actions from the Cau Mau Peninsula in the Mekong
Delta to the DMZ was "fast advance, fast assault, fast clearance, and fast
withdrawal—all based on slow preparation" of the attack.[14]

As the American soldier patrolled week after week, month after month
in a difficult climate and typically hostile territory, encountering booby
traps and an elusive enemy, morale problems inevitably set in on a major
scale. For all their bravery and skill, the US forces were unsuccessful in
uprooting the Communist infrastructure in Vietnam. PAVN headquarters were located underground in vast tunnel complexes. The vast majority
of these complexes survived numerous attempts at destruction. Nor did
American or ARVN units inflict fatal damage on the Communist guerrillas *as a whole,* even granting their success by the criterion of "the body
count." Giap's war against the Americans, when all is said and done, was
a small-unit war supported by big-unit operations. As military analyst
Thomas Thayer writes, most Communist actions against Allied forces

> took the form of standoff attacks, harassment and terrorism which did
> not involve direct contact between their ground forces and those of the
> allies. The communist ground assaults where their troops came into con-
> tact with allied forces accounted for less than five percent of the total
> actions during 1965–1972. More than 95 percent of those assaults were
> attacks by communist units smaller than a battalion. Incessant small
> unit actions truly was [*sic*] the name of their game.[15]

What were the distinguishing characteristics of the PAVN soldier and
the culture in which he operated? The typical regular soldier who made
his way down the Ho Chi Minh Trail was particularly well trained in concealment and night operations. He was disciplined and tenacious. He traveled light. He had to, for the life of a PAVN soldier was a life of constant

movement, of setting up camps and fortifications in one place, only to rest briefly before moving on and repeating the process time and time again. By design, PAVN units marched endlessly and fought rarely. Like the guerrillas, the main-force units benefited greatly from superior ground intelligence, often obtained from operatives who served within Saigon's armed forces, or from sympathetic civilians in close contact with American units working as cooks, in maintenance, delivery, and laundry service.

In preparing his campaigns and operations against the Americans, Giap had to come up with creative solutions to logistical and tactical problems that were far more challenging than what he had encountered against the French—and those had been formidable. American infantry soldiers and Marines developed a great respect for the caliber of their adversaries in the field. Former US Senator James Webb of Virginia, a highly decorated company commander and battalion intelligence officer with the fabled Fifth Marine Regiment, saw heavy combat in I Corps. He describes his adversaries as

> good soldiers.... The NVA [North Vietnamese Army] had great fire discipline and good marksmanship skills. They built excellent fortifications, incredibly impressive trenches and emplacements. They used a "grab and hold" tactic: Their ideal scenario was to wait until we were so close to them that we couldn't use supporting fires for fear of hitting our own men. That required tremendous fire discipline on their part—to hold off until we were so close. They were able to spring very effective and sizeable daytime ambushes in the trenches and tree lines adjacent to wide rice paddies.... When the NVA could control the terrain or when we stayed too long in one spot they were deadly; when we could use maneuver and fire support again, we did a number on them.[16]

By the end of 1967, many close observers of the war judged it a stalemate. After three years of battering each other on battlefields all over South Vietnam, neither side had achieved clear dominance, and it was possible to read the balance of forces in different ways. Yet, if Vietnam could be read as a military stalemate of a sort, the underlying currents of the conflict as a whole seemed to favor the Communist cause. General William Westmoreland did not think so. An apparently serenely confident MACV commander returned to the United States to rally support for the war effort in the fall of 1967. In an address before Congress on November 21, he reported: "We have reached an important point where the end begins to come into view.... The enemy has many problems. He is losing control of the scattered population under his influence. He is losing credibility with the population he controls.... He sees the strength of his forces steadily declining."[17] The gist of his address: Victory was within reach. More of the war was behind the United States than ahead.

Westmoreland was misreading the arc of the war in Vietnam, and badly. In fact, *his* strategy was failing. The elusive "crossover point," the critical juncture where the American army had killed so many Communist troops that they could no longer be replaced, was nowhere in sight. In 1966, 71,000 Communist soldiers had been killed, and at least twice that many wounded. In 1967, 133,000 of Giap's troops died, according to estimates that today seem reasonably on target if one considers figures released by the Vietnamese government long after the war. (In April 1995 Hanoi announced that 1,100,000 of its troops, both guerrillas and main force, died in combat between 1954 and 1975.) Yet Giap remained capable of replacing these losses with relative ease. The steadily more intensive US effort to cut off infiltration through both ground and air operations was failing.

The PAVN order of battle increased steadily from 1965 through December 1967. At the end of 1965, approximately 100,000 regular troops were deployed in South Vietnam. At the end of 1967, some 275,000 Communist troops were either in South Vietnam or its peripheral sanctuaries, capable of engaging in combat operations. Demographics went far in suggesting the crossover point would never be reached, given the strictures Washington had placed on the nature of the war. In 1966, 4 million of North Vietnam's 18 million people were between the ages of fifteen and forty-nine. Half of them were deemed fit for military service. The Americans simply could not bleed North Vietnam out of the South.

By contrast, Giap's understanding of the nature of the war was remarkably astute. From the very beginning of the escalatory stage, he had possessed a realistic understanding of the Americans' liabilities, military and political, in waging a protracted war in South Vietnam. He correctly anticipated that the escalation of combat and expanding American casualty lists would exert strong pressures on the Johnson administration to limit the number of troops in Vietnam: "The American imperialists must restrict the US forces participating in a limited war, because without this restricting their global strategy will encounter difficulties, and their influences over the world will be affected. They must achieve this limitation to avoid upsetting political, economic and social life in the United States."[18]

It was no accident that North Vietnam invested so much energy and effort in its sophisticated propaganda campaign, highlighting the destructiveness of the American way of war on the civilian population, characterizing the conflict to the world press as a "David versus Goliath" contest, "a struggle for the country's survival."[19]

No segment of world opinion received such lavish attention as that of the American people, for Giap knew that popular opposition within the United States was a more important weapon in his war than even the best trained of his PAVN divisions:

> Our people greatly appreciate the struggle of the American people against the aggressive Viet-Nam war of the Johnson administration, considering it a valuable mark of sympathy and support of our people's just resistance.... The U.S. ruling circles have been increasingly opposed by the American people and being isolated politically to a high degree in the international arenas.[20]

The great theorist of modern war, Carl von Clausewitz, wrote memorably that, "The first, the supreme, the most far-reaching act of judgment that the statesman and commander have to make is to establish...the kind of war upon which they are embarking; neither mistaking it for, nor trying to turn it into, something that is alien to its nature. This is the first of all strategic questions and the most comprehensive."[21] It is abundantly clear thirty-five years after the guns fell silent in Vietnam that Giap possessed that "far-reaching act of judgment" in spades. The same cannot be said for his American counterparts. Neither Johnson nor Westmoreland nor the Joint Chiefs of Staff saw Vietnam for what it was: a *revolutionary* guerrilla war, precisely defined by Brigadier General Samuel Griffith, USMC, in his introduction to Mao's *On Guerrilla Warfare.* Such a conflict, he wrote,

> is never confined within the bounds of military action. Because its purpose is to destroy an existing society and its institutions and to replace them with a completely new state structure, any revolutionary war is a unit of which the constituent parts, in varying importance, are military, political, economic, social and psychological. For this reason, it is endowed with a dynamic quality and a dimension in depth that orthodox

wars...lack....In the United States, we go to considerable trouble to keep soldiers out of politics, and even more to keep politics out of soldiers. Guerrillas do the opposite. They go to great lengths to make sure their men are politically educated and thoroughly aware of the issues at stake...The end product is an intensely loyal and politically alert fighting man.[22]

As Giap and his staff developed operational plans for the greatest offensive in the war to date in October 1967, 50,000 Americans, mainly college-age men and women, joined by a growing number of Vietnam veterans, marched on the Pentagon to protest the American prosecution of a war that US Secretary of Defense Robert McNamara had already come to see as an unwinnable tragedy.

9

THE TET OFFENSIVE

Just before 0245 hours on January 31, 1968, amid the boisterous revelry marking the start of the lunar new year holiday known as Tet, a pickup truck and a taxicab bearing seventeen sappers of the PLAF's 11 Commando Team screeched up to the symbol of American power in Saigon, the embassy compound. Within seconds, they blew a three-foot hole in its concrete exterior wall, and raced onto the lawn with automatic weapons ablaze, gunning down four American military policemen who were guarding the compound.

For the next few hours, US Marines, MPs, and a hodgepodge of embassy employees engaged the PLAF commandos in a sharp and chaotic firefight, attempting to prevent their entry into the embassy buildings. The commandos blew off the large seal of the United States hanging above the main entrance to the chancery with a rocket-propelled grenade launcher, but the death of the sapper team's commanders caused the momentum of the attack to slacken, and the entire unit was killed or captured. At 0930, the compound was declared secure. By that point, five GIs had also fallen, and a large contingent of the American press corps had already filed their first stories and video footage for the late afternoon papers and the network newscasts in the United States. Initial reports filed in the heat of the action left the mistaken impression on the public that the embassy had been temporarily seized by PLAF sappers. Strenuous efforts on the part of MACV and the Johnson administration to correct this misconception about the embassy attack were initially lost amid the shock and the confusion of the several hundred spontaneous Communist attacks known to Americans as the "Tet Offensive."

Indeed, fierce attacks seemed to erupt everywhere at once in South Vietnam. Ammo dumps went up in torrents of flame, airbases and scores of base camps were heavily mortared, and hundreds of their defenders were gunned down by apparently fearless sappers and suicide squads. PLAF units took even heavier casualties than the defenders, most of whom were ARVN rather than American troops. The widely dispersed assaults placed crushing demands on US-ARVN headquarters throughout the country: Where and in what strength should their mobile forces deploy in response? Chaos reigned throughout the first night as frantic and contradictory radio messages flooded into headquarters and command posts. American reporters and television crews throughout South Vietnam for the most part reported what they saw and heard without excessive editorializing, but inevitably their reports, the "first draft" of history, were interpreted by the American public as at best a crisis and at worst a catastrophe in the making.

Eighty-four thousand Communist troops were directly engaged in the first waves of the Tet attacks all across South Vietnam. The vast majority of the assault units were PLAF units, not PAVN regulars. The 4,000 specially selected troops who invested Saigon had rehearsed their attacks for three full months, in many cases using detailed replicas of their targets and working with plans that had been revised and refined for several *years*. Communist guerrilla forces had begun to infiltrate the city's porous security checkpoints about a month earlier. In attacks on the presidential palace and five other high-visibility targets in the capital, the initial assaults stunned the defenders, who were partially overrun at several locales. Assault squads overwhelmed the workers in the main radio station and attempted to play audio tapes calling on the populace to rise up and join the fight against the puppets and imperialists.

Giap's initial attacks benefited greatly from the absence of a large percentage of ARVN troops from their installations, and from MACV's failure to detect the extensive preparations for the attack. Westmoreland had been expecting Giap to launch a major offensive close to the DMZ. He had never considered widespread attacks a live option for Communist forces that had suffered so many casualties in recent months. In Quang Tri Province, just below the DMZ, several PAVN divisions had massed in recent weeks. The western anchor of the McNamara Line at Khe Sanh had already been under a formidable siege for a week. As a result, Westmoreland and his intelligence staff had concentrated most of their powerful mobile response units in the northernmost third of the country.

In short, the scope and ferocity of the Tet attacks came as a very unpleasant surprise to the American and South Vietnamese leadership. In the midst of so much carnage and mayhem, surprise turned to dread, and in some cases, to outright panic. Dozens of ARVN installations and GVN-controlled towns and villages were overrun. Communist forces quickly overwhelmed the defenders, dug in, and held their ground against counterattacks with fanatical intensity. Whipped up to a fever pitch by months of intensive indoctrination classes, many PLAF and PAVN troops held out until the last man.

Just outside the capital city, PLAF battalions struck at the huge airbase at Tan Son Nhut, where MACV headquarters was located, from three directions, threatening to overwhelm the entire installation. Other units attacked the massive logistical complex at Long Binh fifteen miles north of Saigon, while an entire Communist division closed in on the Bien Hoa airbase after a mortar and rocket attack. A powerful American relief force punched through a series of road blocks to blunt the attack on Bien Hoa, but it took very heavy casualties in the process. American bases outside Saigon were also attacked, but Giap had known from the outset that his forces were unlikely to overrun them, and indeed, most of the assaults against US forces were beaten back within hours.

The initial American response was as predictable as it was unfortunate. Shocked and angered US commanders unleashed indiscriminate supporting arms fire everywhere they spotted a target. More than 14,000 civilians were killed in the two months following the initial attacks, mostly as the result of overzealous American artillery and air strikes. An American correspondent on the scene with a gift for evoking the peculiar atmospherics of combat in Vietnam described the scene:

> We [the Americans] took a huge collective nervous breakdown, it was the compression and heat of heavy contact generated out until every American in Vietnam got a taste. Vietnam was a dark room full of deadly objects,

the VC were everywhere all at once like spider cancer, and instead of losing the war in little pieces over the years we lost it fast in under a week. After that, we were like the character in pop grunt mythology, dead but too dumb to lie down. Our worst dread of yellow peril became realized; we saw them now dying by the thousands all over the country, yet they didn't seem depleted, let alone exhausted, as the [US] Mission was claiming by the fourth day. We took space back quickly, expensively, with total panic and close to maximum brutality. Our machine was devastating. And versatile. It could do everything but stop. As one American major said in a successful attempt at attaining history, "We had to destroy Ben Tre [a Communist target] in order to save it."[1]

As a result of the ferocity of the US and ARVN counterattacks, virtually all Communist gains were reversed within three or four days.

There were a few notable exceptions. In Cholon, Saigon's sister city, PLAF units held on to the Pho Tho racetrack until February 10, three days after the American command had established a large section of the city as a free-fire zone, and sporadic fighting around the track lasted for several more weeks. The most sustained fighting, though, was in the former capital of Hue, a beautiful city of temples and gardens, flooded with refugees from the heaviest fighting in the war in the northern provinces.

Two PAVN regiments seized most of the city, their path well prepared by local guerrilla forces and political cadres who had been preparing to install a revolutionary government once the city had been seized. A heavily outnumbered force of US Marines and ARVN troops engaged in ferocious house-to-house combat, initially without artillery or air support, to retake first the business and government district south of the Perfume River, and then the formidable Imperial Citadel, a heavily fortified city-within-a-city in the northern section of Hue. Some days the Marines were only able to gain ten or twenty yards, so tough was the resistance.

By the time the South Vietnamese flag went up on the Imperial Palace of Peace within the citadel's grounds on February 25, 150 Marines had died, and 800 had been wounded, while Giap's forces had suffered perhaps 5,000 troops killed in action. In one of the most savage acts of a savage war, the short-lived NLF government in Hue executed some 2,800 "traitors and reactionaries" who had served or supported the GVN. The GVN had initially prohibited air strikes and artillery in order to preserve the beautiful architecture of the city and to limit civilian casualties, but in the end, the progress was so slow that the Marines were granted permission to unleash heavy supporting fire. More than half the city was in ruins by battle's end.

Searing images of the desperate fighting in Hue were broadcast on American television each night, reinforcing the initial shock of the Tet attacks in Saigon and widening further still the "credibility gap"—the disparity between the Johnson administration's sunny reports of progress and the public's growing perception of the war as futile and misconceived. The fighting during Tet, particularly the Battle of Hue, went a long way toward exploiting the "political contradictions" inherent in American war strategy even as the Americans and South Vietnamese were taking back the ground they had lost.

THE DIVERSIONARY CAMPAIGN AT KHE SANH

In classic Giapian fashion, the Tet attacks beginning in late January 1968 had been prefaced in late 1967 by a series of diversionary campaigns near the DMZ at Con Thien and Khe Sanh, in the Central Highlands, and north of Saigon. Far and away the most important of these diversionary operations was the dramatic siege of the Khe Sanh Marine combat base (January 21 to April 1, 1968). Khe Sanh was the westernmost combat base of US forces just below the DMZ, just six miles from the Laotian border. As elements of three PAVN divisions closed in on the 6,000-man Marine garrison, the Marine brass wanted to withdraw to the comparative safety of less isolated strongpoints to the east. They saw no good strategic purpose in remaining at Khe Sanh.

Westmoreland would have none of it. Khe Sanh figured prominently in his future war plans in several ways. It could serve as a jumping-off point for special operations reconnaissance forays into Laos and North Vietnam. It might also function as the staging area for an invasion into Laos that he hoped to convince a skeptical Johnson administration to approve. Westmoreland also described Khe Sanh as the "anchor" of the McNamara Line, protecting its left flank from an invasion by North Vietnam. Finally, the American field commander believed there was a good chance Giap was preparing to engage in something like Dien Bien Phu at Khe Sanh and seizing the northern provinces. If this was indeed Giap's intention, MACV's commander welcomed it. He was confident that, relying heavily on airpower, he could inflict a devastating defeat on the Communists.

Neither Johnson nor the civilian planners in the Pentagon were quite so sure. As PAVN forces closed in and cut Route 9, the only ground road leading to the base, the Marines had to be supplied entirely by air. After Giap launched the first of several ground attacks on the hill outposts outside the base on January 21, Khe Sanh became something of an obsession for Johnson personally. He went so far as to have a detailed replica of the base built in the White House basement for personal daily briefings. Khe Sanh was the object of intense media scrutiny as well. Could the Marines hold? Everywhere, American troops talked of the possibility of another Dien Bien Phu, and copies of Bernard Fall's masterful account of that battle were widely read by correspondents and American officers alike.

Just as Westmoreland misunderstood the main object of the Vietnam War as a whole, mistaking the destruction of Giap's main-force units for the war's true center of gravity—gaining the loyalty of the people of South Vietnam and isolating them from PLAF guerrillas and political cadres—so he misread Giap's intentions at Khe Sanh. The PAVN commander never once made a serious effort to overrun the base. Khe Sanh's similarities to Dien Bien Phu were far less significant than its differences, all of which boded poorly for Communist success in overrunning the Marines.

Giap's Khe Sanh campaign was intended as a ruse, a diversion (albeit a costly one) to draw off US mobile forces to the northern border region, thereby paving the way for the Tet attacks. It may also have been meant to test Westmoreland's reactions to a serious threat near the DMZ—would such a threat prompt him to invade North Vietnam, landing troops behind Giap's forces in the North Vietnamese panhandle? As we have seen, the possibility of an invasion of North Vietnam had been one of Giap's abiding preoccupations since the outset of the American War.

In any case, instead of launching a massive attack on the base itself, the PAVN bombarded the Marines with as many as 1,300 shells a day, much of the fire originating in the mountains of Laos, out of reach of US counter-battery fire. Giap did launch several battalion-sized attacks on the hills protecting the base, but succeeded in overrunning only one hill strongpoint, and that was quickly retaken. In the broad scheme of things, the failure of these ground thrusts mattered little. They succeeded in keeping alive the notion at MACV headquarters that the Big Attack was in the offing at Khe Sanh, and as usual, Giap's heavy casualties had no significant bearing on his ability to wage the campaign in a manner of his choosing.

Another action near the Marine Khe Sanh base that shook MACV and enhanced the believability of Giap's ruse occurred on February 6, when elements of at least two PAVN regiments supported by tanks—their first appearance of the war—overran a Special Forces base, killing most of its Montagnard garrison and a handful of American Green Berets. According to the official history of the PAVN, the Lang Vei attack was "the first combined arms operation that succeeded in destroying an enemy battalion defending a heavily fortified position" in the American War. It "marked a new stage forward in the growth of the combat capabilities of our mobile main force troops."[2] Gradually, very gradually, in the midst of the heaviest combat of the war, Giap's army's capabilities continued to develop.

Did Giap intend to attack the combat base with tanks? Johnson, Westmoreland, and the American people looked on with grave concern and wondered. Khe Sanh was one of the mysteries complicating the larger story of the Tet Offensive. Westmoreland did everything he could to protect the Marines hunkered down in its bunkers. Some 75,000 tons of bombs fell on suspected PAVN positions around the base. There is no question that the siege of Khe Sanh was a costly ruse for the PAVN. American estimates place Communist casualties somewhere between 10,000 and 15,000 in total. Yet the PAVN's ability to bottle up the Marines and inflict such punishment on the garrison for so long tended to reinforce the American public's growing disillusionment with a war that seemed both interminable and futile. Giap welcomed the American high command's intense focus on the Marine base. It fit snugly into his broader campaign plan.

PLANNING TET

We do not know anywhere nearly as much as we would like to about the origins and evolution of the plan for the Tet Offensive. As far back as 1963, the Central Committee of the Politburo had decreed that a general offensive–general uprising (GOGU) would be "the necessary direction of development for the South Vietnamese revolution to achieve victory."[3] The Central Committee and the Central Military Party Committee, Hanoi's two most powerful strategy-making bodies, still believed in the efficacy of the GOGU in January 1967, when the Central Committee's thirteenth plenum called on the PAVN to begin to plan for "a decisive victory in a relatively short period of time."[4] A couple of months later, the Central Committee agreed to launch the GOGU sometime in 1968. General Tran Van Tra, a key figure in the extended planning process and the commander of all forces in the attacks on Saigon, summarized the context of the decision to launch the operation: Hanoi was well aware that

> President Johnson had to make a definite and important decision: either yield to the military and escalate the war, expanding it to the whole of Indochina (including an invasion of North Vietnam) or listen to McNamara and several high-level civilian officials and de-escalate the war and negotiate with Hanoi and the Viet Cong. He could no longer afford to stay at the crossroads any longer.... The United States could not help but sicken of the deadlock in South Vietnam and the fact that the heavy losses in the air war over North Vietnam were not compensated by any tangible political or military results.[5]

A Central Committee resolution issued in mid-1967 makes it clear that Hanoi thought an offensive on an unprecedented scale had a far greater chance of resulting in the latter than the former decision. The same resolution enumerated various objectives, some of which were clearly decisions more realistic than others in the eyes of the operation's architects—a point that appears to be lost on an influential school of American analysts that emerged after the war. (More on this issue follows.) The objectives were summarized by PAVN General Tran Van Tra as follows:

> To break down the bulk of the South Vietnamese army, topple the puppet administration at all levels, and take power into the hands of the people.
>
> To destroy the major part of US forces...and render them incapable of fulfilling their duties in Vietnam.
>
> To break the will of U.S. aggression, force it to accept defeat in the South and put an end to all acts of war against the North.[6]

Sorting out who provided the initial inspiration for Tet and how the plan evolved throughout 1967 until the final operation was formally approved in early January 1968 remains a tricky and speculative enterprise. We may never have a clear understanding of the process, as written documents do not take note of internal debates, and after-the-fact recollections are invariably politically biased. Virtually all reliable sources credit General Nguyen Chi Thanh with presenting the first draft of a plan during the spring 1967, after he visited key commands throughout the South and discussed the strategic situation with his regional commanders there. Thanh may very well have been selected over Giap by the Central Committee to oversee planning in the summer and fall, and even slated to command the entire operation from his headquarters at COSVN.

This is the most likely scenario for three reasons: First, Giap had initially argued against the consensus opinion on the issue of timing. He called for delaying the offensive until late 1968, or even early 1969, fearing that Communist forces would not be sufficiently well prepared by early 1968. Second, Thanh enjoyed the firm support of Le Duan, the most powerful figure sitting on the Politburo at the time. Le Duan had often clashed with Giap over issues of strategic priorities and the timing of military initiatives. Third, Thanh had greater familiarity than Giap did with the conditions of the fighting in the South generally. Be that as it may, after Thanh died in July 1967, "direct responsibility for overseeing the General offensive-General uprising was assumed by Defence Minister Vo Nguyen Giap."[7]

It was on Giap's watch that the offensive took on its distinctive characteristic as a series of "violent surges," beginning with scores of widespread assaults, including attacks on targets of great symbolic significance for the American people. Hanoi deemed it important to launch these attacks at the opening of the American presidential campaign, with a view to sparking divisiveness during the escalation year of 1968.

Two additional offensives were envisaged in May and September—"mini-Tets," as they are described by American historians—to confirm the continued resolve of the revolutionary forces and provide additional incentives for the United States to see that its best course of action would be to pursue negotiations rather than military victory.[8]

In thinking about what Tet could be expected to accomplish, Giap was keenly attentive to "the unpredictability of the Revolutionary process and to the explosive character of popular discontent" in South Vietnam.[9] Another factor heightened the operation's unpredictable outcome: From a strictly military point of view, Tet was radically unconventional, and unconventionality means enhanced risk. No army in twentieth-century history had attempted to conduct simultaneous assaults against so many targets across such a large swath of territory. Tet violated a fundamental precept of offensive doctrine: the need to concentrate forces against a limited number of critical objectives. According to "the book," an offensive should consist of a "main effort" attack, usually supported by diversions or secondary attacks. In Tet, there was no "main effort" in the traditional military sense of the term. The attacks on Saigon were only symbolically more important than the others. Communist forces went after everything, everywhere: cities, towns, rural districts, airfields, and military camps defended in many cases by a mere company or two.

Once the date and provisional plan were approved in October 1967, the PAVN general staff liaised with COSVN as well as the regional and provincial commands, refining and coordinating scores of detailed plans for the attacks on the major cities and towns, while regional military commanders and political cadres worked out the details for secondary and diversionary operations.

Preparations for the big attacks of January 31 at both the national and regional levels were painstaking and laborious to say the least. Infiltration rates throughout 1967 proceeded at a robust pace despite the lavish resources devoted to the American air interdiction and detection. About 75,000 main-force troops made the trek down the Ho Chi Minh Trail during the year, more than in any previous year. Sapper and special attack forces, recently established as a separate branch within the PAVN, were prominently represented among the new arrivals. As General Tran Van Tra recalled,

> different military forces had to be formed to suit different targets....Therefore, it was of the utmost importance that, at a very early stage, we build special mobile attack units and on-the-spot sapper units and pre-assign them to each and every target....Shock battalions of the regular army and local battalions, which were thoroughly familiar with the local terrain and situation—and had their guerrilla bases in the vicinity of their targets—were assigned to approach each main target and provide timely support of the special attack and sapper forces, regular and local. Next in line [i.e., the initial reserve forces] were the regional and main force regiments and divisions which would stand ready to move in to destroy the enemy resistance and repulse any counterattacks.[10]

American and South Vietnamese intelligence organizations were able to penetrate the planning process, but only at the local level. MACV never seriously entertained the idea that the attacks might be countrywide. That the Communists managed to maintain secrecy concerning the basic design of the offensive seems a remarkable feat when one considers the resources of US intelligence in Vietnam and the volume of Communist communications and logistical activity during the preparation phase. Certainly, American intelligence in late 1967 strongly suspected that a major operation was in the works, but MACV was predisposed to believe the offensive would be a conventional one in which Giap would strike very hard against one or perhaps two strategic targets.

AFTER TET

The Communists suffered ghastly casualties in the general fighting in February and March. About 45,000 of the 80,000 troops in the first waves were killed or badly wounded within that time frame. The PLAF guerrilla units had spearheaded the attacks on the cities, where resistance was far stronger than in the hinterlands. So badly were these units mauled that many were never reconstituted. Other PLAF battalions and regiments took on large numbers of replacements, but they were usually North Vietnamese troops, and the fighting for the remainder of the war would be dominated by regular PAVN units trained and equipped in the North.

The infrastructure in the South was badly damaged, but not irretrievably so. The Communists failed to hold on to any of their early territorial gains, largely because once American ground commanders recovered from the shock, they were able to drive comparatively lightly armed, widely dispersed Communist units from their positions with superior numbers of infantry and massive firepower. The South Vietnamese army suffered heavy casualties, though nowhere near as heavy as those suffered by the PLAF, but the people of South Vietnam failed to rise up en masse against the Saigon government, as some of the PAVN and PLAF senior commanders in the field and members of the senior leadership in Hanoi had fervently hoped.

If the allies had more than held their own in the offensive in a tactical sense, beating back Communist forces expeditiously and putting Giap on the defensive militarily, it was equally clear that Tet was a stunning strategic victory for the Communists, and the war's critical turning point. It clearly set into motion a series of events that would lead to the abandonment of America's long quest for military victory and a decision by LBJ to de-escalate the conflict. Week after week following the launching of the offensive, as Johnson and his advisers weighed their policy options, the gruesome images of the fighting in Hue flickered across American television screens. The tenacity of the enemy belied Westmoreland's sunny reports of Hanoi's imminent demise. Public pressure on the Johnson administration to change course escalated sharply, as more and more American opinion makers—national newscasters, business leaders, and academics—joined the ranks of the doubters, and in some cases, the protestors in the streets.

Shortly after the offensive commenced, General Earle Wheeler, chairman of the Joint Chiefs of Staff, attempted to pressure Johnson to call up the reserves to meet worldwide strategic obligations and to send a large number of reinforcements—about 100,000 in all—to Westmoreland in Vietnam, hinting obliquely that if he failed to do so, the United States might soon be faced with a military catastrophe. Wheeler's assessment was disingenuous and manipulative. In no sense was South Vietnam on the verge of collapse, not with half a million American troops spread all around the country, and Wheeler knew it. A public furor erupted when the story of the request for the call-up of 200,000 troops was leaked to the *New York Times* in early March, fueling an already acrimonious debate within the administration over war strategy.

Johnson by this point was agonizing over Vietnam and, according to some accounts, exhausted, on the brink of collapse. Each day it seemed there were new outbursts of public dissent and criticism from the media, the doves in Congress, and the burgeoning antiwar movement. Under growing pressure from all sides, Johnson instructed his new secretary of defense, the urbane moderate Clark Clifford, to undertake a searching re-examination of options in Vietnam. An influential coterie of civilian defense analysts in the Pentagon had already produced a series of trenchant reports and memos, arguing that further escalations were likely to produce more casualties and more public dissent, but no decisive results in Vietnam. One of the most influential of these documents focused on the nub of the problem: "The enemy can control his casualty rate, at least to a great extent, by controlling the number, size and intensity of combat engagements. If he so chooses, he can limit his casualties to a rate that he is able to bear indefinitely. Therefore the notion that we can 'win' this war by driving the VC and NVA from the country or by inflicting an unacceptable rate of casualties on them is false."[11]

By the end of March, Clifford had consulted at length with "the wise men," a group of distinguished American generals and statesmen, including

Omar Bradley, Dean Acheson, and Averill Harriman. After considerable reflection and debate, Clifford and the wise men reached a consensus. The US strategy in Vietnam was not working. The United States could not impose a military solution on the Communists, "at least not in any time the American people will permit," opined Acheson, who served as the group's spokesman.[12] Expanding the war with additional forces would only result in needless death and destruction.

What, then, should be done? The only prudent option, they explained, was to extend an overture to Hanoi to seek negotiations, to begin to draw down US forces, and to gradually shift the burden of fighting over to the South Vietnamese.

Two months after the offensive began, the Johnson administration abandoned an attrition strategy that sought victory through the destruction of Giap's military forces and kicked Westmoreland upstairs to become the Army's chief of staff. Search-and-destroy operations would continue for some time under the command of Westmoreland's successor, General Creighton Abrams, but they would no longer be a core element of US strategy. In a dramatic address on March 31, Johnson spoke in measured tones of "peace in Vietnam." He would take the "first steps to deescalate the conflict" and was prepared to "move toward peace through negotiation." To encourage compromise on the part of Hanoi, he had ordered a bombing halt over all of North Vietnam except for its panhandle, the staging area for infiltration of PAVN forces into South Vietnam. He went on to remark that the "main burden" of defending South Vietnam "must be carried out" by the South Vietnamese themselves. Then came the shocker: he "should not permit the Presidency to become involved in partisan divisions" then enveloping the country, nor would he seek the Democratic Party's nomination for the presidency.[13]

Although seldom mentioned in histories of the Vietnam War written by Americans, Giap did in fact launch two more offensives in 1968, just as his 1967 plan had called for. The attacks in the later offensives of May and September were far fewer in number than in Tet, but generally involved stronger forces. In the northernmost five provinces, the fighting was particularly intense. Here more than half of all American combat forces—fifty-four battalions—squared off against PAVN forces of the same strength in a series of extended, inconclusive engagements. In eastern Quang Tri, the Marines and the PAVN fought throughout the month of May in a brutal engagement around Dong Ha that cost the Americans about 1,900 casualties and Giap's forces 3,600.[14] In total, US forces suffered more men killed in action in May than in February.[15] The second and third offensives reinforced the (correct) impression that Hanoi remained militarily strong enough to carry on fighting, its resolve unbroken by casualty rates that dwarfed those of the Americans. In November 1968 Johnson called a halt to the bombing of *all* North Vietnam, and for the first time the American president indicated that he would be willing to grant the NLF its own seat at the negotiations table, joining Hanoi's, Saigon's, and Washington's delegations. The war was about to enter the "fight and talk" phase the Communists had long sought.

SCHOOLS OF THOUGHT

While there is a clear consensus among serious students of the conflict that Tet was a conventional military defeat but a strategic victory for the Communists, they disagree passionately as to whether its outcome was the result of Giap's brilliance as a strategist, or a misinterpretation of the offensive's results and a regrettable lack of willpower on the part of the United States. The "stab-in-the-back" school is loath to give any credit at all to Giap (and by extension, Hanoi) for America's strategic defeat. The origins of this school lie with General Westmoreland, who would claim as the fighting came to an end in Hue that the Communists had "used up their military chips" in a last "throw of the dice."[16] Westmoreland thought the offensive had been a devastating failure that should have led to a decisive US-GVN counteroffensive, including an "amphibious hook" by US forces into North Vietnam's panhandle to crush Giap's divisions near the DMZ and cut the Ho Chi Minh Trail. He also envisioned thrusts into the sanctuaries in Laos and Cambodia. Instead of pressing on with an aggressive counteroffensive that could very well break the Communists' back once and for all, Washington and the American people lost their nerve.

The media deserved a great deal of the blame, as Westmoreland would explain years after the war had ended, in its biased obsession with the egregiously low estimates by MACV of Communist military strength, and the failure of the attrition strategy implied by the very launching of the Communist offensive. Liberal reporters and editors had distorted the meaning of the offensive, playing up the shocking ferocity of Giap's audacious attacks and MACV's failure to anticipate the scope of the Communist initiative.

In the 1980s and 1990s a number of respected analysts, notably Harry Summers and Lewis Sorley, put forward more nuanced variations of this interpretation, focusing attention not so much on the media, but on the Johnson administration's misreading of what really happened on the ground and on the opportunities the offensive opened up for US military operations. It was not the audacity and superior strategic understanding of the Communist leadership that led to strategic victory, but misperception on the part of the policymakers in Washington and generals in Saigon. Summers believed the United States should have spent less time and effort in pacification and anti-guerrilla actions and instead made a full-bore effort to isolate the PAVN from the battlefields of South Vietnam, causing the Communist forces to wither and die in big-unit battles.[17]

In *A Better War,* Sorely presents the Tet Offensive as a failure for the Communists, for it demonstrated that the people of South Vietnam by and large did not support the revolution's quest for reunification. Quite the reverse, he claims: "One of the great, if unremarked ironies of the war was that the enemy's 'General Offensive/General Uprising' provoked not the anticipated uprising of the population in support of the invaders, but just the opposite—general mobilization in support of the government."[18] Both Sorley and Summers see Giap as having cynically sacrificed PLAF units, holding back North Vietnamese divisions, presumably to enhance the power of Hanoi at the expense of the NLF in the revolutionary enterprise. In their reading, the decimation of the Vietcong exposed the illegitimacy of Hanoi's leadership rather than its audacity or resolve. Phillip Davidson, another prominent historian of the conflict, suggests that Giap launched the offensive not so much after a careful and accurate assessment of the political and military state of play in Vietnam, but because he had to do so. American battlefield successes had forced him to abandon protracted war in favor of "an all-out drive for victory at one stroke."[19]

Lingering beneath the surface of these interpretations, one detects a strong current of hurt pride and humiliation over what transpired in the hellish early months of 1968. (Summers, Sorley, and Davidson all fought in Vietnam as US Army officers.) Davidson, and to a lesser degree Sorley and Summers, seem determined to denigrate the Communist victory because it was won not on the battlefield, but in the living rooms of the

American people and in a series of agonizing conferences over scores of position papers filed by civilian "experts." How could the Communists be said to have won when so many of the objectives they presented to their own soldiers and civilians failed to materialize? Yet, was it not true that what Giap's forces did on the battlefield served as the catalyst for political defeat? Surely it was.

The release of classified documents on both sides since war's end, as well as our growing understanding of Giap's way of war, have gone far in exposing fatal weaknesses in the "stab-in-the-back" school and its variants. While there is no denying that the South Vietnamese people failed to rally in droves to the Communists, which was one of Giap's stated objectives, Sorley's assertion that the people of South Vietnam rushed to mobilize behind the government is wishful thinking, plain and simple. The evidence suggests that the civilian population of South Vietnam hardly rose up in passionate defense of their government in Saigon. Rather, they were traumatized by the heavy combat and, in classic Vietnamese fashion, "sat on the fence," not wanting to attach themselves to one side or the other while the issue was in doubt.

In a sense, the fury of the military action all over the country forced them to do so. Their first concern was to stay alive, and Tet's main effect on civilians was to deepen their despair and war-weariness. The offensive produced over half a million new refugees, mostly the result of the destructiveness of American supporting arms. Never at any phase of the American War in Vietnam did the government of the Republic of South Vietnam enjoy strong support among its own people. True loyalty to Saigon among the South Vietnamese was in as short supply as the belief that the regime had a coherent vision for a brighter future for its peasantry.

Top-secret assessments of the fighting during the offensive among the US Joint Chiefs of Staff reveal they had the same doubts and concerns that were expressed by the American media. For the most part, the media had reported what it had seen and heard in an unbiased fashion. Even the most seasoned and respected journalists in the United States were shaken by Tet and sensed its ominous ramifications for the entire US war effort.[20]

While it is certainly true that Hanoi called on its own people "to overcome all hardships and sacrifices," "overthrow the puppet regime at all administrative levels," and place " all governmental power in the hands of the people," this was hardly the *critical* objective by which Hanoi would judge Tet a victory or defeat.[21] Rather, these were Tet's *optimal* objectives. One seriously doubts that a strategist with Giap's realistic appreciation of the strength of American forces in late 1967 truly expected to achieve them. In his articles assessing the current state of the war in late 1967, Giap cautioned his comrades against excessive optimism. He indicates obliquely that he did not expect a quick or total victory from the next major revolutionary initiative—clearly a reference to Tet.[22] A mid-1967 Central Committee resolution echoes Giap's sentiments, painting the attacks of early 1968 as "*the first stage in a process* involving a very fierce and complex strategic offensive which will combine military and political attacks to be carried out... in combination with the diplomatic offensive [italics mine]."[23]

If the complete collapse of Saigon and a Communist ascension to power were not seen as Tet's crucial objectives by Hanoi, what were? No one really knows for sure because we have no access to detailed discussions of the issue in late 1967 and early 1968. My own belief is that the crucial objective was not outright victory but, as the official history of the People's Army of Vietnam put it, "to crush the American will to commit aggression and force the United States to accept defeat in South Vietnam and end all hostile actions against North Vietnam."[24] Given Hanoi's healthy respect for American military strength, and what little we do know of its pre-launch discussions, it seems far more plausible that this, indeed, was the most important of the several objectives enumerated in the Central Committee resolution. As historian Gabriel Kolko writes, Giap's "main concern was with the impact of military action on the political context of the war, both in South Vietnam and in the United States. That political framework... would prove crucial, and an offensive was an essential catalyst in the process of change... In the largest sense, the primary objective of the offensive was to influence the United States."[25]

If we judge Tet in this light, it was clearly a brilliant success, albeit a costly one in blood. Despite Phillip Davidson's claim that Tet marked the abandonment of protracted war and a quest for "complete victory in a single stroke," neither Giap nor the Communist leadership as a whole thought of it that way. Neither should we. Tet was the continuation of protracted war by other means, an escalation in revolutionary violence, but it hardly marked the abandonment of protracted war strategy.

Of course, this does not mean that Hanoi had *no hope at all* that the attacks would bring about Saigon's collapse, but it seems much more plausible that that lofty objective was meant primarily to inspire revolutionary fervor—the mysterious "power of the masses" that Giap and the other senior leadership believed to be a defining element of people's war—indeed, it might be said to be the distinguishing element of people's war. The popular uprising was more a goal to inspire than a make-or-break objective. As Douglas Pike points out, the idea of the general offensive–general uprising in Vietnamese military thinking had long functioned largely as a "social myth" designed to capture the "Vietnamese imagination, to heighten revolutionary consciousness and rouse the peasant to battle.... Whether the general uprising would ever become a reality was irrelevant, what mattered was that people were willing to act out their lives as if it were a reality."[26]

Johnson's speech confirmed that Giap and Hanoi had achieved Tet's most important objective. Tet turned out to be what Giap had hoped it would from the beginning of the planning process: not the final victory in the American War, but a decisive victory nonetheless. It had set in motion a chain of events that would lead to withdrawal, and it signaled the end of the long phase of American escalation. "For the United States," Gabriel Kolko observes,

> Tet was a long-postponed confrontation with reality; it had been hypnotized until then by its own illusions, desires, and needs. The belated realization that it had military tactics and technology but no viable military strategy consistent with its domestic and international priorities made Tet the turning point in the administration's calculations. Those who had earlier favored the war finally made a much more objective assessment of the balance of forces.[27]

In a 1990 interview with journalist Stanley Karnow, Giap made substantially the same point as Kolko:

> We chose Tet because, in war, you must seize the propitious moment, when time and space are propitious. [The attack's] scope and ardor proved that both our army and people were disciplined and determined. We attacked the brains of the enemy, its headquarters in Saigon, showing it was not inviolable. Our forces destroyed large quantities of other equipment and crushed several of its elite units. We dramatized that we were neither exhausted nor on the edge of defeat, as Westmoreland claimed.

And though we knew most Americans had nothing against us, we wanted to carry the war into the families of America, to demonstrate, *n'est pas*, that if Vietnamese blood was being spilled, so was American blood. We did all this and more, and more Americans denounced the war.[28]

Vo Nguyen Giap's Tet campaign revealed at once his audacity, acute sense of timing, and breadth of thinking about the chemistry of war and politics. Don Oberdorfer writes in his classic account of the Tet Offensive that he "came to the conclusion that Tet was a classic case study in the interaction of war, politics, the press, and public opinion."[29] So it was, and Vo Nguyen Giap was its principal author. In planning and executing Tet, Giap went beyond Mao's doctrine, practicing a way of war that was distinctly his own. For the second time, he had forced a great nation to see the limits of its power and the futility of challenging the Communist revolutionaries on the battlefield. Tet was Giap's second masterpiece as the commander in chief of the People's Army of Vietnam.

10

FIGHTING, NEGOTIATING, AND VICTORY: 1969–1975

Richard Milhous Nixon assumed the presidency of the United States in January 1969. He had made his reputation in the 1950s as a hard-core anti-Communist—a reputation that he hoped would prove advantageous in his dealings with Hanoi. The new president fully accepted the sober conclusions concerning US policy and objectives in Vietnam arrived at by his predecessor: the war could not be won by force of arms, and the United States should seek a political settlement that would secure an independent pro-Western government in South Vietnam. Nonetheless, Nixon was sanguine about American prospects. Defeat was not so much unpalatable as unthinkable. Nixon, aided by his brilliant national security adviser, Professor Henry Kissinger of Harvard, would seek to depart from Southeast Asia with South Vietnam remaining a bulwark against world Communism, and with American credibility restored.

Three core elements of the Nixon administration's strategy as it emerged were inherited from the Johnson administration: a gradual drawdown of American forces; a major effort to expand and improve the South Vietnamese armed forces—dubbed "Vietnamization" by Secretary of Defense Melvin Laird; and the pursuit of negotiations with Hanoi from as strong a politico-military position as possible. Nixon and Kissinger considered themselves shrewd practitioners of realpolitik and believed that, even given the time limitations imposed on their efforts by the pressures of domestic politics, they could achieve "peace with honor."

During his 1968 campaign Nixon claimed he had a "secret plan" to end the conflict. This was disingenuous. In fact, he had no concrete plan, but rather several promising new strategic concepts that he would apply to the problem at hand. Perhaps the most imaginative of the new strategies was enlisting the help of Hanoi's allies in constraining its efforts on the battlefield and in softening its stance in negotiations through great-power diplomacy. In the late 1960s and early 1970s both the Soviet Union and the People's Republic of China were keenly interested in improving their strategic and economic relations with the United States—in large measure to gain certain advantages in their rivalry for dominance of the Communist bloc. Nixon planned on offering both nations a variety of incentives in exchange for promises to pressure Hanoi. The policy was called "linkage."

Kissinger and Nixon believed that their predecessors had exhibited an unfortunate restraint in the application of US military force in order to limit the war's destructiveness, and to wrest concessions from Hanoi in negotiations. They planned on making it clear through overt threats, bluffs, and *selective* escalations of force that they were more than willing, as Nixon would say later, to "bomb the bastards back to the Stone Age" if Hanoi played hardball and attempted to wait out the United States. The notion of threatening Hanoi with outright obliteration was widely known at the time as Nixon's "madman theory"—the idea being that Kissinger, in his negotiations with the North Vietnamese, would obliquely hint that his boss was a fanatical anti-Communist who would go to any lengths, including the use of nuclear weapons, to force North Vietnam to make substantive concessions.

Nixon was also determined to implement his strategy without the encumbrances of congressional, military, or bureaucratic input. The president's penchant for secrecy and deception in shaping Vietnam policy led directly to his downfall and disgrace, and that downfall, of course, stripped the United States of leverage in dealing with Hanoi. So too did Nixon's ironclad commitment to the American people to gradually withdraw all its military forces. Hanoi was under no such pressure.

As a result of these difficulties, a great many historians have come to view Nixon's prosecution of the war as tragically flawed. His intractability in negotiations and willingness to escalate military force to obtain unrealistic concessions from Hanoi needlessly extended the war. Over four years, Nixon's elusive quest for "peace with honor" led to the destruction of hundreds of thousands of lives in Southeast Asia, bitter discord and social upheaval at home, and the collapse of the postwar consensus regarding America's purpose in world affairs. As Walter Isaacson has written, Nixon's effort to preserve American honor "squandered the true sources of [America's] influence—and its credibility—in the world: its moral authority, its sense of worthy purpose and its reputation as a reasonable and sensible player."[1]

ABRAMS'S STRATEGY

Westmoreland's successor, General Creighton Abrams, a tough and aggressive commander who was well respected by his subordinates for his acerbic sense of humor and keen intelligence, was acutely conscious of the complex political dynamics of people's war. He understood and even admired his adversary's strengths: painstaking logistical preparation, defensive prowess, and a striking ability to move entire regiments vast distances undetected. He was well aware of the effectiveness of Giap's indoctrination/education program in producing highly motivated and resilient troops. Referring to the average PAVN soldier, Abrams once remarked to his staff, "Adversity does nothing but strengthen him."[2] In Abrams's estimation the war was "basically a political contest."[3] The NLF infrastructure "permitted the main forces to operate."[4] Thus, the key object of the war was to break down Hanoi's control over the villages and its ability to mobilize the energies of the people. "In the whole picture of the war," Abrams commented wisely, "the battles don't really mean much."[5]

The new MACV chief warmly endorsed a thoughtful army study arguing, in repudiation of Westmoreland's approach to the war, that the critical developments in the contest were "those that occur at the village, district and province level. This is where the war must be fought; this is where the war...must be won."[6] For Abrams the critical index of success was population security. Without it, the GVN could not begin to develop the responsive governmental institutions and policies that would earn it long-term popular support and survival. The expansion of South Vietnamese Regional and Popular Forces for local defense (as opposed to offensive operations against powerful enemy forces carried out by the ARVN) was an indispensable element of this effort. Accordingly, Abrams gradually shifted US forces away from attrition to a "one war" strategy, integrating clear-and-hold combat operations, in which US forces rooted out guerrillas and then turned security over to South Vietnamese Regional and Popular Forces, with a revamped pacification program.

The upgrading of the South Vietnamese armed forces so that they could take over complete responsibility for the conduct of the war was at the very center of Abrams's effort, as he had been told by his superiors to expect all American troops to be withdrawn by mid-1972. Yet Vietnamization went considerably beyond professionalizing and expanding South Vietnam's armed forces. If the GVN were to survive after the Americans departed, it simply had to undertake political and social reforms that it had resisted for years.

Meanwhile, the unwieldy collection of GVN-US pacification and intelligence-gathering programs aimed at gaining the support of the population were efficiently streamlined through the Accelerated Pacification Campaign by William Colby, a hard-driving, ruthless CIA operative. Without question, the revamped pacification program created enormous difficulties for the revolutionary forces; venal GVN local officials were replaced by councils of village elders elected by the villagers themselves, and civic improvement programs were placed under the direction of better-trained and more responsive GVN administrators under the watchful eye of Colby and the CIA.

The CIA-run Phoenix Program, designed to identify and neutralize the Communists' political infrastructure through assassination, terrorism, and torture, had a particularly devastating effect on mid- and low-level political cadres, as US special forces and ARVN commandos adopted the ruthless population control methods used for so long by the revolution's own special agents. It succeeded in denying revolutionary forces access to thousands of villages where they had previously obtained recruits, funds, and provisions. The CIA claimed that Phoenix resulted in the capture or killing of 40,000 cadres in 1969 and 1970.[7]

HANOI'S GRAND STRATEGY

From early April 1968, when Hanoi accepted Johnson's invitation to open negotiations, until January 1973, when Hanoi and Washington signed the Paris Peace Accords, Hanoi continued to pursue an ingeniously flexible and eclectic protracted war strategy. For twenty-five years, Giap had been adapting and experimenting with the Maoist three-stage model of protracted war to meet his needs. As we have seen, however, Hanoi did not so much follow Mao's model to the letter as use it as an analytical tool to make judgments about the changing balance of forces, the timing of operations, the relationship between political and armed struggle, and the relative merits of fighting spirit and military technology.

Giap understood that in taking on a power as vast as the United States, Mao's model posited too rigid a trajectory from the defensive to a state of equilibrium, and finally to victory through the means of a general offensive carried out only after one had military forces stronger than those of the enemy. Giap had long refused to be fenced in by the theory. He simultaneously adapted tactics appropriate for stage one warfare in one area, and stage two and stage three in others.

Hanoi referred to the variant of protracted war it practiced between the spring of 1968 and the spring of 1973, when the United States departed Vietnam for good, as "fighting while negotiating." It might better have been called "fighting, waiting, waiting some more, and then negotiating." In fact, Hanoi had little incentive to engage in serious negotiating at all until the balance of military and political power in South Vietnam had shifted significantly in its favor. The shift could not happen until Nixon withdrew substantial numbers of American troops, especially US ground combat divisions, and Nixon agreed to make several critical concessions the United States was determined to resist on the grounds that they could be read as a prelude to an American defeat.

The first of these concessions was an unconditional halt to the bombing of North Vietnam. Hanoi refused to negotiate on any issue whatsoever until it had wrung out this concession, for continued bombing would have severely retarded its war-production facilities and its ability to move men down the Ho Chi Minh Trail. At the end of October 1968, after five months of no progress in negotiations, Johnson called off the bombing. Hanoi also demanded that, in exchange for its agreement to halt the fighting, the United

States agree to form a coalition government in South Vietnam and dissolve Nguyen Van Thieu's regime in Saigon, on the theory that it had no standing with the Vietnamese people and was therefore an illegitimate product of American colonialism. Hanoi was even more adamant that no agreement would be forthcoming until the Americans agreed to the removal of all "foreign" forces in South Vietnam, by which the Communists meant American and allied forces (Australian, Korean, etc.), but without a concurrent withdrawal of the formidable array of regular PAVN units that had come down the Ho Chi Minh Trail to the battlefields in the South.

After three more years of war, after Giap had achieved significant gains in the military balance—albeit at a frightful cost in casualties—Hanoi saw its way clear to dropping the demand for the removal of Thieu. By that point it was a painless concession to make. Meanwhile, the Americans failed utterly to move the Communists on the most important issue for Saigon and Washington: the removal of PAVN regulars from South Vietnam wherever they stood at the time of the agreement.

Thus, the essence of the "fighting and talking" strategy was that Hanoi's negotiators would stonewall at the conference table, prolonging the fighting and dragging out the war. Hanoi was reasonably confident that the contradictions between Washington's war policy and the desires of the American public for peace would grow deeper. So would the friction between ARVN and American forces in the field and between Washington and Saigon over how to prosecute the conflict. Ever the realist, Giap fully expected that the war would continue for a considerable period of time. A captured 1969 COSVN document reflected this view, advising the faithful that revolutionary "victory will not come suddenly, but in a complicated and tortuous way."[8] And so it would.

GIAP'S NEW STRATEGY FOR THE GROUND WAR

The Communist "mini-offensives" of May and August 1968 were directed at American targets to a far greater extent than had the Tet attacks of February and March. In launching these two offensives, Hanoi wanted to reinforce the impression in Washington and among the American public that the force of the Revolution could not be defeated outright militarily, given the limitations placed on US operations by domestic politics.

Without a doubt, the so-called mini-offensives further attenuated domestic support for the war effort in the United States, but Giap paid

a heavy price. For all their political success, the offensives of 1968 were
so costly in blood that they substantially constricted the scope of Giap's
combat operations for about two years. Having suffered 75,000 combat
deaths between Tet and September 1968, Giap had to all but abandon high-
intensity big-unit combat and return to guerrilla warfare. The "stand and
fight" tactics of the latter two 1968 offensives were put aside in favor of
the PAVN's traditional fighting style of "slow plan, quick attack, strong
fight, quick withdrawal."[9] Offensive operations in 1969 and 1970, a captured document for field commanders explained, should occur "simultaneously, continuously, widespreadedly [sic]"—meaning that sustained,
massed attacks should be avoided whenever possible.[10] A very high percentage of Communist-initiated combat in this period was carried out by independent companies and battalions rather than regiments or divisions. In
addition to wearing down US infantry units with harassment actions and
ambushes, PLAF and PAVN units were tasked with frustrating increasingly
well-coordinated allied pacification efforts.

If PAVN regiments and divisions were used very sparingly in 1969 and
1970, just what were they doing? Some units were withdrawn to North
Vietnam, and others remained in their sanctuaries along South Vietnam's
western border. The vast majority of Giap's main forces were refitted with
an impressive array of state-of-the-art weaponry, motorized vehicles of
various functions and sizes, tanks, and communications equipment provided by the People's Republic of China and the USSR. Moscow and Beijing
read President Johnson's post-Tet decisions as auguring very well indeed for
the Vietnamese revolutionaries, and they responded with unprecedented
largesse. With the help of several thousand advisers and military aid from
China and the Soviet Union, Giap transformed the PAVN between 1969
and 1971 from a fine light-infantry organization with limited punching
power and mobility into one of the largest and most formidable armies in
the world, with a combined arms capability Giap could only have dreamed
of during the War of Resistance. PAVN's divisions were being prepared for
use against the South Vietnamese in conventional warfare once the United
States had withdrawn the lion's share of its combat forces.

It seems reasonably clear that Giap saw 1969 and 1970 as a time to
alter the psychological and military balance of forces in his favor, as one
Communist document at the time put it, "bit by bit."[11] The morale of
American troops was sure to suffer as a result of frequent and inconclusive
engagements against guerrillas and sapper units that attacked at a place

and time of their choosing. Remarkably, in his pronouncements during this difficult phase of the conflict, Giap continued to display unalloyed confidence in eventual victory even as he admitted that Abrams's new strategy was inflicting serious damage on the revolution's infrastructure, and making gains in pacification reforms. He had faith that, in time, the South Vietnamese people's disillusionment with American neocolonialism and with the incompetent and corrupt Saigon regime would lead to a reinvigorated revolutionary political presence.

Giap made it clear that the reversion to what might be called "proto-guerrilla" operations was only temporary, as the iron law of revolutionary war required a return to conventional operations once the Americans turned over the bulk of the fighting to the fractious ARVN forces. A few months after the first withdrawal of US forces—Nixon ordered 25,000 troops to return home in July 1969— Giap wrote that the Revolution had to "incessantly develop the guerrilla war into a regular war. Only through *regular war* in which the main force troops fight in a concentrated manner and the armed services are combined and fighting in coordination with the regional troops, militia guerrillas, and the political forces of all the people, can they annihilate important forces of the enemy...and create conditions for great strides in war."[12]

The abandonment of big-unit combat had the salutary effect of diminishing Communist casualties precipitously. Combat deaths dropped from 208,000 in 1968 to 132,000 in 1969, and then to 86,000 in 1970, but the significant diminution of combat also opened the door for US/GVN gains on the pacification front and permitted the ARVN to expand and modernize at a pace of growing concern to Giap and his colleagues on the Central Committee. Political struggle had to fill the gap left by the depletion of armed forces—at least to some degree. To that end, the NLF formed an alliance with a "third force" of political parties hostile to the policies of Saigon and pronounced the formation of a provisional Revolutionary Government. The clear intention of this maneuver was to diminish the prestige and standing of the GVN in the eyes of the world, and to undercut President Thieu's authority among the South Vietnamese people.

Even today, despite the passage of almost forty years and the release of thousands of documents from all the adversaries, all statistics concerning the Vietnam War must be viewed with caution, for they are all rough approximations at best. Yet it is clear from captured NLF documents that

1969 and much of 1970 were extremely hard on Communist guerrilla units and political cadres. One authoritative study on pacification by an American scholar concluded that revolutionary political infrastructure operatives were reduced from 84,000 in January 1968 to 57,000 in February 1972, while the percentage of the population living in GVN-controlled hamlets rose from 42 percent to 80 percent in 1972.

The difficulties encountered in the South as a result of the revamped pacification programs and clear-and-hold operations led to extreme hardships for all of Giap's forces. Rice was often in perilously short supply, and main-force units were often denied access to friendly villages and districts by General Abrams's screening operations, in which highly mobile US troops were quickly inserted between populous areas and PAVN forces moving in their direction. The "ink blots" representing liberated base areas on the maps in Giap's headquarters began to shrink in number and size. As a result, comments the official history, "our most important work became the education of cadre and soldiers operating deep behind the enemy lines in moral character and in the revolutionary traditions... [thereby] building a will to fight and a spirit of resolution...to endure."[13]

As far as the 1969 guerrilla war campaign went, a PLAF internal document reported important gains and a number of successful attacks in the Mekong Delta, but "generally speaking, our campaign was not strong or continuous."[14] But the PAVN's commander in chief remained undaunted, looking beyond adversity to a brighter future. There had been setbacks aplenty in twenty-five years of revolutionary history. There would be others ahead. Nonetheless, in January 1970, the Central Committee's eighteenth plenum projected that more aggressive, mobile warfare attacks would resume by late 1970 or early 1971.[15]

Lewis Sorley joins a number of other historians and participants in suggesting obliquely that had the success of the American strategic initiatives of 1969 and 1970 been fully appreciated by the US media and the public, the war might not have ended with the fall of South Vietnam and American defeat. Sorley's "what might have been" scenario is both thought provoking and controversial, if for no other reason than that his conclusion is belied by his own assessments of the particulars. As Sorley tells it, Abrams's initiatives in ground tactics, pacification, and Vietnamization made startlingly impressive progress initially, but as time went on, Communist countermeasures and the old bugaboos that afflicted the US/GVN war effort started to rear up yet again. As the NLF infrastructure began to rebound, the ARVN lacked the expertise to deploy its new arsenal of sophisticated weapons effectively in combat operations. This was an ominous sign that the ramped-up ARVN training program was running into serious obstacles.

Not surprisingly, signs of morale and leadership problems began to surface in US Army and Marine ground units. In part this was the result of the changed political context of the war. Victory was no longer the objective, and increasing numbers of US servicemen saw no point in risking their lives for a cause that was no longer supported by the American people. Other factors in declining American military performance were counterproductive rotation and replacement policies. Combat unit commanders typically served only six months in the field before rotating out to staff jobs. They were often replaced by "cherry" junior officers whose judgment was questionable in the eyes of experienced noncommissioned officers and enlisted men. Incidents of fragging—the killing of inexperienced, excessively "gung ho"officers by their own men—reached alarming proportions. The widespread use of drugs, and growing rancor between black and white servicemen, severely damaged unit cohesiveness in all but the most elite units.

As astute and effective as Abrams's initiatives were in the short run, Sorley's book reveals dramatically that they failed to induce the changes in the South Vietnamese regime that would give Saigon a fighting chance if it had to go it alone against an invasion by the People's Army of Vietnam. Sorley (like virtually every other serious historian) depicts South Vietnamese president Nguyen Van Thieu as hopelessly inept and intransigent. Thieu himself remarked well into Abrams's tenure that the military formed his major political constituency and that it was "the only cohesive force" holding the country together.

Pacification operations *were* more effective than they had ever been in the American War, but that was not saying a great deal. Callousness and indifference on the part of hostile American and Vietnamese troops toward Vietnamese civilians in the countryside persisted. Many so-called secure areas were in fact vast refugee camps populated by thousands of miserable peasants relocated from "free-fire zones" and areas controlled by the Communists. In other words, they were rural slums.

The camps and the relocation operations that precipitated them heightened what Giap so often described as the "contradictions" between the peasantry and the US/GVN administration. In fact, it seems clear that widespread civilian dislocation and despair accompanied the evanescent gains in the 1969–1970 period. Frances Fitzgerald's prize-winning 1972 critique of the war, *Fire in the Lake*, contains a devastating critique of the lingering effects of American pacification programs and combat operations.

> In the refugee camps and isolated villages people die of malnutrition and the children are deformed. In the cities, where there is no sanitation and rarely any running water, the adults die of cholera, typhoid, smallpox, leprosy…and their children die of the common diseases of dirt, such as scabies and sores.…The land and the family were the two sources of [Vietnamese] national as well as personal identity. The Americans have destroyed these sources for many Vietnamese, not merely by killing people but by forcibly separating them, by removing the people from the land and depositing them in the vast swamp-cities.[16]

In retrospect—as Sorley and others make clear—it seems that the legions of overly optimistic MACV reports heralding progress in South Vietnam in the war's last years were tainted by enormous pressure from the White House for good news to discredit its growing number of detractors. The revolutionary forces operating during the Nixon years proved far more resilient than the contemporary reports claimed. Surely this was both a result of the effectiveness of Giap's indoctrination campaign, which by this point had reached the level of high art, and the toughness of men and women who were unbending in their desire to hang tough and outwait the Americans.

According to one authoritative source, by June 1971 the infrastructure was bouncing back in many provinces. Cadres were conducting mobilization and proselytizing among two-thirds of the population.[17] Post-1968 GVN gains in the villages began to collapse in late 1970 in more than a few strategically important provinces where the Communist infrastructure had once flourished.

In December 1970 MACV hailed recently completed Operation Washington Green, a clear-and-hold pacification operation in Binh Dinh Province, as a great success, but a senior US adviser in the province remarked a few months after the operation that "as the U.S. forces pull out of areas where they alone are responsible for security, the place reverts to communist control."[18] As one American historian observed, Washington Green "offered little reason for optimism" about the pacification program generally.[19] It was the same story in most of the contested provinces of South Vietnam.

Despite intensified B-52 strikes on the infiltration routes and the employ-
ment of recently developed electronic sensors and laser-guided ordnance,
the North continued to infiltrate replacements and ample quantities of food
and ammunition into the South. Group 559, the organization responsible
for managing and defending the Ho Chi Minh Trail, became an independent military command with its own static and mobile forces in 1970. More
than 30,000 civilians, soldiers, and engineers built or upgraded six main
north-south roads through the mountains and hundreds of kilometers of
connecting roads and bypasses at choke points between 1970 and 1971. In
March 1971 work commenced on a secret or "green road" from the North
Vietnamese panhandle to southern Laos—about 1,000 kilometers in length,
replete with fake fortifications and vehicles to draw interdiction fire.[20]

Perhaps the most impressive engineering feat on the trail was a fuel
and oil pipeline running 1,000 kilometers from the panhandle deep into
southern battlefields. These improvements reduced the transport time of
the average trip down the trail to only twenty days, and losses along the
route dropped from 13.5 percent in 1969 to 2.07 percent in 1971. Between
1970 and 1971, 195,000 troops entered the South.[21] During 1969, PAVN sent
no fewer than ten sapper battalions and one hundred sapper companies
and platoons from North Vietnam to southern battlefields. The sapper
units formed the nucleus of the small-unit combat effort between 1969 and
early 1971.

By mid-1970, Giap's elite guerrilla-sapper units, many of which had
been formed by breaking down main force PAVN regiments into independent companies and battalions, were inflicting very heavy casualties in the
villages against the territorial and popular forces trained for their defense.
(After 1968, Saigon's popular and regional forces suffered more casualties
than regular ARVN units.)

THE CAMBODIAN INCURSION
AND THE WAR ON THE HO CHI MINH TRAIL

While Giap built up the strength and capabilities of his regular forces,
Nixon initiated a dramatic effort to attenuate Communist military power.
In April 1970, he ordered a force of 20,000 American and South Vietnamese
troops to invade the PAVN's network of sanctuaries in eastern Cambodia
with a view to destroying the considerable threat those forces posed and

seizing COSVN headquarters, which had been located near the Cambodia-Vietnam border. Nixon claimed that the expansion of the ground war was necessary to maintain the security of American forces and to buy time for Vietnamization to work. He also hoped this dramatic and quite unexpected attack might intimidate Hanoi into a more flexible stance in negotiations in Paris. Giap responded to the enemy's drive into the sanctuaries by ordering his divisions there to withdraw deeper into Cambodia and to buttress the Cambodian Communist movement with his political cadres.

The incursion resulted in the capture of hundreds of tons of PAVN weapons and supplies, but inflicted only marginal damage on PAVN forces, which soon returned to their old sanctuaries and began preparations for a major combined arms offensive slated initially for late 1971. That offensive was ultimately postponed, and some analysts have conjectured that the losses and disruption of the Cambodian incursion were the cause. The evidence of this claim is sketchy at best.

Meanwhile, the incursion into previously off-limits Cambodia set off a firestorm of protest in the United States, resulting in the largest antiwar protests in the United States up to that point. Some 400 colleges and universities were closed as a result of the protests. ROTC buildings were vandalized, and at Kent State University, nervous National Guardsmen opened fire on student protestors, killing four. An outraged Congress passed legislation prohibiting further operations in Cambodia and Laos by American forces. In short, the incursion surely heightened rancor between the US government and the American people and therefore worked in Giap's favor in the long run.

In mid-November 1970 General Abrams submitted an astute analysis of Giap's strategy to the Joint Chiefs of Staff and the president. Hanoi's war could be broken down into seven interrelated conflicts. Each was important, "but the logistics war of southern Laos and northern Cambodia now stands as the critical conflict for the VC/NVA."[22] Because the PAVN supply route called the Sihanouk Trail leading from Laos to South Vietnam had been closed by Laotian General Lon Nol, the Revolution was completely dependent for supplies on the Ho Chi Minh Trail. Giap almost certainly concurred with Abrams's assessment for, as the official history of the PAVN has it, in June 1970 the Central Party Military Committee "laid out many urgent measures aimed at expanding…[and] consolidating the strategic supply route."[23]

We have already described the massive effort to improve the Ho Chi Minh Trail in 1970 and 1971. In Hanoi it was universally agreed that whatever reverses Communist forces had to suffer on the ground in South Vietnam, the trail had to be kept open, and the modernization of the army in North Vietnam had to proceed as fast as possible so it could go down the trail in strength to resume big-unit fighting. Giap's forces had been fighting against an increasingly sophisticated CIA-led effort to use Thai and Laotian troops to interdict the trail in Laos since 1969. By October 1970 Giap had a new asset to throw into this critical struggle—the first truly operational corps-level force in PAVN history, an armored mobile entity consisting of three divisions, including the 320th, with its newly acquired T-54 Soviet tanks.

OPERATION LAM SON

In early 1971, Abrams attempted to cut the trail in Laos with a dramatic ground-air armored operation. Because the 1970 Cooper-Church Amendment forbade the use of US troops in Laos, ARVN ground forces could not be accompanied by US advisers on the ground. Thus, Operation Lam Son would serve as a critical test of the effectiveness of Vietnamization.

Supported by armor and artillery, ARVN troops punched into Laos west of Khe Sanh via Route 9. Giap decided to counter the attack by deploying his new corps in support of the 10,000 PAVN troops of Group 559 that were already protecting the trail. The ARVN scheme of maneuver called for a drive on Tchepone along Route 9 in Laos, a broken track of road running through low hills that soon gave way to rugged jungle. Supporting forces would meanwhile march north and south of the main axis of advance, setting up a string of mobile fire-support bases after clearing PAVN forces in a series of search-and-destroy thrusts.

PAVN resistance was light initially. On February 12, the ARVN mobile column bogged down twelve miles inside Laos, apparently because of a secret order from Thieu, who feared that heavy ARVN casualties might further erode support for his regime in Saigon. But Thieu was not the only problem. ARVN senior commanders were simply out of their depth in undertaking such a complex operation, and the deficiencies that plagued the South Vietnamese army throughout the war began to tell, as timid subordinate commanders disobeyed or misconstrued their orders.

As the ARVN bogged down, 60,000 PAVN troops began to converge on the ARVN units from the north, south, and west, attacking ARVN fire-support bases with 103mm and 122mm artillery fire and well-executed tank-infantry assaults. Whole ARVN companies were annihilated in the ensuing melee. A huge fleet of US helicopters and fighters attempted to relieve the pressure, but PAVN units "hugged the belt" of the ARVN infantry, and antiaircraft fire limited the effectiveness of US air support.

President Thieu soon lost his nerve and countermanded the orders of his senior commanders in the field. He began ordering the withdrawal of his overmatched forces after briefly "taking" Tchepone with a token air assault force that managed to capture a few small caches of weapons and supplies against token Communist resistance. It was a hollow victory, a face-saving measure that fooled no one. The ARVN withdrawal soon turned into a rout; *Life* magazine photographers shot haunting images of terrified ARVN soldiers clinging to the skids of overburdened helicopters.

Lam Son revealed in glaring fashion the deficiencies of the ARVN in combined arms offensive operations without American advisers on the ground. As one seasoned US adviser in the operation observed, ARVN commanders had been ordered "to execute an operations order much of which they did not understand."[24] Reflecting on Lam Son long after the fact, Henry Kissinger remarked that "the operation, conceived in doubt and assailed by skepticism, proceeded in confusion."[25]

PAVN forces, however, performed very well indeed. Preparation of the battlefield had been first-rate, as Group 559's battalions organized formidable defense positions; PAVN armored forces deployed after the ARVN had penetrated Laos linked up with Group 559 seamlessly while under ground and air attack, deploying their artillery and antiaircraft capabilities to good effect. As the ARVN units withdrew, PAVN antiaircraft forces downed at least three hundred helicopters—an amazing feat—and severely damaged hundreds of others, while expertly laid ambushes harried ARVN troopers in retreat. The victory in Laos was a decisive event in the history of PAVN. As one PAVN historian put it, the clash along Route 9 "was proof that the PAVN could defeat the best ARVN units."[26]

THE NGUYEN-HUE OFFENSIVE

Giap's staff studied and refined their doctrine for combined arms operations in light of their experiences during Lam Son as they prepared for their most ambitious operation of the war: a conventional offensive by virtually all the main force units under Giap's command, supported by guerrilla action. The broad objective of the new initiative was to achieve "a decisive victory in 1972."[27] On March 30, 1972, after a massive buildup of forces in the North Vietnamese panhandle and in the sanctuaries in Laos and Cambodia, Giap launched the Nguyen-Hue Offensive, a powerful offensive drive along three axes of advance. Several infantry divisions spearheaded by tanks were deployed in each thrust—in South Vietnam's two northern-most provinces, in the Central Highlands, and out of Cambodia, heading in the direction of Saigon. The strongest attack by far was directed against ARVN defenses in Quang Tri Province. There, three reinforced PAVN divisions slammed into the ARVN Third Division's string of strongpoints along the DMZ from both the west and the north. Their ultimate objective was to rout ARVN defenses rapidly and seize the lion's share of South Vietnam's two northern provinces. The attack up north had long been expected, but the two thrusts farther south came as nasty surprises to General Abrams and the ARVN ground units deployed in both those areas of operations.

About a day after the offensive began in Quang Tri, PAVN's 320th Division, supported by tanks, pressed east in the Central Highlands in an effort to wipe out a dozen ARVN outposts southwest of Kontum, seize that town, and cut Routes 14 and 19, effectively severing the country in two. Then, on April 2, PAVN forces jumped off from their Cambodian sanctuaries, swept the ARVN back from its first line of defense in western Binh Long Province, took Loc Ninh, and encircled An Loc, the province's capital. As these attacks developed in early April, Giap would deploy a total of eleven infantry divisions, seven artillery divisions, and twenty-two independent regiments supported by a few squadrons of MiG fighters, surface-to-air missiles, and T-54 tanks.

Preparations for the Easter Offensive, as the Nguyen-Hue Offensive (see map, page xix) was soon christened by the Americans, had begun in earnest in 1969, when Hanoi made (or perhaps was forced to make?) the strategic decision to lower the level of combat in South Vietnam, revert to guerrilla warfare, and withdraw most of PAVN's divisions from active operations. As we have seen, in the wake of Tet, Giap never for a moment doubted that a return to "regular war" would prove essential to achieving complete victory.

To understand the offensive as Giap and the Central Committee conceived it, one must recall the thinking behind the fighting-while-negotiating strategy that Hanoi had adopted after Tet. The essence of that strategy was to forestall concessions at the negotiating table on all fundamental issues while Giap's forces engaged in protracted warfare to grind down the will of the United States and to demonstrate the bankruptcy of Vietnamization so clearly that the United States would have no choice but to concede two critical points: First, to permit all Communist forces to remain in place within South Vietnam once all American forces had withdrawn. Second, as one Communist document put it, to agree to the formation of "a broad national democratic coalition regime" in South Vietnam with "the South Vietnamese NLF at its core," after the Thieu government had been dissolved.[28]

Giap had stated repeatedly since the mid-1960s that these concessions could be obtained only through a major conventional offensive supported by widespread guerrilla action. Just a few days before Nguyen-Hue was launched, Giap published an article confirming his belief that only a major conventional offensive could bring about a "clear change on the battlefield."[29]

Nixon and Kissinger's brilliant efforts to exploit Sino-Soviet rivalry by offering both powers diplomatic and strategic incentives in exchange for the application of pressure on the DRV to make concessions—the "linkage" strategy—showed signs of success in 1970, making a Communist offensive to alter the military balance in the South something of an urgent necessity as the end of the year approached. Hanoi had to use military force, observes a prominent American historian, to convince "the United States of the hopelessness of its positions and further accelerate the military, economic and psychological decline of its RVN dependents."[30] Thus, as General Abrams observed at the time, the offensive was essentially a test of "whether Vietnamization had been a success or failure."[31] At the time of its launch, only 90,000 American troops were deployed in Vietnam, and fewer than 10,000 of them were combat troops. It was also a test run for a larger conventional offensive envisaged by Hanoi to conquer all of South Vietnam after it felt reasonably confident that domestic politics in the United States would prevent Washington from coming to the rescue of the faltering regime in Saigon.

Within three days after the attacks in Quang Tri Province commenced, all the vital strongpoints adjacent to the DMZ save Dong Ha on the eastern end of the line were in the hands of the People's Army. The entire ARVN Third Division had collapsed as Giap's tank-infantry assaults broke through one defense line after another. A few ARVN divisions would perform heroically in defense over the next few weeks, but far more would bend and then break in mass confusion and panic under PAVN pressure.

The attacks in the north continued unabated until April 9, when ARVN's shattered forces managed to regroup into tight perimeters around Dong Ha and Quang Tri City. Meanwhile, the 324B Division had moved out of the Ashau Valley to threaten Hue. Quang Tri City fell on May 1, as ARVN forces defending the town panicked and fled south toward Hue along with thousands of civilians along Route 1. Perhaps 10,000 soldiers and civilians were killed by heavy artillery fire along the "highway of death."

A genuine sense of crisis swept over MACV and the presidential palace in Saigon, as equally grim reports came in from the Central Highlands area of operations. There PAVN forces had taken most of Binh Dinh Province on the coast, besieged Kontum, and were on the verge of wresting Dak To from a dispirited 22nd ARVN Division. The PAVN was once again on the verge of cutting South Vietnam in half.

To the north of Saigon, Giap's forces took Loc Ninh, the capital of Tay Ninh Province, on April 7. Then PAVN armored forces surrounded five ARVN regiments at An Loc, a mere seventy miles from Saigon. The siege at An Loc was an extremely bloody and protracted engagement and was one of those rare battles where the South Vietnamese ground forces acquitted themselves well. Still, it is doubtful that An Loc could have held out were it not for extensive "Arc Light" strikes by American B-52s directed against PAVN units ringing the town. Once again, the Americans had to use a strategic bomber for horrendously destructive tactical air strikes. The siege of An Loc was not fully broken until early June. When the ARVN 21st Division in the Mekong Delta rushed north to join in the relief effort at An Loc, several PAVN regiments led by sappers slipped into the Mekong Delta from Cambodia and inflicted heavy damage on the pacification program in the Delta with more than one hundred attacks on lightly defended outposts.

In early May, General Abrams summarized the seriousness of the situation in a communication to his superiors. "Enemy staying power is his most effective battlefield characteristic.... An enemy decision to attack carries an inherent acceptance that the forces involved may be expended totally.... In summary of all that has happened here since 30 March 1972, I must report that as pressure has mounted and the battle has become brutal the senior [ARVN] military leadership has begun to bend and in some cases to break. In adversity it is losing its will and cannot be depended on to take the measures necessary to stand and fight."[32]

Enraged at the audacity and success of the initial phase of the Easter Offensive, Nixon in early April ordered a rapid deployment of American tactical air assets to Southeast Asia from all over the world, adding 35 fighter squadrons to the 39 already in theater, along with more than 120 B-52s and the naval airpower afforded by two aircraft carriers. On May 10, around-the-clock bombardment of PAVN units began to blunt the momentum of all three prongs of the drive. On May 11, 1972, all US B-52 assets in theater were thrown against the attacking forces ringing An Loc for twenty-four hours straight, breaking PAVN's drive toward Saigon. At An Loc, Giap lost most of his armor and suffered 10,000 casualties in the costliest battle of the offensive. On May 12 the B-52s struck with similar force at PAVN units pressing in on Kontum, inflicting frightful casualties and blunting that attack. The next day, the massive fleet of US strategic bombers pummeled PAVN divisions in the northern Tri-Thien front. Giap's drive just below the DMZ was stopped cold at the My Chanh River, the southern boundary of Quang Tri Province. A shrewd ARVN tactician, General Ngo Quang Truong, having blunted PAVN's attack on Hue, mounted a counteroffensive that succeeded in recovering about half of Quang Tri Province and Quang Tri City by September 15, but only after weeks of costly street fighting.

General Abrams had remarked to a State Department official during the battle that "it's very clear to me that...[the South Vietnamese] government would have fallen and this country would be gone...if it hadn't been for the B-52s and the tac air."[33] But it was Nixon's decision to launch Operation Linebacker (May 10 to October 23, 1972) that truly broke the back of the Nguyen-Hue Offensive. Probably the most effective interdiction campaign in military history up to that point, Linebacker destroyed huge quantities of war matériel and production facilities in North Vietnam, including power plants, supply depots, and barracks. Communist antiaircraft efforts were stymied by electronic jamming. The Ho Chi Minh Trail was severely damaged by precision attacks against bridges, roads, and railroads with laser-guided bombs, used for the first time in history, and Haiphong Harbor was mined, sealing off the flow of seaborne Soviet high-tech weapons and desperately needed war matériel. The PAVN official history makes it clear beyond all doubt that Linebacker effectively stanched the flow of troops and supplies to the battlefield.[34]

American estimates have it that PAVN losses in the Nguyen-Hue Offensive were roughly 40,000 killed and 60,000 wounded. About half of

Giap's armor and heavy artillery assets were lost. Factoring in the enduring American tendency to exaggerate casualty figures, the true losses were probably more like 25,000 killed and 45,000 wounded.

Many Western historians describe the offensive as another of Giap's strategic gaffes, confirming his habit of wasting tens of thousands of troops for no good end. They point to the survival of the ARVN and the GVN as decisive evidence of the failure of Hanoi's big push.

Yet, as was the case with Tet, it is quite unlikely that Hanoi expected the Easter Offensive to achieve a complete collapse of South Vietnam's army and government. Its true objectives, surely, were ambitious but more modest. They had to be. By early 1972 no competent Communist planner, certainly not someone with Giap's uncanny ability to gauge the strengths as well as the weaknesses of his enemies, could possibly have believed that President Nixon would permit the outright collapse of South Vietnam in an election year. Although Nixon was increasingly under siege from the antiwar movement and a growing body of detractors in Washington, he still had the wiggle room to unleash decisive US air power to prevent South Vietnam's collapse. If the American people had long ago tired of Vietnam, they were not yet willing to suffer the humiliation of the first major defeat in the history of American warfare. Of course, Hanoi would hope for the best, but it would be enough if the offensive changed the political and military balance of forces substantially in favor of the Revolution. That would indeed be the "decisive victory" Hanoi had hoped to achieve in the planning phase of the operation.

Giap had not abandoned protracted war on March 30, 1972, in favor of a conventional campaign to crush ARVN and the GVN once and for all as many American historians claim. It was no "last gasp" effort. Rather, *he used conventional operations in the service of protracted war.* The offensive ratcheted up congressional and popular opposition to Nixon's war strategy in the United States, further constricting his military options to prevent the fall of South Vietnam in the future, and placing enormous pressure on Washington to come to an agreement in Paris. The uproar over the continuation of the war four years after Nixon had begun his elusive search for "peace with honor" was a clear sign that the American people had had about all they could stomach of the Vietnam War.

The Nguyen-Hue Offensive was costly, but it went far in establishing the "correct conditions" for a favorable peace agreement with the United

States. It left the Communists substantially stronger in the South, with more than 140,000 hardened regulars on South Vietnamese soil. They were the nucleus of the force that would inflict a humiliating defeat on the ARVN a mere two years after the Americans departed for good in March 1973. The offensive left Communist forces in full control of large swaths of territory in Quang Tri and along the border with Cambodia, in addition to a number of smaller "liberated areas" of strategic significance. These could be used as springboards by Armed Propaganda Units to recoup lost ground in the political struggle movement.

Having said that, it must be admitted that both the planning and the execution of the Nguyen-Hue campaign were seriously flawed. The logistical system could not sustain the furious pace of the attacks, causing disruptive halts in advances, giving the ARVN and American air power golden opportunities to stanch the attacks, inflicting heavy casualties in the process. The combined arms attacks (tank-infantry attacks supported by artillery) generally lacked coordination. And unquestionably, any Western general who sustained such high casualties would have been summarily sacked. But in fighting the Americans, neither the Communists nor Giap should be judged by conventional Western military criteria of success. This was not a conventional conflict; Communist Vietnam was not an industrialized military power, and its military performance should not be judged as if it were. In the end, a fair-minded observer should recognize that Giap's accomplishments in Nguyen-Hue as a strategist and a commander were far more impressive than his failures, or those of his army. How could one reasonably expect the Communists to sustain logistics for 200,000 troops over hundreds of miles against the world's most powerful air force? Indeed, it seems to me that the very fact that Giap could mount such an offensive at all was itself a sterling military achievement.

Finally, the offensive essentially confirmed—to Giap at least—that the ARVN could not defend South Vietnam in a sustained campaign against PAVN conventional forces once the Easter Offensive losses had been replaced. The most charitable assessment of the ARVN's performance was that it was uneven. Despite the official pronouncements that the offensive showed how far the ARVN had come, more candid private appraisals soon proved to be on the mark: the ARVN had a great deal of firepower, but it was too poorly led and trained to use its combat power effectively, and most of its units clearly lacked the fighting spirit to take on highly motivated PAVN units.

THE PARIS PEACE TALKS

In the wake of the offensive and the subsequent withdrawal of all US combat troops, the sense of bitterness and betrayal on the part of South Vietnam toward Nixon and the United States was palpable, and even as the talks marched tortuously to a peace settlement in fall 1972, a sense of foreboding, even doom, pervaded Saigon, and it was clear to everyone but the most naïve optimists that Hanoi had more chips to play at the bargaining table than did Washington. The war by this point was both a cause and a symbol of political divisiveness, racial unrest, and cultural clashes that threatened to tear the country apart at the seams. Vietnam had become the nightmare that would not end.

In early May 1972, Kissinger, in secret talks with long-time Central Committee member and Hanoi's chief negotiator, Le Duc Tho, dropped the demand for mutual withdrawal of US and PAVN forces from South Vietnam. By fall Tho was in a position to make a concession himself because of the gains of the Nguyen-Hue Offensive. Hanoi would accept the Thieu government into a coalition with the NFL to work out the political future of South Vietnam. Le Duc Tho explained his thinking in doing so in 1985: "Since the military balance of forces had been fundamentally altered, no puppet administration could remain firmly in place" in South Vietnam."[35] In other words, Hanoi was fully confident that Thieu would be marginalized in a coalition government.

It seemed in October that Washington and Hanoi had reached an understanding, with only the details left to be resolved, but Thieu understandably balked at the provision allowing PAVN forces inside the South to remain in place after the Paris Peace Accords were signed, for he understood what Washington knew but could never admit at the time: that this provision all but guaranteed the resumption of conflict under conditions that greatly favored the Revolution. If it did not amount to a death warrant for the Government of Vietnam, it came very close to one. Hanoi, for its part, felt betrayed when Kissinger presented Thieu's objections and called for the Communists to address them. Its delegation walked out of the negotiations in Paris, claiming, quite rightly, that the United States had already agreed in principle to leave PAVN forces where they were at the effective ceasefire date.

In an effort to bring the North Vietnamese back to the table, Nixon once again unleashed US airpower over North Vietnam in the most destructive attacks of the entire air war. Operation Linebacker II wreaked havoc on Hanoi's war-making facilities and transport grid. It depleted its surface-to-air missile (SAM) inventory to the point where the country was rendered almost defenseless against further attacks.

North Vietnam returned to the table, but it refused to agree to Thieu's demand that PAVN troops return to North Vietnam. Nixon then privately promised Thieu substantial additional aid packages and gave his personal assurance that he would respond with sufficient air power to obliterate future Communist offensives if they posed an imminent threat to Saigon's survival. But Nixon also issued Thieu an ultimatum: either he could sign the accords as negotiated, or he would have to reach a separate agreement with Hanoi. In other words, he left Thieu no choice but to step in line.

The Paris Peace Accords, signed on January 27, 1973, called on the United States and all other countries to respect the independence, sovereignty, unity, and integrity of Vietnam as recognized by the 1954 Geneva Agreements on Vietnam; required the withdrawal of all US forces and an exchange of prisoners within sixty days; and imposed strict limitations on US military assistance to South Vietnam and on infiltration of additional North Vietnamese forces to the South. A toothless international commission was put in place to oversee the ceasefire.

Most importantly, the political future of South Vietnam was left up in the air. Since the adversaries could not even approach a congenial solution or a set of procedures to determine the country's long-term political identity, the accords merely indicated that its future would be determined by a vaguely defined "national council of reconciliation," in which the GVN, the NLF, and representatives of neutral parties would "end hatred and enmity, prohibit all acts of reprisal," and move "step by step" toward reunification by peaceful means. It seemed to assume, as one scholar puts it, that "miracles could be accomplished by decree," and in fact marked "only a new phase of the war for the Vietnamese."[36]

Nixon and Kissinger claimed that they had achieved "peace with honor," but the claim was groundless in 1973, and is now rightly dismissed out of hand by virtually every serious student of the war, regardless of political persuasion. The Paris Accords ended direct American involvement, but they had failed to obtain even tacit recognition of South Vietnam as an independent entity that could determine its own fate without Communist interference. The agreement provided no enforceable mechanisms to ensure that politics, not military operations, would determine South Vietnam's fate. In fact, Nixon had "conceded to the Communists an active political and military role in South Vietnam."[37]

In the wake of the Paris Accords, domestic politics in the United States cast grave doubt on the proposition that the United States would come to the rescue of Saigon if Hanoi was able to marshal another major conventional offensive. Indeed, American aid packages to the GVN were predictably slashed from $2 billion in 1973 to $1 billion in 1974. Nixon's resignation in August 1974 all but guaranteed that South Vietnam would have to go it alone if attacked by revolutionary forces. In the end, it is impossible to quarrel with William Duiker's conclusion that Hanoi had gotten the better part of the deal.[38]

SOUTH VIETNAM STANDS ALONE

Giap had long viewed the American War as a two-stage process: first, the removal of US military power from South Vietnam; second, the unification of Vietnam through political struggle if possible, and through armed struggle if necessary. But who can believe that he and his comrades in Hanoi had any intention of letting the Paris Accords stand in the way of the prize they had sought for so long? In fact, *neither* North or South Vietnam had any intention of honoring the ceasefire, or even much incentive to do so. Blatant violations on both sides commenced within a few weeks, and the faint hope that Vietnam's fate would be determined by peaceful means vanished very quickly indeed.

Initially, Communist forces in South Vietnam operated at a disadvantage because they were exhausted and depleted by the Easter Offensive and were heavily outnumbered by Saigon's armed forces, which numbered about 300,000 ARVNs and 600,000 Regional and Popular Force troops. Yet in the year following the signing of the accords, Giap infiltrated 120,000 regulars into the South, acquired hundreds of replacement tanks and artillery pieces from China and the Soviet Union, and methodically built up the Ho Chi Minh Trail in preparation for another major conventional attack. In 1973 alone, PAVN shipped 27,000 tons of weapons and 6,000 tons of petroleum products to the south. In the first half of 1974, another 80,000 troops made their way into the South. Giap summarized the consensus that emerged from a series of conferences in June 1973 in restating his strategic mantra, his iron law: "The Politburo concluded that a strategic opportunity would soon present itself....Whatever the developments, we realized that the revolution could win victory only through war."[39]

Meanwhile, Thieu had resorted to draconian measures to maintain his personal dominance south of the 17th parallel. All government officials were required to join Thieu's own political party and pledge their allegiance to the powers that be in Saigon. Thieu reversed land reform measures in the countryside. Peasants and the intelligentsia alike resented Thieu's repression of political opposition. On the military front, he foolishly spread ARVN units widely across the country instead of developing a coherent plan to repulse the inevitable Communist invasion by deploying his forces in strength in areas of strategic vulnerability. The economy of South Vietnam had long been dependent on American spending and investment, and soon after the accords, it was in dangerous decline, heightening a general sense of malaise and unrest, which prompted additional oppressive measures on the part of Saigon.

By the summer of 1974, Giap joined other senior leaders in Hanoi in believing that its adversary in the South could not survive a major PAVN offensive without massive American aid, and that such aid was unlikely to be forthcoming. The People's Army was judged capable of executing a "final offensive" to crush the ARVN and the GVN and establishing a revolutionary administration over all Vietnam. This time, at last, the PAVN was going for broke. The balance of forces clearly favored the Revolution.

In March and April 1974, at two top-level conferences in Hanoi, it was concluded that for the first time since the Easter Offensive of 1972, the revolutionary forces had gained the initiative on the battlefield. Giap believed that the time had come to begin planning the final campaign. As he would write after the war's end, "Confronted with the formidable strength of the people's war, the other side found itself being pushed with increasing swiftness into a relentlessly downward course. The enemy's 'pacification' and encroachment schemes had been clearly defeated....The 'leopard-skin' ["oilslick"] pattern, far from being contained, was growing. The puppet army had been driven to the defensive on numerous battlefields."[40]

After reviewing a May 1974 PAVN General Staff study of a plan to win the war, Giap called upon General Hoang Van Thai to develop a detailed campaign plan for total victory by the end of 1976 at the very latest—before the results of the next US presidential election could potentially reverse the American decision to stay clear of Vietnam. It would unfold in two stages:

first, a major attack in the Central Highlands in the spring of 1975, and then, after widespread guerrilla operations to disrupt and further disperse Saigon's armed forces, a multipronged drive on Saigon in late 1975 or early 1976. Virtually every PAVN division would join in the attack.

While many Western accounts have it that Giap played little or no role in the formation of the plan for the Ho Chi Minh Campaign as a result of illness and the loss of his position as commander in chief to Senior General Van Tien Dung in 1973—Giap remained minister of defense—the most reliable sources we have make it clear that Giap was "very much involved in the planning and overall command of the offensive from its inception through its final victorious conclusion."[41] The General Staff then refined the plan several times before it was fully approved by the Politburo sometime in October 1974. By that point, Giap had also developed a contingency plan for a truncated campaign ending in 1975 should the opportunity present itself.

In December, the plan for the Ho Chi Minh Campaign was once again revised after General Tran Van Tra, the COSVN military commander, made a successful pitch for wresting all of Phuoc Long Province from the ARVN as a stepping-stone to a rapid drive on Saigon in the spring of 1975. In early January 1975, Tra's forces crashed through the ARVN's defenses along the Cambodian border into Phuoc Long. ARVN forces bent and then broke. Within a few days the PAVN had succeeded in gaining control of the entire province. Much to Giap's relief, the administration of President Gerald Ford rebuffed frantic requests from Saigon for direct intervention. It was then clear that, for all intents and purposes, South Vietnam had been abandoned by its superpower ally.

According to General Hoang Van Thai, a key member of the planning staff, Tran's success prompted the senior command to approve the truncated campaign plan with the objective of taking Saigon by the early summer of 1975.[42] While the battle of Phuoc Long (December 1974–January 1975) marked a critical turning point in the war "by demonstrating the impotence of both the ARVN and the United States," observes Phillip Davidson, "it was the ARVN's loss of Ban Me Thuot which marked the beginning of the end for the RVN."[43]

On March 10, twelve regiments of the PAVN converged on Ban Me Thuot, a target of critical strategic and psychological significance in the Central Highlands. In attacking this lightly defended city, as historian

Merle Pribbenow points out, Giap employed B.H. Lidell Hart's strategy of the "indirect approach." PAVN's main attack was "directed not at the enemy's main army deployed in the Tri-Thien front and around Saigon and the Mekong Delta, but instead at a weakly defended strategic point which the enemy could not afford to lose."[44]

Giap hoped to deceive Saigon into thinking he planned to move on Pleiku and Kontum to the north, when in fact his objective was to seize Ban Me Thuot, lure substantial ARVN forces into a counterattack, and destroy them in detail. Within two days, the PAVN took the town and its environs after heavy fighting. Meanwhile, a massive PAVN force of more than 70,000 troops with ample armor and artillery began to close off the road net within the highlands. Thieu fell into the trap, ordering that Ban Me Thout be retaken at all costs, and airlifted several regiments into jumping-off points for a counterattack.

Launched on March 15, the attack quickly broke down and turned into a South Vietnamese rout. The ARVN was outnumbered, outgunned, and outfought. As it happened, thousands of families of the ARVN troops who were slated for the counterattack lived in the vicinity of Ban Me Thuot; rather than forming up for the drive on the city, the troops scattered in a frantic rush to their families, threw away their weapons, and began to move en masse to the east toward Nha Trang and the coast.

Now desperate, Thieu decided to exchange territory for time to regroup. He ordered a withdrawal of all forces in the Central Highlands behind a straight horizontal line running from the Cambodian border to Tuy Hoa on the coast, about sixty miles south of Qui Nhon. Meanwhile, in the Tri-Thien front, all ARVN forces were ordered to withdraw eastward to coastal enclaves around Hue and Danang, surrendering vast swaths of territory to PAVN units pressing in on them from the north and west.

In the highlands, the column of ARVN troops moving east along a secondary road in bad repair toward Nha Trang was repeatedly attacked, causing the column to break up and disintegrate. Perhaps 20,000 of the 60,000 ARVN troops in the retreat reached the comparative safety of Nha Trang, on the South China Sea coast. In the Tri-Thien front, Giap attacked the coastal enclaves with the equivalent of eight divisions on March 19. As they crushed one South Vietnamese line of defense after another, the ARVN corps commander attempted to withdraw all his forces into the three strongest enclaves at Hue, Danang, and Chu Lai.

About the same time, Thieu ordered the withdrawal of his elite ranger and Marine forces deployed in I Corps Tactical Zone south in the hopes of forming a new defensive line extending from the Cambodian border through Cu Chi, Bien Hoa, and Xuan Loc. Terrified civilians and soldiers in the vicinity of Hue now fled south by the thousands along Route 1 toward Danang. There the ARVN commander attempted an evacuation by sea on March 24. That operation, too, turned into a disaster, as the port came under heavy shelling, and all weapons and other military equipment were abandoned to the enemy. On March 29, Danang, flooded with more than one million refugees, fell to the PAVN. All of I Corps was now under Hanoi's control.

After a week of regrouping and replenishment, the People's Army began its drive on Saigon. In the final attack on the capital, there would be no logistical breakdowns along the lines of those in the Nguyen-Hue campaign of 1972. Everywhere except at Xuan Loc, thirty-five miles northeast of Saigon, which Giap aptly described as the "iron door" to the massive Bien Hoa airbase and to Saigon itself, South Vietnamese troops folded up. At Xuan Loc the ARVN 18th Division fought with great valor and skill against four PAVN divisions between April 9 and April 23. They gave way only when Communist forces were able to cut off all reinforcements.

After Xuan Loc fell, a force of about thirteen PAVN divisions tightened the noose around Saigon, encountering only desultory resistance. In Hanoi, Giap and the rest of the Politburo and Central Military Committee had spent a sleepless night at the PAVN command center before convening on the morning of April 28. According to Giap's account, "the atmosphere was one of elation." A map of Saigon was spread across a large table. "The red arrows on our map were now clustered in the direction of the inner city. Slash-marks indicated successively captured targets. Nearly every hour—at every instant, it seemed—a new report was received.... The enemy soldiers were like beheaded snakes. American military and civilian personnel fled by helicopter from the rooftops of high-rise buildings in a 'whirlwind' operation."[45]

Thieu had resigned on April 21 and fled to Taiwan. On April 29, 1975, the United States began a dramatic evacuation of Americans and a limited number of their South Vietnamese allies, as seventy Marine helicopters flew between landing pads in central Saigon and a fleet of aircraft carriers off the coast. By the early morning of April 30, PAVN columns swept down from Bien Hoa into the heart of the city. A tank squadron made its way down Hong Thap Tu Street and turned left onto Thong Nhut Boulevard. Around 1100 hours, its lead tank crashed through the gates of the presidential palace. Jubilant PAVN soldiers jumped off their tanks and headed through the courtyard into the palace proper.

General Duong Van Minh, who was thought to be a titular head of state acceptable to the Communists, was waiting with his cabinet in a second floor reception room. Colonel Bui Tin, People's Army of Vietnam, was then serving as a journalist covering the war's final campaign. As the senior officer attached to the tank squadron, it fell to him to take the surrender. "I have been waiting since early this morning to transfer power to you," said General Minh. Colonel Tin replied, "There is no question of you transferring power. Your power has crumbled. You cannot give up what you do not have."[46]

Within minutes, the senior comrades at the command post received the news of the surrender. Giap recalled the moment: "Tears of joy filled everyone's eyes.... The Ho Chi Minh Campaign was ended in total victory. Mixed with the sounds of the loudspeaker applause resounded in all the streets.... [That night] I took a drive around Hanoi and discovered that the city had been transformed into a sea of flowers and flags. The streets were full of people festively celebrating. That night Hanoi and all of Vietnam rejoiced, together with Saigon and the whole south."[47]

Many Western historians describe the Ho Chi Minh offensive as a conventional invasion in which the PLAF guerrillas played only a marginal role, the implication being that Giap's people's war strategy had been effectively defeated, leaving him no option but to resort to a conventional invasion aimed at the conquest of a hostile nation. In fact, PLAF regional and local guerrilla forces performed a number of critical roles, seizing many objectives that had been bypassed in the attacks in the Tri-Thier Front and the Central Highlands. They protected the rear as PAVN forces drove southward on Saigon, tying down ARVN units and preventing GVN forces, including the regional and popular force units that remained in strength, from cutting PAVN lines of communication. Moreover, local guerrilla forces had prepared clandestine supply depots along the lines of advance into Saigon for several months before the drive commenced. Finally, Tran Van Tra had directed an impressive guerrilla campaign in the densely populated Mekong Delta in 1973 and 1974, resulting in substantial territorial gains in that region. In March and early April 1975, the intensity of guerrilla activity in the Mekong Delta was so great that Thieu ordered reinforcements of the three divisions then deployed in the region. As historian Rod Paschall points out, had these divisions been able to redeploy to the defensive line north of Saigon, the battle for the city might well have been a much more costly and time-consuming event than it was.[48] In the end, the victory of the Revolution was achieved not by the abandonment of Vo Nguyen Giap's protracted war strategy in favor of conventional warfare, but by the methodical and imaginative application of that strategy, and by the resilience and resolve of millions of Vietnamese—soldiers and citizens alike—who believed the Revolution offered them the only path to freedom and to a brighter future in a postcolonial world.

11
REFLECTIONS

After the Communists' great victory in 1975, Senior General Giap's influence in national policy and military affairs gradually diminished. In April 1973 he had relinquished his title as commander in chief of the People's Army to his protege, Van Tien Dung. Dung also succeeded him as minister of defense in 1980. In March 1982, Giap's tenure as a member of the Politburo came to an end. Most accounts have it that the "architect of victory" over France and the United States was forced to resign from these posts, or was at best strongly pressured. Yet it wouldn't be unreasonable to surmise that Giap may have welcomed a diminished role in Vietnamese affairs after more than thirty years of service in the revolutionary struggle.

Since his departure from the Politburo, government officials have referred to Giap as a "national treasure." Certainly most Vietnamese would agree. This designation makes his mysterious absence from public events marking the anniversaries of Vietnam's crucial battles with France and the United States all the stranger. His absence might be explained as the result of prohibitions issued by the leadership intended to prevent the emergence of a "personality cult" that might challenge the collective leadership paradigm that worked so effectively during the war years. The health problems that have dogged the general on and off since the late 1960s may also have contributed to his low profile in public life. We can only speculate on these questions. We do know that at the time of the publication of this book, Giap is more than a century old. He is the last of Hanoi's founding leaders, and his passing will mark the end of a pivotal era for the Vietnamese people.

This book has presented an account of Vo Nguyen Giap's campaigns, an exploration of his unique way of war, and his contribution to the Vietnamese Communists' long struggle to establish a society and government congenial to their own ideas and values. It is appropriate here to close with some reflections on Giap's place among the great commanders of history, as well as the relevance of his experience to contemporary military affairs. These issues have been much on my mind as I wrote about the man over the last three years, and I expect that they have emerged in the minds of many of the book's readers as well.

On the first issue, Giap's career in large measure speaks for itself. He defeated two major Western powers in anticolonial wars. It is indisputable that colonialism and the struggles against it have been seminal forces in shaping the modern world. These subjects remain an abiding preoccupation for serious students of politics and military history today, and will surely remain so for some time. So the Vietnamese and their revolution matter, and Giap and his ideas matter as a part of this global story.

"Over the years, Giap would make his share of mistakes on the battlefield," observes Professor Logevall, "but his record as a logistician, strategist, and organizer is nevertheless extraordinary and ranks him with the finest military leaders of modern history—with Wellington, Grant, Lee and Rommel. He proved spectacularly adept, in particular, at using the often-limited means at his disposal as well as the terrain, which he knew better than his adversaries because it was his own."[1] I cannot quarrel with a single word of that assessment, but in my estimation it does not go far enough. Giap's achievements are more dazzling in scope than those of most of the other great captains of modern war, few of whom, it seems to me at least, fought against such great odds and prevailed.

Over the thirty years of his career as commander in chief, Giap not only frustrated the designs of two nations far stronger than his own both militarily and technologically, but also continuously built up the strength and capabilities of his own military forces, seamlessly integrating them into a resilient political infrastructure that he himself had no small hand in creating. Few generals in history have been able to integrate so many different forms of warfare—guerrilla insurgency, guerrilla-style war waged by independent regular companies and battalions, mobile operations, sieges, and conventional offensives—to forward their broad strategic objectives.

As for the second issue, Giap's relevance to contemporary warfare and military strategy is profound, but it cannot be easily summarized into a neat set of maxims and precepts. He did not develop an original theory of guerrilla war or protracted war. Rather, he deftly synthesized a number of classic strategies to the varied circumstances he faced in Vietnam. So varied were those circumstances, so great the challenges, and so eclectic Giap's responses to them, that it is no exaggeration to say that his career is worthy of study by all serious students and practitioners of warfare today. What follows below is a modest attempt to summarize elements of his approach particularly relevant to contemporary conflict.

Like Mao, Giap was intensely concerned with the role of experience and knowledge in strategic decision making. Again and again in his writings, Giap called attention to the importance of continually re-examining what could be learned from the ever-expanding reservoir of one's political and military experience, and how these experiences could inform future decisions. Only when such re-examination became a deeply ingrained habit of mind could one arrive at what Giap and the other Communists refer to as "correct thinking." War, according to Giap, is a protean thing, and those who seek success must constantly examine their own actions and attitudes with unflinching honesty, as well as those of their adversaries, in an effort to improve performance in the present and the future.

One wellspring of Giap's unshakeable confidence was his conviction that, while the military capabilities of his adversaries were qualitatively superior to his own, their *assessments* of the broad strategic realities on the ground were precisely the opposite. "The Communist Party's leadership ability to analyze and adapt, to relate its resources to reality, and to avoid a sense of omnipotence as well as excessive caution was the link between its existing and potential forces and the future," Gabriel Kolko wisely observes.[2] "The Communist Party's genius was its ability to survive and adapt and to fulfill the [social and political] vacuum the United States and its dependents created."[3] This, too, was part of Giap's genius. As Giap saw it, the French and the Americans were bound to fail in the long run because they did not engage in rigorous re-examination of their experiences, or those of their adversary. Thus, they failed to grasp the true nature of the balance of forces—military, political, social, psychological—that prevailed on the battlefield.

The power of the US military machine posed immense challenges to Giap as a commander. He knew that the conflict would result in horrific losses, but he also realized that those casualties were the inevitable cost of victory, and neither the reality of those casualties, as regrettable as they were, nor the destructive capacity of American forces, would prove to be decisive factors in the war's outcome. The Americans came to the opposite conclusion. They were sublimely confident that the immense capabilities of their armed forces, coupled with Giap's mediocrity—he was seen more as a stubborn butcher than a competent commander—would lead Communist forces first to despair and then to collapse. Yet, in the end, the Americans failed in Vietnam because proper understanding of the balance of forces proved more important than military capability.

Giap was first and foremost a *revolutionary war* strategist, which is to say he conceived of war primarily as a social struggle by people committed to breaking down the status quo and replacing it with a new set of power relationships and institutions, not as a strictly military activity carried out by full-time soldiers and guerrillas. Of course, the struggle had a very prominent military component. The military aspect of the conflicts with France and the United States was at times the most important, but the Communists never lost sight of the fact that their wars were political struggles for control of the energies and allegiance of the Vietnamese people as a whole. Such a conflict required a flexible and disciplined *social* strategy that could mobilize large numbers of highly motivated individuals committed to breaking down the old order and constructing a new one. As such, the work of building a powerful political infrastructure that could challenge French and American efforts was far more important than achieving victory in a series of conventional military battles and campaigns.

Giap saw with far greater clarity than did his adversaries that the balance of forces could be fundamentally altered by ideas, events, and passions far from the battlefield. He was acutely conscious of the way domestic politics in France and the United States could be shaped and manipulated to drive a wedge between the people and the governments that claimed to represent them. By protracting the conflicts against France and America, inflicting substantial casualties, and portraying his enemies' war policies as unjust through the Revolution's varied propaganda programs, Giap believed that he could sap the will of his adversaries to a point where their military victory would become impossible. He was entirely correct.

He also believed that he could instill a sense of futility and exhaustion in the French and American armies by avoiding large-scale combat engagements in favor of harassing tactics, including ambushes, booby traps, and luring the enemy into patrolling forbidding mountainous terrain and steamy jungles where his own troops were more at home. For Giap, military operations were often planned and executed to achieve specific psychological and political effects.

Giap never doubted that the power of his soldiers' and citizens' commitment to the Vietnamese revolutionary vision would compensate for the inferiority of their military forces. It was only necessary to instill the same level of belief and determination he himself possessed for the cause into the Revolution as a whole, and to direct that energy toward victory. Giap, the man and the general, came to embody the spirit of invincibility built into the fabric of the entire revolutionary enterprise—the PAVN, the PLAF, the political cadres, the aspirations of the people. Much of the revolution's allure stemmed from Giap's dexterity in presenting the Communist revolution as the only vehicle for achieving national liberation and unification, as the only way to give the people power to shape their own history and destiny. Whether this was true or not in some objective sense—and of course the French, the Americans, and many of their Vietnamese allies did not think it was—hardly mattered. What did matter was that the people and the soldiers loyal to the Revolution believed it was true.

When all is said and done, Giap's enduring importance lies in recognizing that he was a successful general largely because he could see with extraordinary clarity all the factors and forces that shaped the trajectory of the wars in which he fought, and how each element related to all the others. He understood that the relative importance of each element was constantly in a state of flux, and that one's strategy, and one's tactics, must be constantly recalibrated in light of those changes.

The hallmarks of Vo Nguyen Giap's way of war were, then, tactical flexibility, pragmatism, and a gift for seeing conflict as it was, not as he wished it to be. The diminutive history professor turned soldier from the tiny village of An Xa in Quang Binh Province, Vietnam, humbled first the French and then the Americans. Giap himself once said he had learned his trade in the bush. In thirty years of fighting, he learned well—well enough to provide his adversaries with a very costly education in warfare simply by doing what worked.

NOTES

CHAPTER 1

1. Hoài Thanh, ed., *Days with Ho Chi Minh* (Hanoi: Foreign Languages Publishing House, 1962), p. 181.
2. Robert F. Turner, *Vietnamese Communism: Its Origins and Development*, Hoover Institutions Publications, 143 (Stanford: Hoover Institution Press, 1975), p. 5.
3. Ibid, p. 6.
4. Ibid., endnote, p. 5.
5. Cecil B. Currey, *Victory at Any Cost: The Genius of Viet Nam's Gen. Vo Nguyen Giap* (Washington, DC: Brassey's, 1997), p. 100.
6. Douglas Pike, *PAVN: People's Army of Vietnam* (Novato, CA: Presidio Press, 1986), p. 18.
7. William J. Duiker, *The Communist Road to Power In Vietnam*, 2nd ed. (Boulder, CO: Westview Press, 1996), p. 22.
8. Currey, p. 10.
9. Hoài, p. 185.
10. Currey, p. 32.
11. Ibid.
12. Duiker, p. 57.
13. Ibid., p. 62.
14. Ibid., p. 74.
15. Phillip B. Davidson, *Vietnam at War: The History: 1946–1975* (Novato, CA: Presidio Press, 1988), p. 15.
16. Samuel B. Griffith, tr., *Mao Tse-tung: On Guerrilla Warfare* (New York: Praeger, 1961), p. 8.
17. Ibid., pp. 42–46.

CHAPTER 2

1. Fredrik Logevall, *Embers of War: The Fall of an Empire and the Making of America's Vietnam* (New York: Random House, 2012), p. 71.
2. Logevall, p. 73.
3. Currey, p. 51.
4. See ibid., p. 52.

5. Ibid., p. 54.
6. Logevall, p. 35.
7. Duiker, p. 74.
8. Pike, pp. 27–28.
9. Võ Nguyên Giáp, *The Military Art of People's War* (New York: Monthly Review Press, 1970), p. 57. Hereafter cited as *MAPW*.
10. See John T. McAlister, Jr., *Viet Nam: The Origins of Revolution* (New York: Alfred A. Knopf, 1969), pp. 263–264.
11. Giáp, p. 65.
12. Ibid., p. 64.
13. Ibid., p. 67.
14. Pike, p. 29.
15. Democratic Republic of Viet Nam, Central Committee of Propoganda of the Viet Nam Lao Dong Party and the Committee for the Study of the Party's History: *Thirty Years of Struggle of the Party*, Book One (Hanoi: Foreign Languages Publishing House, 1960), p. 91, quoted in McAlister, p. 158.
16. McAlister, p. 269.
17. Logevall, p. 71.
18. Democratic Republic of Viet Nam, *Thirty Years of Struggle of the Party*, p. 88.
19. McAlister, pp. 155–156.
20. Ibid., pp. 156–159.
21. Logevall, p. 149.

CHAPTER 3

1. Logevall, p. 115.
2. Ibid., p. 118.
3. Ibid., p. 133.
4. Ibid., p. 151.
5. Quoted in Logevall, pp. 149–150.
6. Bernard B. Fall, *The Two Viet-Nams: A Political and Military Analysis* (New York: Frederick A. Praeger, 1967), p. 73.
7. Logevall, p. 144.
8. Duiker, p. 126; Davidson, p. 42.
9. Duiker, p. 128.
10. See ibid., pp. 134–137.
11. Ibid., p. 136.
12. Pike, p. 215.
13. Joseph Buttinger, *A Dragon Defiant* (New York: Praeger, 1972), vol. 2, p. 1023.
14. Bernard Fall, *Street without Joy: The French Debacle in Indochina* (Harrisburg, PA: Stackpole Co., 1964), p. 30.
15. Ibid., p. 54.
16. Ibid., p. 27.
17. Giáp, pp. 87–88.
18. George K. Tanham, *Communist Revolutionary Warfare: From the Vietminh to the Viet Cong*, rev. ed. (New York: Praeger, 1967), p. 25.
19. Davidson, p. 76.
20. Giáp, p. 11.
21. Robert J. O'Neill, *General Giap: Politician and Strategist* (New York: Praeger, 1969), p. 66.
22. Duiker, p. 142.
23. Davidson, p. 59.
24. Pike, p. 220.
25. Giáp, *MAPW*, pp. 168–176.
26. Pike, p. 24.
27. Edgar O'Ballance, *The Indo-China War, 1945–1954: A Study in Guerilla Warfare* (London: Faber and Faber, 1964), p. 105.
28. Logevall, p. 147.

CHAPTER 4

1. Stanley Karnow, *Vietnam, a History* (New York: Viking, 1983), p. 181.
2. Lucien Bodard, *The Quicksand War: Prelude to Vietnam* (Boston: Little, Brown, 1967), p. 247.
3. Võ Nguyên Giáp, *People's War: People's Army* (Hanoi: Foreign Languages Publishing House, 1961), 49. Hereafter cited as *PWPA*.
4. Ibid., pp. 108–109.
5. Bodard, p. 174.
6. Ibid., p. 279.
7. O'Neill, p. 76.
8. Logevall, p. 238.
9. Davidson, p. 80.
10. Bodard, p. 241.
11. Ibid., p. 57.
12. Davidson, p. 83.
13. United States Marine Corps, *Warfighting* (New York: Doubleday, 1994), p. 1.
14. Fall, *Street*, p. 33.
15. Logevall, p. 250.
16. Fall, *Street*, p. 34.
17. Ibid.

CHAPTER 5

1. Duiker, p. 151.
2. Fall, *Street*, pp. 39–40.
3. Davidson, pp. 123–125.
4. Fall, *Street*, p. 5.
5. Ibid., pp. 52–53.
6. Giáp, *PWPA*, p. 109.
7. O'Ballance, p. 177.
8. Fall, *Street*, p. 71.
9. Ted Morgan, *Valley of Death: The Tragedy at Dien Bien Phu that Led America into the Vietnam War* (New York: Random House, 2010), p. 158.
10. Joseph R. Starobin, *Eyewitness in Indo-China* (New York: Greenwood Press, 1954), pp. 158–159.
11. O'Ballance, p. 187.
12. Ibid., pp. 191–192.
13. Logevall, p. 345.
14. Morgan, p. 151.

CHAPTER 6

1. Giáp, *PWPA*, p. 159.
2. Morgan, p. 178.
3. Logevall, p. 388.
4. Ibid., pp. 388–389.
5. Ibid., p. 389.
6. Giáp, *PWPA*, p. 206.
7. Logevall, p. 382.
8. Fall, p. 44.
9. Logevall, p. 394.
10. Giáp, *PWPA*, pp. 166–169.
11. Fall, *Street*, p. 67.
12. Ibid., p. 72.
13. Morgan, p. 248.
14. Logevall, p. 412.

15. Ibid.
16. Morgan, pp. 260–261.
17. O'Neill, p. 150.
18. Fall, *Street*, pp. 45–46.
19. Morgan, p. 218.
20. Ibid., p. 154.
21. Logevall, p. 446.
22. Võ Nguyên Giáp , *Dien Bien Phu*, rev. ed. (Hanoi: Foreign Languages Publishing House, 1964), pp. 124–126.
23. Giáp, *PWPA*, pp. 180–181.
24. Ibid., p. 182.
25. Quoted in Bernard B. Fall, *Hell in a Very Small Place: The Siege of Dien Bien Phu* (Philadelphia: Lippincott, 1967), p. 354.
26. Ibid., p. 462.
27. John Prados, "Assessing Dien Bien Phu," in *The First Vietnam War: Colonial Conflict and Cold War Crisis*, Mark Atwood Lawrence and Fredrik Logevall, eds. (Cambridge, MA: Harvard University Press, 2007), p. 228.
28. Quoted in George C. Herring, *America's Longest War: The United States and Vietnam, 1950–1975*, 4th ed. (New York: McGraw-Hill), pp. 54–55.
29. Ibid., pp. 55–56.

CHAPTER 7

1. Herring, p. 53.
2. *The Military History Institute of Vietnam*, Merle L. Pribbenow, tr., *Victory in Vietnam: The Official History of the People's Army of Vietnam, 1954–1975* (Lawrence: University Press of Kansas, 2002), p. 32.
3. Herring, p. 75.
4. Logevall, p. 682.
5. Karnow, p. 235.
6. Pribbenow, *Victory*, p. 18.
7. Ibid., p. 43.
8. J. J. Zasloff, "Origins of the Insurgency of South Vietnam, 1954–1960: The Role of the South Vietminh," Rand Corporation Memorandum, May, 1968, author's collection.
9. Pribbenow, *Victory*, pp. 43–44.
10. Ibid., p. 43.
11. Logevall, p. 689.
12. Pribbenow,*Victory*, p. 53.
13. Ibid., p. 68.
14. Duiker, pp. 226–228.
15. Kolko, p. 257.
16. Ibid., p. 254.
17. Duiker, p. 213.
18. Herring, p. 97.
19. Duiker, p. 221.
20. Ibid., p. 237.
21. Ibid., p. 240.
22. Quoted in Turner, p. 248.
23. Pribbenow, p. 103.
24. Võ Nguyên Giáp, *South Vietnam People Will Win*, reprinted from 1965 ed. (Honolulu, HI: University Press of the Pacific, 2001), pp. 33–36. Hereafter cited as *SVPWW*.
25. Giáp, *SVPWW*, p. 26.
26. Ibid.
27. Ibid., p. 22.
28. Ibid., pp. 46–47.
29. Karnow, p. 423.

30. Ibid., p. 421.
31. Ibid.
32. Ibid., pp. 421–422.
33. Karnow, p. 390.
34. Ibid., p. 229.

CHAPTER 8

1. Giap, *MAPW*, p. 177.
2. Giap, *Big Victory*, p. 53.
3. See Davidson, pp. 311–313, Prados, pp. 191–195.
4. Brigham in Gilbert, p. 109.
5. Summers, *Atlas of the Vietnam War*, p. 106.
6. CIC Intelligence Memorandum, "The Vietnamese Communists Debate Military Strategy," 25 August 1966. Author's collection.
7. Quoted in Larry H. Addington, *America's War in Vietnam: A Short Narrative History* (Bloomington: Indiana University Press, 2000), p. 99.
8. "Ho Chi Minh Trail," in Spencer C. Tucker, ed., *Encyclopedia of the Vietnam War: A Political, Social, and Military History* (New York: Oxford University Press, 2001), p. 176.
9. Ibid.
10. Prados, p. 373.
11. Ibid., p. 374.
12. Marc Jason Gilbert, ed., *Why the North Won the Vietnam War* (New York: Palgrave, 2002), p. 163.
13. Addington, pp. 101–102.
14. Michael Lee Lanning and Dan Cragg, *Inside the VC and the NVA: The Real Story of North Vietnam's Armed Forces* (College Station: Texas A&M University Press, 2008), p. 173.
15. Thomas C. Thayer, *War without Fronts: The American Experience in Vietnam* (New York: Westview Press, 1986), p. 45.
16. Quoted in Lanning, p. 217.
17. Quoted in Tucker, p. 516.
18. Vo Nguyen Giap, *Big Victory, Great Task* (New York: Praeger, 1968), pp. 23–24.
19. Ibid., p. 47.
20. Ibid., p. 56.
21. Carl von Clausewitz, *On War* (Princeton, NJ: Princeton University Press, 1976), pp. 88–89.
22. Griffith, pp. 7–8.

CHAPTER 9

1. Michael Herr, *Dispatches* (New York: Alfred A. Knopf, 1977), pp. 68–69.
2. Pribbenow, p. 222.
3. Merle L. Pribbenow, "Vo Nguyen Giap and the Mysterious Evolution of the Plan for the 1968 Tet Offensive," *Journal of Vietnamese Studies*, Vol. 3, No. 2 (Summer 2008), p. 3.
4. Duiker, p. 288.
5. Tran Van Tra, "Tet: The 1968 General Offensive and General Uprising," in *The Vietnam War: Vietnamse and American Perspectives*, Jayne S. Warner and Luu Doan Huynh, eds. (Armonk, NY: M.E. Sharpe, 1993), pp. 38–39.
6. Ibid., p. 40.
7. Ang Chenq Guan, "Decision-Making Leading to the Tet Offensive (1968) - The Vietnamese Communist Perspective,"*Journal of Contemporary History*, Vol. 33, No. 3 (July, 1998), p. 346.
8. See Duiker, pp. 288–291.
9. Duiker, p. 290.
10. Tran, pp. 43–44.
11. Thayer, p. 91.
12. Don Oberdorfer, *Tet!* (Garden City, NY: Doubleday, 1971), p. 314.

13. Ibid., pp. 320–323.
14. Ronald Spector, *After Tet: The Bloodiest Year in Vietnam* (New York: Free Press, 1993), p. 155.
15. Ibid., p. 319.
16. William S. Turley, *The Second Indochina War: A Short Political and Military History, 1954–1975* (Boulder, CO: Westview Press, 1986), p. 108.
17. See Summers, *On Strategy,* for the most detailed elaboration of his thinking.
18. Lewis Sorely, *A Better War: The Unexamined Victories and Final Tragedy of America's Last Years in Vietnam* (New York: Harcourt Brace & Co., 1999), p. 15.
19. Davidson, p. 441.
20. Anderson, p. 67.
21. Tran, p. 41; Pribbenow, *Victory*, p. 214.
22. Turley, p. 100.
23. Tran, p. 40.
24. Pribbenow, *Victory*, p. 215.
25. Kolko, p. 303.
26. Pike, pp. 218–219.
27. Kolko, p. 335.
28. Karnow, p. 557.
29. Oberdorfer, p. xviii.

CHAPTER 10

1. Herring, p. 275.
2. Lewis Sorley, *A Better War: The Unexamined Victories and Final Tragedy of America's Last Years in Vietnam* (New York: Harcourt Brace, 1999), p. 45.
3. Ibid., p. 192.
4. Ibid., p. 85.
5. Ibid., p. 59.
6. Ibid., p. 6.
7. Prados, p. 327.
8. Duiker, p. 304.
9. Lanning, pp. 178–179.
10. Duiker, p. 304.
11. Ibid., p. 316.
12. Ibid., p. 306.
13. Pribbenow, *Victory*, p. 249.
14. Duiker, p. 304.
15. Ibid., p. 307.
16. Frances Fitzgerald, *Fire in the Lake: The Vietnamese and the Americans in Vietnam* (Boston: Little, Brown), pp. 428–429.
17. Thomas C. Thayer, *War without Fronts: The American Experience in Vietnam* (Boulder, CO: Westview Press, 1985), p. 206.
18. Richard A. Hunt, *Pacification: The American Struggle for Vietnam's Hearts and Minds* (Boulder, CO: Westview Press, 1995), p. 226.
19. Ibid., p. 227.
20. Ibid., pp. 262–263.
21. Ibid., p. 264.
22. Sorley, p. 273.
23. Pribbenow, *Victory*, pp. 261.
24. Sorley, p. 257.
25. Ibid., p. 265.
26. Turley, p. 138.
27. Ibid.
28. Quoted in Duiker, p. 307.
29. Ibid., p. 319.

30. Kolko, p. 422.
31. Henry Kissinger, *White House Years* (New York: Simon and Schuster, 1979), p. 1100.
32. Sorley, pp. 329–330.
33. Ibid., p. 328.
34. Ibid., p. 300.
35. Duiker, p. 325.
36. Turley, p. 151.
37. Duiker, p. 325.
38. Ibid.
39. Vo Nguyen Giap, *The General Headquarters in the Spring of Brilliant Victory: Memoirs* (Hanoi: Thế Giới Publishers, 2002), p. 55.
40. Ibid., pp. 74–75.
41. Merle Pribbenow, "North Vietnam's Final Offensive: Strategic Endgame Nonpariel," *Parameters,* Winter 1999–2000, http://www.proquest.com.
42. Pribbenow, "Final Offensive."
43. Davidson, p. 769.
44. Pribbenow, "Final Offensive."
45. Giap, *General Headquarters,* pp. 246–247.
46. Karnow, p. 683.
47. Giap, *General Headquarters,* pp. 253–255.
48. Rod Paschall, "Victor's Final Strategy," *Vietnam Magazine*, Vol. 12, No. 6 (April 2000), http://www.proquest.com.

CHAPTER 11

1. Logevall, *Embers of War,* p. 147.
2. Kolko, p. 551.
3. Ibid., p. 552.

SELECTED BIBLIOGRAPHY

Addington, Larry H. *America's War in Vietnam: A Short Narrative History.* Bloomington: Indiana University Press, 2000.

Anderson, David. The *Columbia Guide to the Vietnam War.* New York: Columbia University Press, 2002.

Andrews, William R. *Vietnamese Communist Revolutionary Activities in Dinh Tuong Province, 1960–1964.* Columbia: University of Missouri Press, 1973.

Bodard, Lucien. *The Quicksand War: Prelude to Vietnam.* Boston: Little, Brown, 1967.

Bui Tin. *Following Ho Chi Minh: Memoirs of a North Vietnamese Colonel.* Judy Stow and Do Van, translators. Honolulu: University of Hawaii Press, 1995.

Buttinger, Joseph. *A Dragon Defiant.* New York: Praeger, 1972.

CIA. "The Vietnamese Communists Debate Military Strategy," August 25, 1966. Memorandum. Author's collection.

Clausewitz, Carl von. *On War,* revised edition, edited and translated by Michael Howard and Peter Paret. Princeton: Princeton University Press, 1984.

Colvin, John. *Giap: Volcano Under the Snow.* New York: Soho, 1996.

Currey, Cecil B. *Victory at Any Cost: The Genius of Viet Nam's Gen. Vo Nguyen Giap.* Washington, DC: Brassey's, 1997.

Davidson, Phillip B. *Vietnam at War: The History, 1946–1975.* Novato, CA: Presidio, 1988.

Democratic Republic of Viet Nam, Central Committee of Propaganda of the Viet Nam Lao Dong Party and the Committee for the Study of the Party's History. *Thirty Years of Struggle of the Party,* Book One. Hanoi: Foreign Languages Publishing House, 1960.

Duiker, William J. *The Communist Road to Power in Vietnam,* second edition. Boulder: Westview Press, 1996.

———. *Ho Chi Minh.* New York: Hyperion, 2000.

Elliott, David H. P. *The Vietnamese War: Revolution and Social Change in the Mekong Delta, 1930–1975,* concise edition. Armonk, NY: ME Sharpe, 2007.

Fall, Bernard B. *The Two Viet-Nams: A Political and Military Analysis.* New York: Frederick A. Praeger, 1967.

———. *Hell in a Very Small Place: The Siege of Dien Bien Phu,* second edition. New York: Da Capo Press, 2002.

———. *Street Without Joy: The French Debacle in Indochina.* Mechanicsburg, PA: Stackpole Books, 2005.

Fitzgerald, Frances. *Fire in the Lake: The Vietnamese and the Americans in Vietnam.* Boston: Little, Brown, 2002.

Gilbert, Marc Jason, ed. *Why the North Won the Vietnam War*. New York: Palgrave, 2002.

Herr, Michael. *Dispatches*. New York: Alfred A. Knopf, 1977.

Herring, George C. *America's Longest War: The United States and Vietnam, 1950–1975*, fourth edition. Boston: McGraw Hill, 2002.

Hoài Thanh, ed., *Days with Ho Chi Minh*. Hanoi: Foreign Languages Publishing House, 1962.

Hunt, Richard A. *Pacification: The American Struggle for Vietnam's Hearts and Minds*. Boulder: Westview Press, 1995.

Irving, R. E. M. *The First Indochina War: French and American Policy, 1945–1954*. London: Helm, 1975.

Karnow, Stanley. *Vietnam: A History*. New York: Viking, 1983.

———. "Giap Remembers." *New York Times Magazine*, June 24, 1990, pp.22–62.

Kim Khanh Huynh. *Vietnamese Communism, 1925–1945*. Ithaca, NY: Cornell University Press (Published under the auspices of the Institute of Southeast Asian Studies, Singapore), 1982.

Kolko, Gabriel. *Anatomy of a War: Vietnam, the United States, and the Modern Historical Experience*. New York: The New Press, 1994.

Lanning, Michael Lee, and Cragg, Dan. *Inside the VC and the NVA: The Real Story of North Vietnam's Armed Forces*. College Station, TX: Texas A&M University Press, 2008.

Le Duan. *On the Socialist Revolution in Vietnam*. Hanoi: Foreign Languages Publishing House, 1967.

Liddell Hart, B. H. *Strategy*, second revised edition. New York: Meridian, 1991.

Logevall, Fredrik. *The Origins of the Vietnam War*. Harlow, England: Pearson Education, 2001.

———. *Embers of War: The Fall of an Empire and the Making of America's Vietnam*. New York: Random House, 2012.

MacDonald, Peter. *Giap: the Victor in Vietnam*. New York, WW Norton, 1993.

Maclear, Michael. *The Ten Thousand Day War: Vietnam, 1945–1975*. New York: St. Martin's Press, 1981.

Mao Tse-tung, *On Guerrilla Warfare*. Reprint of the 1961 edition. Translated by Samuel B. Griffith II. Urbana, IL: University of Illinois Press, 2000. McAlister, John T. *Viet Nam: The Origins of Revolution*. New York: Knopf, 1969.

McGarvey, Patrick J., comp. *Visions of Victory: Selected Vietnamese Communist Military Writings, 1964–1968*. Stanford, CA: Hoover Institution on War and Peace, Stanford University, 1969.

Military History Institute of Vietnam. *The Official History of the People's Army of Vietnam, 1954–1975*. Translated by Merle Pribbenow. Lawrence, KS: University Press of Kansas, 2002.

Morgan, Ted. *Valley of Death: The Tragedy at Dien Bien Phu that Led America into the Vietnam War*. New York: Random House, 2010.

Nguyen Khac Vien. *Tradition and Revolution in Vietnam*. Washington, DC: The Indochina Resource Center, 1974.

O'Ballance, Edgar. *The Indo-China War: A Study in Guerilla Warfare*. Faber & Faber, 1964.

Oberdorfer, Don. *Tet!* Garden City, NY: Doubleday, 1971.

O'Neill, Robert J. *General Giap: Politician and Strategist*. New York: Praeger, 1969.

Paret, Peter. *French Revolutionary Warfare from Indochina to Algeria: the Analysis of a Political and Military Doctrine*. Published for the Center of International Studies, Princeton University. New York: Praeger, 1964.

Paret, Peter, ed. *Makers of Modern Strategy from Machiavelli to the Nuclear Age*. Princeton, NJ: Princeton University Press, 1986.

Pike, Douglas. *Viet Cong: The Organization and Techniques of the National Liberation Front of Vietnam*. Cambridge, MA: MIT Press, 1966.

———. *War, Peace, and the Viet Cong*. Cambridge, MA: MIT Press, 1969.

———. *PAVN: People's Army of Vietnam*. Novato, CA: Presidio, 1986.

Porter, Gareth, ed. *Vietnam: The Definitive Documentation of Human Decisions*, two volumes. Stanfordville, NY: Earl M. Coleman Enterprises, Inc. Publishers, 1979.

Prados, John. *The Blood Road: The Ho Chi Minh Trail and the Vietnam War*. New York: Wiley, 1998.

———. "Assessing Dien Bien Phu," in *The First Vietnam War: Colonial Conflict and Cold War Crisis*, Mark Atwood Lawrence and Fredrik Logevall, eds. Cambridge, MA: Harvard University Press: 2007.

Pribbenow, Merle L., "Vo Nguyen Giap and the Mysterious Evolution of the Plan for the 1968 Tet Offensive" *Journal of Vietnamese Studies*, Vol. 3, No. 2 (Summer 2008).

Race, Jeffrey. *War Comes to Long An: Revolutionary Conflict in a Vietnamese Province,* updated and expanded edition. Berkeley: University of California Press, 2010.

Sorley, Lewis, *A Better War: The Unexamined Victories and Final Tragedy of America's Last Years in Vietnam.* New York: Harcourt Brace & Co., 1999.

Spector, Ronald. *After Tet: The Bloodiest Year in Vietnam.* New York: Free Press, 1993.

Starobin, Joseph R. *Eyewitness in Indo-China.* New York: Greenwood Press, 1968.

Summers, Harry G. *On Strategy: A Critical Analysis of the Vietnam War.* Novato, CA: Presidio, 1982.

Tanham, George K. *Communist Revolutionary Warfare: From the Vietminh to the Viet Cong.* New York: Praeger, 1967.

Thayer, Thomas C. *War without Fronts: The American Experience in Vietnam.* Boulder: Westview Press, 1985.

Tran Van Tra. "Tet: The 1968 General Offensive and General Uprising" in *The Vietnam War: Vietnamese and American Perspectives,* Jayne S. Warner and Luu Doan Huynh, eds. (Armonk, NY: M.E. Sharpe, 1993).

Truong Chinh and Vo Nguyen Giap. *The Peasant Question, 1937–1938.* Translated by Christine Pelzer White. Ithaca, NY: Cornell University Press, 1974.

Tucker, Spencer C., ed. *The Encyclopedia of the Vietnam War.* New York: Oxford University Press, 2001.

Turley, William S. *The Second Indochina War: A Short Political and Military History, 1954–1975.* Boulder: Westview Press, 1986.

Turner, Robert F. *Vietnamese Communism: Its Origins and Development.* Stanford: Hoover Institution Press, Stanford University, 1975.

United States Marine Corps. *Warfighting.* New York: Doubleday, 1994.

United States State Department. *A Threat to the Peace: North Viet-Nam's Effort to Conquer South Viet-Nam.* Washington, DC: Dept. of State, 1961.

Vo Nguyen Giap. *People's War, People's Army: The Viet Cong Insurrection Manual for Underdeveloped Countries.* New York: Praeger, 1962.

———. *Big Victory, Great Task: North Viet-Nam's Minister of Defense Assess the Course of the War.* New York: Praeger, 1968.

———. *Banner of People's War, The Party's Military Line.* New York: Praeger, 1970.

———. *The Military Art of People's War.* Russell Stetler, ed. New York: Monthly Review Press, 1970.

———. *National Liberation War in Viet Nam: General Line-Strategy-Tactics.* Hanoi: Foreign Languages Publishing House, 1971.

———. *To Arm the Revolutionary Masses to Build the People's Army.* Hanoi: Foreign Languages Publishing House, 1975.

Vo Nguyen Giap and Van Tien Dung. *How We Won the War.* Philadelphia: Recon Press, 1978.

———. *The South Vietnam People Will Win.* Reprint of the 1965 edition. Honolulu: University of Hawaii Press, 2001.

———. *Unforgettable Months and Years.* Hanoi: Goi Publishers, 2004.

———. *Dien Bien Phu: Rendezvous with History.* Hanoi: Goi Publishers, 2008.

———. *The General Headquarters in the Spring of Brilliant Victory.* Hanoi: Goi Publishers, 2011.

Zasloff, J. J. "Origins of the Insurgency of South Vietnam, 1954–1960: The Role of the South Vietminh Cadres." Rand Corporation Memorandum, May, 1968.

INDEX